Victims' Rights and Victims' Wrongs

Critical Perspectives on Crime and Law

Edited by Markus D. Dubber

Victims' Rights and Victims' Wrongs

COMPARATIVE LIABILITY IN CRIMINAL LAW

Vera Bergelson

Stanford Law Books
An Imprint of Stanford University Press
Stanford, California

Printed in the United States of America on acid-free, archival-quality paper

Library of Congress Cataloging-in-Publication Data

Bergelson, Vera.
Victims' rights and victims' wrongs : comparative liability in criminal law / Vera Bergelson.
p. cm. — (Critical perspectives on crime and law)
Includes bibliographical references and index.
ISBN 978-0-8047-5538-2 (cloth : alk. paper)
1. Criminal liability—United States. 2. Victims of crimes—Legal status, laws, etc.—United States. 3. Criminal law—Philosophy. I. Title. II. Series: Critical perspectives on crime and law.
KF9235.B47 2009
345.73'04—dc22 2008055815

Typeset by Westchester Book Group in 10/14 Minion

To my parents, Boris and Nadezhda Bergelson.

CONTENTS

ACKNOWLEDGMENTS

I AM INDEBTED to many extraordinary people who were generous with their time, ideas, and good humor. Their comments made my work on this book much more challenging and interesting. Among these people are: Lawrence Alan Alexander, Norman L. Cantor, Meir Dan-Cohen, Sherry F. Colb, Donna Dennis, Joshua Dressler, Markus D. Dubber, Gerald Dworkin, Kimberly Kessler Ferzan, George P. Fletcher, Gary L. Francione, Anna Gelpern, Stuart P. Green, Alon Harel, Adil Haque, Kyron J. Huigens, Heidi M. Hurd, Douglas N. Husak, Howard A. Latin, John Leubsdorf, Boris Lokshin, Gregory A. Mark, Stephen J. Morse, Iñigo Ortiz de Urbina Gimeno, Elizabeth Rapaport, Kenneth W. Simons, George C. Thomas III, Mark S. Weiner, Peter Westen, Ekow N. Yankah, and Leo Zaibert.

Several of them should be mentioned twice: Markus D. Dubber without whose help and encouragement this project would have never been accomplished; George C. Thomas III who has continuously followed and supported the development of my manuscript; and Alon Harel, Heidi M. Hurd, Douglas N. Husak, Kenneth W. Simons, and Iñigo Ortiz de Urbina Gimeno whose insightful commentaries significantly deepened my understanding of criminal law theory and prompted me to rethink and sharpen many of my arguments.

I am also grateful to the Deputy Director of Rutgers Law Library Paul Axel-Lute for his outstanding research and advice; my research assistants Joshua M. Gaffney, Eric Finkelstein, Melody He, Rebecca Klein, Elina Leviyeva, Linda Posluszny, Melanie L. Ryan, and Kathleen Wells for their expert help throughout my work on this book; participants of the Victims and Criminal Justice System symposium at Pace Law School and members of faculty colloquia at Rutgers School of Law-Newark and Benjamin Cardozo School of Law for their thought-provoking comments; and to Dean's Research Fund of Rutgers School of Law-Newark for its financial support.

Finally, my very special thanks go to my family who were there for me through all the ups and downs of this project.

None of these people are liable, comparatively or otherwise, for the contents of this book.

Victims' Rights and Victims' Wrongs is based, in part, on the following previously published works: "Victims and Perpetrators: An Argument for Comparative Liability in Criminal Law," *Buffalo Criminal Law Review* 8 (2005): 385–487; "Conditional Rights and Comparative Wrongs: More on the Theory and Application of Comparative Criminal Liability," *Buffalo Criminal Law Review* 8 (2005): 567–97; "Rights, Wrongs, and Comparative Justifications," *Cardozo Law Review* 28 (2007): 2481–2503; "The Right to Be Hurt: Testing the Boundaries of Consent," *George Washington Law Review* 75 (2007): 165–236; "Consent to Harm," *Pace L. Rev.* 28 (2008): 683–711; and also in *The Ethics of Consent: Theory and Practice*, edited by Alan Wertheimer and Franklin G. Miller (Oxford University Press, 2009).

Victims' Rights and Victims' Wrongs

INTRODUCTION

THIS BOOK is about the "penal couple,"[1] the two individuals most directly involved in a criminal act—the victim and the perpetrator. What roles do they play in a criminal episode? How should we evaluate their participation in it and attribute liability for the resulting harm? Should the perpetrator always be the single culprit or should his responsibility depend on the conduct of the victim? These questions are at the center of *Victims' Rights and Victims' Wrongs: Comparative Liability in Criminal Law.*

It is common to think of crime as something that "bad guys" do to "good guys" and of criminal adjudication as "us" against "them." This thinking is reflected even in the way we identify criminal cases: "People v. John Doe." We, "the People," prosecute John Doe. If he is wrong, then we—all of us, including the victim—are right. The guilt of the perpetrator presumes the innocence of the victim. In fact, perception of victims as innocent has a long history, which significantly predates our legal system. In numerous cultures, as evidenced by linguistics, the notion of victimhood is tied to the religious sacrifice. Most Semitic, Germanic, Romance, and Slavic languages have the same word for the victims of sacrifice and the victims of crime.[2] This homonymy is rooted in the dichotomous vision of the world as split into two categories, the guilty and the innocent. Those who were to serve as victims of sacrifice had to be pure, without blemish, and today too we continue to associate victimhood with innocence.[3]

It is also natural to think of the victim in the passive voice, as someone who was harmed, someone who was an object rather than a subject of an offense. Perhaps this image has historical and religious connotations as well.

Recall, for instance, the biblical story of the binding of Isaac and its depiction by Rembrandt: a young man is bound to an altar, motionless and helpless.

Yet, no matter what are the psychological, anthropological, or linguistic reasons for our separating the victim from the crime, they are largely misleading. In reality, victims are often co-authors of the harm they suffer. They may participate in risky activities; agree to infliction of pain or injury; attack or provoke others. Sometimes, they do not take necessary precautions against criminals; sometimes, they are criminals themselves. Frequently, yesterday's offenders become today's victims. For example, in Newark, New Jersey, where I am writing this book, approximately 85 percent of victims killed in the first six months of 2007 had criminal records.[4] In many instances, complex interpersonal dynamics between the victim and the perpetrator invoke a question of shared responsibility. Consider the following examples:

> A motorist driving ten miles per hour in excess of the speed limit hits and kills a pedestrian who intentionally threw himself in front of the car. Had the motorist not been speeding, he would have been able to avoid the collision. Is the motorist guilty of criminal homicide?
>
> Three drivers participate in a drag race. One loses control of his car and is killed. The other two are charged with manslaughter. Should the surviving drivers' culpability be reduced because of the decedent's own recklessness?
>
> A man agrees to be killed and eaten by another man. Should his voluntary consent to the homicide be a factor mitigating the killer's criminal liability?
>
> After years of abuse, a woman lashes out and, during a nonviolent confrontation, kills her husband. Should she be punished as severely as if there were no history of domestic violence?

In other words, should the victim's own acts ever be taken into account when we evaluate the criminal liability of the perpetrator? The law seems to be clear on the point: "Victim fault is not a defense, either partial or complete, to criminal liability."[5]

"Don't blame the victim" is one of the cornerstone maxims of Anglo-American jurisprudence, frequently quoted by judges, trial lawyers, and scholars. But is that maxim true—does the law in fact ignore the victim's behavior in determining the level of the defendant's criminal liability? Even more importantly—*should* the law ignore it? And if the answer depends on the circumstances, how should we decide when the victim's behavior is a mitigating factor and when it is irrelevant? To answer these questions, we need to integrate the victim into the theory of criminal law.

In recent years, as a result of the victims' rights movement, victims have become active participants in the American criminal justice system.[6] Today, thirty-two states have Victims' Rights Amendments, and all states have Victims' Bills of Rights that guarantee crime victims notice of important legal proceedings; participation in those proceedings, including victim impact statements at the time of sentencing, and restitution.[7] The increased role of victims in criminal law has raised new questions about their rights and responsibilities. However, most academic debates have focused on the victims' position in the criminal process rather than substantive criminal law.[8] This is not surprising in view of the fact that, until relatively recently, "there has been virtually no consideration of the victim's participation in the wrongdoing, or of any other interaction or interrelationship between criminal and victim."[9] As one commentator phrased it, the "analysis of victim conduct in substantive criminal law could be said to represent the dark side of the moon of the victims' rights movement."[10]

Both legal and nonlegal scholars agree that criminal law has developed "without paying much attention to the place of victims in the analysis of responsibility or in the rationale for punishment."[11] Some authors have pointed out that there is a need for a comprehensive theory that would assign victims and perpetrators their proper places in each aspect of criminal law.[12] Despite a number of insightful works that have discussed victims in connection with various areas of criminal doctrine,[13] such a comprehensive theory is yet to be written. This book is a step in that direction. It takes the position that each criminal episode must be viewed in its complexity, as an interaction of victims and perpetrators. If the victims voluntarily (by consent or assumption of risk) or involuntarily (by an attack on legally recognized rights of others) change their moral and legal status vis à vis the perpetrators, the perpetrators should be entitled to a defense of complete or partial justification, which would eliminate or diminish their criminal liability.

The book consists of three parts and six chapters. Part I, "Reality Check: Can Victims Be Partly Responsible for the Harm They Suffer?" challenges the accuracy of the proposition that the perpetrator's liability does not, and should not, depend on the conduct of the victim. I start in Chapter 1 with a review of criminological and victimological studies, which strongly suggest that criminal liability may be properly evaluated only in the context of the victim-perpetrator interaction. I then turn attention to criminal law itself and show that a number of criminal doctrines, such as consent, self-defense, and provocation, do in fact include victims' actions in the determination of perpetrators' liability. In Chapter 2, I make a normative claim that victims' actions should be considered a liability mitigator in all appropriate cases and not merely in the context of a few distinct defenses. My main arguments draw on the following:

1. The just desert principle, based on which perpetrators should be responsible for the harm caused only by them and not by the victim;
2. The efficiency principle, pursuant to which, in order to preserve the moral authority of criminal law, penal sanctions should not be overused and the law should develop in a dialogue with community perceptions of right and wrong;
3. The consistency principle, which mandates that punishment-justifying considerations be applied systematically;
4. The analysis of mitigating factors recognized at the penalty stage of a criminal trial; and
5. Considerations underlying the apportionment of liability in torts.

In Part II, "Toward a Unifying Theory of Comparative Criminal Liability," I propose a basis for developing a theory of comparative responsibility in criminal law and suggest a method allowing us to determine when the victim's conduct should provide the perpetrator with a complete or partial defense and when it should be legally irrelevant. Specifically, in Chapter 3, I revisit the doctrines of consent, self-defense, and provocation and consider some of the most problematic cases in each of these areas of law. Such cases include consensual homicide, sadomasochism, and gladiatorial contests; attacks by "innocent aggressors"; and killings provoked by spousal infidelity. I suggest that the doctrines of consent, self-defense, and provocation need to be revised to account properly for these cases. At the same time, as I argue in Chapter 4, these doctrines are based on a common principle, the principle of *conditionality of rights*. Pursuant to it, the perpetrator's liability may be mitigated or eliminated if the victim, by his own acts, has waived or reduced his right not to be harmed. With a view of putting it in the foundation of the defense of comparative criminal liability, I examine the principle of conditionality of rights in the context of a broader theory of rights and address a number of specific questions, such as: Should the defense be grounded in people's moral rights or legal rights? Do people have rights only against actual harm or against a risk of harm as well?

In Chapter 5, which opens Part III, "Incorporating the Principle of Conditionality of Rights into Criminal Law," I consider the temporal application of the principle: assuming the victim has reduced his right not to be harmed, how long does it remain reduced? To illustrate the issue, I discuss the effect of remote consent in the context of living wills; revocation of consent in connection with the law of rape; and "imminence" of threat in cases of killing of abusers in nonconfrontational circumstances. The final chapter of the book, Chapter 6, analyzes specific factors that may play a role in determining the scope of the perpetrator's liability—such as the magnitude of the affected rights of the perpetrator and the victim; the comparative causative impact of their conduct; and their respective culpability—and offers some thoughts about practical implementation of the principle of conditionality of rights and comparative liability in criminal law. I conclude with a proposition that the victim's rights-reducing conduct should function as an affirmative defense. In some circumstances, it would provide the defendant with complete justification, whereas in other circumstances it would only mitigate the defendant's liability. The new defense is sorely needed to reflect the realities of human interaction and bring the theory of liability in accord with fundamental principles of justice.

Part 1

REALITY CHECK

Can Victims Be Partly Responsible for the Harm They Suffer?

1 VICTIMS' CONDUCT IN CRIMINAL LAW AND CRIMINOLOGY

CRIMINOLOGICAL STUDIES OF VICTIMS AND VICTIM-OFFENDER RELATIONSHIPS

For years, social scientists have been calling attention to the incomplete, decontextualized approach taken by the law—with respect not only to the victim-offender relationship but also to other aspects of criminal behavior relevant to the concept of personal responsibility, the overarching concept of criminal justice.[1] This narrowness has been the source of great frustration among social scientists whose work has been systematically excluded from the lawmaking process. A scholar complained: "Much that a social scientist would want to know about the historical, social, contextual, and even immediate situational influences on criminal behavior—knowledge that otherwise would be crucial to meaningfully analyze and truly understand the actions of a criminal offender—is deemed irrelevant by the criminal law."[2] One of the major shortcomings of criminal law, in their view, is that penal statutes do not adequately reflect the variations of human interactions. Criminal law has been criticized because

> [i]t introduced abstraction as a domineering force, it introduced the rule of the paper, and it made criminal justice merely the interpretative machinery of the printed law: the goddess Justicia probably was impartial and knew the law very well, but her blindfold deprived her of the sight of complex interactions, group characteristics, and social problems. The criminal-victim relationship, like many other aspects of crime, therefore remained unknown to her.[3]

Of course, as a normative code, the law ought to be selective in choosing relevant facts; however, to be fair and effective, it may not ground its doctrines in an erroneous vision of the world. Criminological studies represent an important source of information about victim-perpetrator interaction. Thus, it may be helpful to start discussion of respective responsibility of victims and perpetrators with a brief overview of criminological research and findings.

Social scientists began to study criminal-victim interactions in the late nineteenth century,[4] and by the middle of the twentieth century victimology emerged as a free-standing branch of criminology[5] with a focus on the victim-offender relationship and the harm suffered by the victim as a result of the offense.[6] Two people are usually recognized as its founders—Benjamin Mendelsohn and Hans von Hentig.[7] A practicing attorney, Mendelsohn conducted a questionnaire study of his clients and formulated a typology that encompassed several degrees of victim culpability, ranging from the "completely innocent victim" (e.g., a child) to the "victim who is guilty alone" (e.g., an aggressor killed by the target of his attack in self-defense). Between these two extremes, Mendelsohn placed the "victim with minor guilt," the "victim as guilty as the offender," and the "victim more guilty than the offender."[8] Approximately at the same time, Hans von Hentig suggested that there is an interconnection between the "killer and killed, duper and dupe."[9] According to von Hentig, the victim was not merely a passive figure but rather an "activating sufferer" who played a part in the creation of the criminal act yet who was barely considered by our legal system.[10] Von Hentig wrote:

> I maintain that many criminal deeds are more indicative of a subject-object relation than of the perpetrator alone. There is a definite mutuality of some sort. . . . In the long process leading gradually to the unlawful result, credit and debit are not infrequently indistinguishable.[11]

Mendelsohn's and von Hentig's works were followed by numerous other typologies that used sociological, psychological, biological, and other criteria to measure the level of a victim's susceptibility to, and involvement in, a criminal act.[12] A contemporary sociologist has commented that "[b]y raising questions about victim proneness, vulnerability, and accountability, [the first victimologists] put forward a more complete but also more controversial explanation about why laws are broken and people get hurt."[13]

The essence of the controversy was the idea of shared responsibility, which implied that some victims as well as offenders did something wrong. Ever since the rise of the victims' rights movement in the 1970s, that idea and its implications have been hotly debated among victimologists. The "victim-blaming" and "victim-defending" tendencies clashed on a number of issues. However, as a recent influential work shows, victimologists cannot be simply divided into victim-blamers and victim-defenders. Advocates of both approaches often switch sides, depending on the facts of the case, the nature of the crime, and the parties involved.[14] The same people may criticize one group of victims (e.g., abusive husbands who get killed by their wives) but defend another (e.g., women who have been raped by acquaintances).

The victims' rights movement and the "discovery" of the victim by sociologists resulted in an important change: crime victims stopped being invisible. The enormous volume of research data collected and analyzed by victimologists is an invaluable source of information regarding crime, community standards, values, ethics, prejudices, and allegiances.

The first comprehensive empirical study of "victim-precipitated" crimes focused on homicides committed in Philadelphia from 1948 to 1952.[15] The study showed that in approximately 25 percent of all murders, the deceased was the first to use force, by drawing a weapon, striking the first physical blow during an argument, or in some other way initiating violence. Situations that resulted in violence included charges of infidelity, arguments over money, drunken brawls, and confrontations over insults and "fighting words."[16]

In the late 1960s, the National Commission on the Causes and Prevention of Violence (NCCPV) was formed to investigate, among other things, the victim's role in several types of street crime.[17] After reviewing police files from seventeen American cities, the commission concluded that instances of victim-precipitated behavior were not uncommon in cases of homicide and aggravated assault, less frequent but still empirically noteworthy in robbery, and least relevant in cases of rape.[18]

Further studies have expanded on the results of the NCCPV and other research.[19] A 1988 survey of nearly 10,000 homicide cases indicated that 19 percent of the victims were armed with a gun, a knife, or another deadly weapon. "Some armed victims used the deadly weapon to provoke the defendant. Others provoked the defendant with a nonlethal weapon or their fists or by pushing the defendant. Altogether, 19 percent of the victims in some way provoked the defendant."[20]

When victim precipitation was defined more broadly as any situation in which provocative behavior of the victim played an important role in the perpetrator's decision to act[21] or encouraged the offender into a progression of violence,[22] the victim precipitation rates were found to be as high as 49 to 67 percent. In an examination of homicides preceded by "hard drinking, weapon possession, insulting banter, and displays of physical toughness,"[23] a researcher concluded that "distinctions between victims and offenders are often blurred and [are] mostly a function of who got whom first, with what weapon, how the event was reported, and what immediate decisions were made by the police."[24]

In cases of violent crimes, distinctions between victims and offenders may be particularly distorted. Thus, recent years have witnessed a startling spike in killings of victims with criminal histories. For example, in 2007, 91 percent of murder victims in Baltimore had criminal records, up from 74 percent a decade ago. In Philadelphia, that number went up from 71 percent in 2005 to 75 percent in 2007. In Milwaukee, the homicide commission created after the number of murders increased by 39 percent in 2005 found that 77 percent of homicide victims in the past two years had an average of nearly twelve arrests.[25] Police and crime analysts agree that understanding interpersonal dynamics is critical to driving crime back down. "If you are trying to look at prevention, you need to look at the lives of the people involved," says Mallory O'Brien, director of the Homicide Review Commission in Milwaukee.[26]

In addition to academic research and investigations of reported crimes, victimologists conducted numerous polls of public opinion. The polls—predictably—found that people in general, and jurors in particular, assign significant weight to victims' behavior prior to the offense.[27] According to a famous study of juries, one of the main instances in which juries apply the power of nullification to acquit the defendant is when they take into account the contributory fault of the victim.[28] Moreover, research has shown that evidence of the victim's conduct affects all stages of a criminal proceeding:

> Offenders who kill the victim in response to a physical attack are less likely to be prosecuted; if they are prosecuted, they are less likely to be indicted; and if they are indicted, they are less likely to be convicted of the most serious indictment charge rather than a reduced charge.[29]

As an illustration, consider statistics collected by the Department of Justice. In 1988, approximately 540 people in the nation's seventy-five most populous counties were charged with killing their spouses.[30] Of these defendants, 43 percent pleaded guilty, 44 percent pleaded not guilty and stood trial, and 13 percent were not prosecuted.[31]

Spouse Murder Defendants in Large Urban Counties

Cases in Which Perpetrators Were Not Prosecuted[a]

Dallas. The wife (the victim) is eighty-nine and has been married sixty-five years. A recent stroke leaves her in terrible pain. She pleads with the doctor to kill her. The doctor refuses. The eighty-seven-year-old husband goes to the hospital and shoots her. He is immediately arrested.

New Orleans. For years, the forty-three-year-old husband (the victim), a dry cleaner operator, has beaten his thirty-five-year-old wife. At the time of the murder the two are fighting and the husband stabs her in the back. She grabs the knife and stabs him, causing him to bleed to death. She is arrested the same day. She claims self-defense and the victim's family voices no objection.

New Orleans. The twenty-eight-year-old husband (the victim) has a long history of assaulting his twenty-five-year-old wife. At the time of the murder a witness sees the husband in the kitchen chasing the wife with a machete in his hand. The fight ends when the wife stabs the husband once. She is arrested the same day and claims self-defense.

Los Angeles. During an argument, the fifty-year-old wife (the victim) pulls out a gun and threatens to kill her thirty-nine-year-old unemployed husband. The two struggle. He flees the house and gets in his car. She moves in front of the car, raises the gun, and takes aim. He runs over her. He is arrested a day later.

Orlando, FL. The husband comes home drunk and demands money from his wife. She refuses and he attacks her with a metal pipe. She gets a butcher knife from the kitchen and stabs him once through the heart.

Cases in Which Perpetrators Pleaded Guilty[b]

New Haven, CT. The wife, a twenty-eight-year-old secretary, suffers years of physical and sexual abuse at the hands of her thirty-year-old husband (the victim). Several times he tries to kill her. She stays with him at first because she thinks he will stop, then because she fears he will find her wherever she goes, and then because she fears losing her kids. At some point she buys a gun to defend herself. On the night of the murder she thinks he is possibly going to kill her. In the middle of a beating she grabs the gun from under the mattress and shoots him. She pleads guilty to negligent manslaughter and is sentenced to straight probation (no confinement in prison or jail).

Pittsburgh. The husband (the victim) has a history of beating his wife. On the night of the murder, the husband comes home and begins ordering her around, as he frequently does. The wife leaves the room. When she returns she notices him looking through the closet for the gun. The wife earlier hid it under the bed. While he is searching, the wife retrieves the gun and shoots him repeatedly. She claims she was tired of the abuse. She pleaded guilty to nonnegli gent manslaughter and was sentenced to straight probation (no confinement in prison or jail).

Dayton, OH. The husband (the victim) and his common-law wife are arguing about a variety of things. Throughout the argument the husband beats her. When the husband comes after her in the kitchen, she grabs a knife. She stabs him in the back as he is walking away. She pleaded guilty to negligent manslaughter and was sentenced to two years in prison.

Cases in Which Perpetrators Were Acquitted[c]

Miami. The couple has an on-again, off-again relationship for twenty years. Several weeks prior to the murder, she sees her common-law husband (the victim) leave a motel with another woman. Subsequently, the couple has several violent confrontations until one day she shoots him. The jury acquitted her of all charges.

Chicago. The couple is arguing when the sixty-four-year-old husband (the victim) swings a pipe at his thirty-four-year-old wife. She gets a knife and stabs him to death. The jury acquitted her.

Chicago. The forty-nine-year-old husband (the victim) is drunk and gets into an argument with his fifty-year-old wife. According to her, at some point he throws a fan at her. She gets a knife and lunges at him, cutting his abdomen. The jury acquitted her.

Philadelphia. The thirty-five-year-old husband (the victim) comes home drunk after work and begins fighting with his thirty-one-year-old common-law wife over money he is missing. The husband is throwing things at the wife and her children until she gets a knife and stabs the husband once in the chest. At a bench trial the judge acquitted her.

SOURCES: (a) U.S. Department of Justice, *Spouse Murder Defendants in Large Urban Counties*, 5; (b) ibid., 13–14; (c) ibid., 9.

The disposition of these cases, as indicated by the facts summarized in the table above, largely depended on whether the victim had initiated or provoked violence. Specifically, the study revealed a lower conviction rate of wife defendants compared to husband defendants and hypothesized that this disparity was, in part, a function of the higher frequency of provocation by husbands rather than wives. Based on the information contained in prosecutor files, 44 percent of wife defendants (compared to 10 percent of husband defendants) had been assaulted by their spouses (beaten or threatened with a weapon) at or around the time of the homicide.

According to the study, the victim's aggressive conduct was considered at all stages of the prosecution. Sixteen percent of all women arrested on a charge of spousal homicide were not prosecuted; most of them were screened out because prosecutors concluded that the killing happened in self-defense. In those cases in which wife defendants pleaded guilty, provocation provided grounds for a reduced charge. Finally, in the cases that reached the trial, only 56 percent of the provoked wife defendants were convicted. This number was significantly lower than either the 86 percent conviction rate for unprovoked wife defendants or the 88 percent conviction rate for unprovoked husband defendants.[32] The study concluded that victim provocation may have reduced the likelihood of prosecution and conviction.[33]

It thus appears that sociological theories, factual findings, and the views equally prevalent among the public and members of the criminal justice system all reflect the same intuition, namely, that the victim's own behavior matters. It is often a relevant "but for" cause and even a proximate cause of a crime. In short, victims may be *partly responsible* for their own injury or loss. What about the law? Does it account for victims' conduct, and does it weigh the fault of the defendant against the fault of the victim?

In private law, the answer is clearly "yes." In contracts, a material breach by one party serves as a complete defense to the following breach by the other. In property, an owner's failure to eject an adverse possessor from the estate may result in the owner's loss of the title to that estate. In torts, the closest relative to criminal law, long-established doctrines of comparative fault, consent, and assumption of risk[34] effectively provide that the scope of the defendant's liability depends on the injured party's own acts. The development of tort law doctrine from contributory to comparative fault has eliminated the unfairness of denying recovery to a partially faulty victim and marked a big step toward a more contextualized view of the victim-perpetrator interaction.

Tort "no duty" rules, as applied to plaintiffs, guard against penalizing the victim in a situation in which the victim might have acted stupidly or reprehensibly but did not violate a legal duty to the defendant.[35] For instance, a driver owes no duty to a car thief to lock his car (even though he may owe the same duty to the public).[36] Therefore, the fact that the plaintiff carelessly left his keys in the ignition does not diminish his recovery against the car thief.

Criminal law, on the other hand, has explicitly rejected the idea of comparative liability. It has been said that, according to a nearly universal rule, a victim's own negligence is not a defense in a criminal prosecution.[37] Courts are unanimous in stating that unless it is *the sole* proximate cause of the resulting harm, the victim's conduct is irrelevant.[38] This declaration, however, is not quite accurate. Several criminal law doctrines depart from the declared paradigm. The most prominent among those are the doctrines of consent, self-defense, and provocation. All three condition the scope of the perpetrator's responsibility on the conduct of the victim. Let us examine these doctrines and the role the victim-perpetrator interaction plays in judicial determination of the defendant's fault.

VICTIMS IN CRIMINAL LAW

Consent

The victim's consent to a perpetrator's act is one situation in which the victim's behavior dramatically changes the nature of the perpetrator's criminal liability.[39] The law looks upon the same actions very differently depending on whether they are consensual or not:

> What is called a "fond embrace" when gladly accepted by a sweetheart is called assault and battery when forced upon another without her consent; the act of one who grabs another by the ankles and causes him to fall violently to the ground may result in a substantial jail sentence under some circumstances, but receive thunderous applause if it stops a ball carrier on the grid-iron.[40]

In most instances, valid consent either negatives an element of the offense or justifies what would otherwise be a criminal act.[41] A person is not guilty of rape, kidnapping, theft, or many other serious crimes if what he did was based on a legally valid consent.[42] This rule, however, has exceptions, and in this section I will focus on those with the view of assessing their legitimacy and desirability from the perspective of the philosophy and policies underlying the general theory of consent.

A commentary to the *Model Penal Code* (MPC) lists a number of offenses to which an individual may not give valid consent. The most prominent among them is homicide—the victim's consent to being killed does not justify the perpetrator.[43] Other offenses include riot, escape, breach of the peace, bribery, and bigamy.[44] Interestingly, the reasons for denying the defense of consent in the case of homicide have little in common with the reasons for denying the defense in the other cases. If we look closely at the group of offenses from riot to bigamy, it will be clear why consent may not work as a defense. There is simply no identifiable victim who would be able to give consent and thus legitimize the defendant's conduct. Or, put differently, the victim is the general public, and the general public has already spoken out by adopting a law proscribing the respective behavior.

Homicide is unlike that. There is a specific victim in each act of homicide, the person who was killed. Therefore, it is not the lack of a subject capable of waiving his rights that explains why homicide may not be consented to. The reasons are probably partly historical and partly pragmatic. Historically, the nonrecognition of consent to killing can be explained by the influence on criminal law of Christianity and the Christian moral philosophy that did not view the life of an individual as his own. Blackstone, for example, postulated that one's natural life, being "the immediate donation of the great Creator, cannot legally be disposed of or destroyed by any individual, neither by the person himself, nor by any other of his fellow-creatures, merely upon their own authority."[45] Suicide was a crime; therefore, the victim of a consensual killing was, in fact, the perpetrator's coconspirator and accomplice. Naturally, consent of a cofelon did not suffice to obliterate the criminal nature of the act. This logic, however, holds little force today because, in the overwhelming majority of states, suicide is no longer a crime.[46] Accordingly, there is a strong argument that assisting in a legal act should not be a crime either.

The other explanation for invalidating consent to homicide is not entirely compelling either. It deals with the fear of abuse and manipulation of people in a situation or state of mind when they are not capable of making rational choices of that magnitude. These concerns ought not to be lightly discarded. It is well known, for example, that prolonged ailment or pain makes one feel vulnerable and insecure. Some scholars have opposed physician-assisted suicide, in part, because of the influence physicians may exert over their patients:

"Through their tone, the encouragement they provide or withhold, and the way they present the information available, physicians can often determine the patient's choice."[47] Needless to say, the problem of undue influence and abuse is not limited to the physician-patient relationship. And the state certainly has an interest in protecting "vulnerable groups—including the poor, the elderly and disabled persons—from abuse, neglect, and mistakes."[48]

It is, however, important to distinguish a rule from abuse of that rule. The abuse is something that is *not* the rule, that is *outside* the rule. After all, anything, even a good thing, can be abused and turned into a bad thing, but this is not a reason to prohibit the good thing itself. Sexual abuse, for instance, is a bad thing, but we do not criminalize sex as a result. In other words, when the need for a law stems from the uncertainty regarding the validity (voluntariness and rationality) of an individual's consent, the law should be directed at that uncertainty by demanding persuasive proof of the valid consent and not by taking away the very opportunity to give it.[49]

One could argue that, by criminalizing assisted suicide, we significantly reduce the number of instances when suicide is actually committed.[50] That may be true, but while welcoming this result, we ought to acknowledge that it comes with a price: by reducing the sheer number of harmful incidents, we impose substantial pain and indignity on the ultimate victims—those whose exercise of autonomy is infringed. The Supreme Court signified that an individual has no constitutionally protected right to assisted suicide,[51] yet he may have the right to starve himself to death.[52] It is plausible that fewer people choose this torturous way of dying compared to the number of those who would choose death by a lethal injection. But does this disparity justify continued criminalization of assisted suicide? To answer this question, suppose that a legislature considers a bill promoting a new level of capital punishment for particularly egregious crimes: death by starvation. Assume further that the bill is accompanied by a convincing study, which shows that by this simple change in the form of the death penalty we can reduce the violent crime rate by 50 percent. Deterrence is one of the main priorities of criminal justice; however, it is highly unlikely that the reduction of crime (and even the accompanying reduction in the number of death penalties) would make us adopt such a law. And if we are unwilling to make criminals suffer a painful and degrading death despite any potential decrease in the number of crimes and executions, how can we use the same numerical argument to prohibit humane forms of dying to noncriminals?

Finally, denying an individual the right to suicide leads to absurd results in any jurisdiction that recognizes the death penalty. A person wishing to die can achieve his goal only by murdering someone else and thus forfeiting the right to life which he cannot alienate voluntarily. And a person wishing to die with someone else's help can receive that help from one person only, his executioner. Joel Feinberg correctly warned:

> Those who believe in the inalienability of the right to life . . . might well think twice before enforcing its forfeitability. . . . Whenever the right in question can be thought of as burdensome baggage, it cannot be made inalienable *and* forfeitable without encouraging wrongdoing—the pursuit of relief through "error, fault, offense, or crime."[53]

But even without homicide, there remains a group of offenses to which a person may not consent. For instance, one may not lawfully agree to be maimed or severly tortured. Consent to a fight is not a good defense either, but under the MPC, a consensual fight is a lesser offense than nonconsensual.[54] Very few jurisdictions, however, have followed the mitigation envisioned by the MPC.[55] Some states, while adopting the general language of the provision, did not include the mitigation afforded by the MPC.[56] Other states explicitly rejected the mutual character of combat as a partial defense.[57]

As a complete defense, consent to physical harm is recognized even more reluctantly. Under the MPC, for example, consent of the victim exonerates the perpetrator only in three sets of circumstances: (1) when the injury is not serious,[58] (2) when the injury or its risks are "reasonably foreseeable hazards" of participation in a "lawful athletic contest or competitive sport or other concerted activity not forbidden by law,"[59] and (3) when the bodily harm was inflicted for the purpose of a "recognized form of treatment" intended to improve the patient's physical or mental health.[60] Unfortunately, this definition, which reflects the law in the majority of states,[61] does not give much practical guidance. What harm is not serious? What harmful "concerted activities" are "not forbidden by law"? And what can be viewed as a "recognized" form of treatment? Let us examine these questions one by one.

What Harm Is "Not Serious"? Today's penal statutes classify a bodily injury as serious if it "creates a substantial risk of death or . . . causes serious, permanent disfigurement, or protracted loss or impairment of the function of any bodily member or organ."[62] As this definition indicates, "serious harm" may be deemed to result from two kinds of actions—those that caused permanent debilitating injuries and those that caused *any* bodily injury, if such injury creates a "substantial risk of death." The second category leaves so much room for interpretation that courts have frequently made use of this opportunity to inflate the risk of death in order to denounce an unwanted activity.

For example, in *In re J.A.P.*, a group of eighth graders played the game of "passout," the object of which was for one player to make a fellow player faint.[63] The defendant grabbed his friend around the neck and proceeded to choke him for a few seconds until that boy lost consciousness and fell on the ground. The victim suffered a few facial lacerations and chipped teeth. By the time of the trial, all his injuries had been treated and healed. Nevertheless, the juvenile court concluded that the defendant had engaged in delinquent conduct by committing aggravated assault, an offense which required a finding of "serious bodily harm."[64]

On appeal, the *J.A.P.* court opined that in determining whether the evidence supports a finding of such harm, "the relevant issue is the quality of the injury as it was inflicted, not after the effects are ameliorated by medical treatment."[65] The court concluded that a rational juror could determine that the act of choking presented a substantial risk of death; thus the "serious harm" element of the charged offense was established. Accordingly, because one may not give valid consent to "serious harm," whether or not the victim had consented to the choking was irrelevant for the defendant's liability. What the court apparently overlooked is that, under the state law, a "serious injury" was defined as an *injury* that created a substantial risk of death, not merely an *activity* that created such a risk.[66] Otherwise, following the court's logic, a driver who exceeded the speed limit and was stopped by the police before he had a chance to get into any accident would be automatically guilty of causing serious injuries to his passengers even though none of them had suffered a scratch.

In one particular context, courts have managed to find "serious harm" in virtually every case, irrespective of the extent of injuries. Those are cases arising out of consensual sadomasochistic sexual activities. As the MPC Commentary acknowledges, the "iniquity of the conduct involved" tends to affect judicial assessment of the seriousness of the harm.[67] In *State v. Collier*, for instance, the victim's injuries consisted of "a swollen lip, large welts on her ankles, wrists, hips, buttocks, and severe bruises on her thighs."[68] The defendant was convicted of assault resulting in a serious injury, and the appellate court agreed with the verdict even though, as the dissenting judge pointed out, the inflicted bodily harm did not constitute a serious injury within the meaning of the state statute.[69]

The MPC and some state penal codes include physical pain in the definition of "bodily harm."[70] In *State v. Guinn*, for example, the defendant was convicted of inflicting "serious physical injury" in the course of a sexual encounter.[71] There was no evidence that the victim "ever required any medical attention or suffered any wounds of any sort."[72] Yet the appellate court sustained the assault conviction, reasoning that the sadomasochistic paraphernalia the defendant used must have caused serious physical pain—the candle wax was "hot and it stung" and the nipple clamps were "tight and cutting"—and "serious physical pain" satisfied the definition of "serious physical injury."[73] Naturally, under a statute of this type, practically any sadomasochistic activity automatically qualifies as criminal.

Even in the rare instance when a court feels compelled to give weight to the victim's consent, the opinion still tends to reiterate the traditional rule. In *People v. Jovanovic*, for example, the New York Appellate Court held:

> Indeed, while a meaningful distinction can be made between an ordinary violent beating and violence in which both parties voluntarily participate for their own sexual gratification, nevertheless, just as a person cannot consent to his or her own murder, as a matter of public policy, a person cannot avoid criminal responsibility for an assault that causes injury or carries a risk of serious harm, even if the victim asked for or consented to the act.[74]

Consequently, the court ignored the requirements of basic logic and did both: declared that consent of the victim may not serve as a defense to the charge of assault and, at the same time, reversed the defendant's assault conviction on the grounds that the trial judge had improperly excluded evidence indicating the victim's consent.[75] Still, this decision is unique in its recognition of a difference between consensual and nonconsensual brutality. As a general matter, courts habitually exaggerate the seriousness of injury or pain and the risk of death in order to condemn an unwanted activity. Like in other instances when an argument is used not for its own sake but as a proxy for an unspoken consideration, these decisions frequently reveal conceptual manipulation and poor reasoning.

What Harmful "Concerted Activities" Are "Not Forbidden By Law"? Originally, MPC section 2.11(2)(b) recognized consent as a defense for the harmful conduct of the perpetrator and bodily injuries of the victim only when those harms were "reasonably foreseeable hazards of joint participation in a lawful athletic contest or competitive sport."[76] In 1962, this provision was expanded to add at the end "or other concerted activity not forbidden by law."[77] According to the MPC Commentary and materials of the American Law Institute (ALI) proceedings, the new language was intended to cover activities that are "more appropriately characterized as exhibitions than as sports or athletic contests."[78] But did the drafters intend to limit "other concerted activity not forbidden by law" only to exhibitions? The ALI reporters explicitly excluded certain events, such as a duel or a scuffle, from the protection of the new language in section 2.11(2)(b).[79] It is likely, although not specifically provided, that other harmful hostile activities, such as hazing, are not covered by the revised section either.[80] What is less clear is whether *nonhostile* consensual private encounters, such as religious mortification, sadomasochistic sex, or voluntary contracting of HIV, may be entitled to legal protection.

Historically, courts have viewed religious flagellation as a lawful activity.[81] In an 1847 Scottish case, the court said: "In some cases, a beating may be consented to as in the case of a father confessor ordering flagellation; but this is not violence or assault, because there is consent."[82] The practice still exists in a number of nations with a strong Roman Catholic tradition. The Philippines, for example, is famous for its bloody crucifixion reenactment ceremonies that happen every year on Good Friday and attract large crowds of local and foreign tourists.[83] Opus Dei, a conservative Catholic movement, encourages "corporal mortification," which can include flagellation done by another person.[84] "Such acts are said to help bolster self-discipline and recall the suffering of Christ."[85]

In the United States, religious flagellation is practiced mainly in southwestern states.[86] Although courts have said that the law "may prohibit religiously impelled physical attacks,"[87] research has revealed no legal cases, which suggests that religious flagellation has not been subject to criminal prosecution. Moreover, some states have statutes regulating ritual mutilation. The Illinois Criminal Code, for instance, provides that

> [a] person commits the offense of ritual mutilation, when he or she mutilates, dismembers or tortures another person as part of a ceremony, rite, initiation,

> observance, performance or practice, *and the victim did not consent or under such circumstances that the defendant knew or should have known that the victim was unable to render effective consent.*[88]

The italicized language implies that if the religious mutilation, dismemberment, or torture is done *with* the consent of a legally competent victim, such activity should be lawful. In its consultation paper, the Law Commission of England and Wales sympathetically describes a woman who belongs to the liberal edge of the Roman Catholic Church and "takes her religion seriously":[89]

> For many years she has occasionally found self-mortification the appropriate penance, if she has behaved in a way that falls gravely short of what a committed Christian faith involves. . . . Now that she is married, her husband helps her. He inflicts an adequate level of pain to ensure that the punishment is full and effective. As she put it, the threshold for "actual bodily harm" is clearly exceeded.[90]

People may approve or disapprove of the way this couple practices religion. However, under the current law, both in theory and in practice, the "religious" husband is not guilty of any offense. At the same time, if his primary motive for the infliction of pain were not religious but sexual gratification, he most likely would be convicted of assault.[91] Any attempts to present sadomasochistic sex as "other concerted activity" have failed. In *State v. Collier*, for example, the court held that the legislature did not intend to include sadomasochistic goings-on in the list of "sport, social or other activity" under the Iowa Code.[92]

The different treatment of the two kinds of flagellation is disturbing: in both instances the perpetrator may perform the exact same acts, with consent of the victim, and for the purpose of satisfying the emotional need of the victim. Yet, if that emotional need has a sexual undertone, the perpetrator is likely to be convicted of a felony. It appears that this rule is a typical example of morals legislation intended to punish the perpetrator for causing a "wrong" kind of satisfaction.

While consensual infliction of pain during a sadomasochistic encounter constitutes assault, boxing remains entirely legal, despite the often severe battering caused by the fighters to each other. One court aptly described the sport as an "activity, in which participants excel by injuring their opponents. Indeed, the very acme of achievement for a boxer is to so batter the opponent as to induce a temporary coma—otherwise known as a knockout."[93] The court pointed out that permanent injuries and even death sometimes result from those fights and that, in any other context, "such an activity would be unacceptable, indeed, criminal."[94] Another judge in a British case made a similar observation finding it "very strange that a fight in private between two youths where one may, at most, get a bloody nose should be unlawful, whereas a boxing match where one heavyweight fighter seeks to knock out his opponent and possibly do him very serious damage should be lawful."[95]

Even more surprisingly, consensual intentional transmission of HIV is not punishable in a significant number of states. The phenomenon, known as "bug-chasing," involves "bug-chasers" (HIV-negative men who actively seek out infection by having unprotected sex with infected partners) and "gift givers" (HIV-positive men willing to infect "bug-chasers"). According to a source, this practice is the cause of 25 percent of all new infections among American gay men.[96] These statistics have been questioned, but even if they are not entirely accurate, there is a general consensus that "bug-chasing" and "gift-giving" present a serious problem for the gay community.[97] Nevertheless, out of twenty-four states that have statutes criminalizing the act of knowingly exposing another human being to HIV, eight states explicitly recognize consent of the victim as an affirmative defense,[98] and another ten reach the same outcome by making failure to disclose one's HIV status an element of the crime.[99] The discrepancy and inconsistency in the treatment of different kinds of harmful behavior highlight the need for a more coherent rule of consent.

What Is a "Recognized Form of Treatment"? Just as it is not easy to distinguish "serious" and "nonserious" harm, it is hard to differentiate between recognized and experimental forms of treatment.[100] Sometimes judicial characterization depends on the "regulatory status of a product or the novelty of a procedure, while in other instances an established product or procedure may become experimental simply because a research protocol aims to investigate its use."[101] A few courts have invalidated—as unconstitutionally vague—state statutes that criminalized certain medical procedures characterized as "experimental."[102]

The existing rules are often puzzling as to why the line between the lawful and unlawful conduct was drawn where it was. For example, a woman who carries a breast cancer gene may choose to have a preventive mastectomy.[103] Such a radical surgery is considered to be controversial in medical literature:

there is little proof that for purposes of cancer prevention it is superior to less extreme and less disfiguring alternatives.[104] For women with "familial breast cancer syndrome," a condition indicating a high risk for developing breast cancer,[105] the main advantage of the surgery is that it helps to relieve chronic stress and anxiety over the substantial likelihood of developing the disease.[106]

Yet no amount of emotional pain legitimizes an elective surgery on a patient with Body Integrity Identity Disorder (BIID), a rare ailment whose victims seek to become amputees.[107] The limited statistics seem to indicate that if BIID patients succeed in their pursuit, their quality of life improves dramatically.[108] A surgeon who agrees to perform such an amputation, however, opens himself up to criminal liability because his patients' consent is legally invalid.[109] The BIID patients often compare themselves to those suffering from Gender Identity Disorders (GID), describing the common experience as "being trapped in the wrong body."[110] The law, however, treats the two groups very differently: the GID patients can consent to a sex change operation, which often involves removal of healthy sexual organs,[111] whereas the BIID sufferers cannot consent to amputation of an arm or a leg.[112] Rejected by the medical community, some BIID sufferers turn to self-help or illegal practitioners in order to achieve their goal—the amputation of unwanted limbs:

> In May of 1998 a seventy-nine-year-old man from New York traveled to Mexico and paid $10,000 for a black-market leg amputation; he died of gangrene in a motel. In October 1999 a mentally competent man in Milwaukee severed his arm with a homemade guillotine, and threatened to sever it again if surgeons reattached it. That same month a legal investigator for the California state bar, after being refused a hospital amputation, tied off her legs with tourniquets and began to pack them in ice, hoping that gangrene would set in, necessitating an amputation. She passed out and ultimately gave up. Now she says she will probably have to lie under a train, or shoot her legs off with a shotgun.[113]

To what extent all these restrictions are justified is an open question. On the one hand, the liberal tradition with its emphasis on personal autonomy opposes criminal limitations on the decision-making power of rational adult citizens if their choices do not directly harm others.[114] On the other hand, considerations of moral dignity support the intuition shared by many that not every consensual injury should be permitted. This conflict of fundamental human values has been the subject of political, public, and academic debates in a number of countries. Consider two recent cases, one from Germany and the other from Great Britain, which have attracted a lot of publicity in their own countries and far beyond.

The German case started in late 2000, when Armin Meiwes, a forty-two-year-old computer technician, posted a message in an Internet chat room devoted to cannibalism: "[S]eeking well-built man, 18–30 years old, for slaughter."[115] A few months later, Bernd Juergen Brandes, a forty-three-year-old microchip engineer, replied: "I offer myself to you and will let you dine from my live body. Not butchery, dining!!"[116]

The two men exchanged numerous e-mails, discussing details of the prospective killing and dining. Brandes even joked about their both being smokers: "Good, smoked meat lasts longer."[117] On March 9, 2001, Brandes arrived at Meiwes's place.

> Brandes swallowed twenty sleeping tablets and half a bottle of schnapps. Then Meiwes cut off part of his body and fried it as a snack for them both. Brandes was bleeding to death, but still not dead when Meiwes stabbed him in the neck after a goodbye kiss. Then Meiwes butchered him and froze the flesh. Eventually he ate about 20kg, washing it down with a South African red.[118]

At his trial, Meiwes admitted to killing, dismembering, and eating Brandes. His principal defense was the victim's consent. Meiwes was convicted of manslaughter and sentenced to eight and one-half years in prison. The three-judge German court rejected the prosecution's plea for murder on the grounds that Meiwes had followed the victim's instructions.[119] Both the prosecution and the defense appealed the verdict, and the Federal Court of Justice, Germany's highest criminal court, ordered a retrial, saying that Meiwes's manslaughter conviction was too lenient. In 2006, Meiwes was convicted of murder and sentenced to life in prison.[120] The new verdict was affirmed by the Federal Court of Justice in 2007.[121]

The events that led to *Regina v. Brown*, the British case, happened a few years earlier in London. In the course of a very high-profile "Operation Spanner," several men were prosecuted for their involvement in sadomasochistic activities. Those activities were conducted in private between willing adult members of a gay club and were subject to certain rules including a code word by which the masochistic participants could stop infliction of pain whenever they wanted to. Although no member of the group had ever filed a police complaint or suffered an injury requiring medical attention, the defendants were charged with assault and unlawful wounding and pleaded guilty after the trial judge ruled that they could not raise consent of their partners as a defense.

The defendants were convicted and sentenced to prison terms ranging from several months to several years. The verdict was appealed first to the Court of Appeal and then to the House of Lords. Both appeals failed as the courts refused to recognize "satisfying of sado-masochistic libido"[122] as a reason to expand an individual's power to consent to injury.[123] The case was then appealed to the European Court of Human Rights, but "in a disappointing, poorly argued judgment, the Strasbourg Court simply endorsed the reasoning of the majority in the House of Lords, and unanimously rejected the applicants' complaint."[124]

The court decisions in *Brown* provoked numerous discussions and publications, most of which were critical of the judicial reasoning and the outcome of the case. The Law Commission of England and Wales, an independent governmental organ responsible for the systematic development of criminal legislation, issued two consultation papers, which analyzed the law of consent and called for its reform.[125] In the words of the commission, *Brown* "cast fresh light on the unprincipled way in which [the rules of consent] had developed, and revealed considerable disagreement about the basis and policy of the present law, its detailed limits and its scope for future development."[126] The commission has assembled and analyzed numerous cases, attempting to work out general principles of the law of consent, but the attempt proved to be largely unsuccessful.[127] No legislative recommendations were issued and no reforms followed.[128] Eventually, in 2001, the commission admitted its inability to reach consensus and terminated the consent project.[129]

Similarly, in the United States, the rules governing individuals' ability to consent to bodily harm remain largely uncertain and outdated. On the one hand, even when harm is as grave as death, the victim's cooperative conduct often reduces the perpetrator's criminal liability. For example, the victim's consent is viewed as a mitigating circumstance for the purposes of capital punishment by both the MPC and the majority of jurisdictions that impose the death penalty.[130] On the other hand, serious bodily harm has been largely excluded from the defense of consent. This rule needs to be revised to balance the interests of individual autonomy and collective dignity and to be consistent with the general theory of consent, pursuant to which, in all instances where (1) there is an identifiable victim (2) capable of giving legally valid consent and (3) in fact, voluntarily consenting to the perpetrator's act that infringes on some legally recognized right of the victim, the law, at least partially, takes that consent into account to reduce the perpetrator's liability.

Self-Defense

A whole group of defenses (self-defense, defense of another, and defense of property) are predicated on the unlawful harm about to be inflicted on the defendant or a third person by the putative victim. Just like the defense of consent, these defenses reveal the fallacy of the statement that the victim's conduct may have a bearing on the perpetrator's liability only when the victim is *the sole* proximate cause of the resulting harm. The aggressor-turned-victim is certainly not the proximate cause of his own death or injury. It is the target of his attack (or someone acting on his behalf) who intentionally chose to use preventive force against the perceived harm or threat of harm. Nonetheless, all state laws as well as the MPC completely exonerate the person who reasonably defended himself or another. Since this group of defenses is based on a single rationale, I will focus on self-defense as a characteristic representative.

What a person may do in self-defense depends to a large degree on what the aggressor attempted to do to that person—in other words, the scope of justified behavior is fundamentally determined by the acts of the victim. For instance, under the MPC, the use of deadly force is permitted only in the face of death, serious injury, forcible rape, or kidnapping.[131] It would be clearly inappropriate to use deadly force in order to prevent shoplifting. In allocating rights between the person acting in self-defense and the victim-aggressor, the law looks at the conduct of both parties. Most states, for example, deny the initial aggressor the right to defend himself even when his initial, minor attack was met with a grossly excessive response.[132]

What matters for self-defense is the kind of threat posed by the victim-aggressor, not his moral or legal culpability. Thus, an unoffending party may be justified if he kills a child or an insane assailant attacking him with a handgun.[133] He may be justified even if he kills a sleepwalking aggressor, that is, someone who has committed no voluntary act at all.[134] Of course, each of these cases assumes that no less drastic alternative was available.

Although a person may be justified in killing an innocent *aggressor*, he is never justified in killing an innocent *bystander*—even if this is the only way to save his own life. In fact, he may not defend himself against a deadly aggressor if by doing so he will also have to kill an innocent bystander.[135] These examples show that what distinguishes permissible self-defense from impermissible is the actions of the victim—the defendant's liability depends on whether or not the victim has attacked him.

The case of innocent aggressors should be distinguished from the case of innocent actors who are mistakenly perceived by the defendant as aggressors. All criminal codes grant a mistaken defender justification, so long as the mistake was "reasonable."[136] In addition, many states recognize "imperfect self-defense" and partially excuse actors who killed another under an unreasonable belief that the circumstances justified the killing.[137] The MPC justifies all acts of self-defense, reasonable or unreasonable, based on mistaken but sincere beliefs, although the defender may be liable for the negligent or reckless use of force if his beliefs were held negligently or recklessly.[138] Yet it is far from obvious that the MPC is correct in characterizing mistaken self-defense as justification.[139]

Justification means that, in addition to having the required state of mind, the actor was *objectively right* in what he did, whereas excuse focuses on the actor's inability to make the right choice under the circumstances and forgives him for the wrong he has committed. The victim's conduct may be a mitigating consideration primarily under the justificatory rationale—we look to the victim's conduct to determine whether the defendant was right in his response to it. Specifically, in self-defense, we assign the responsibility for the resulting harm to the aggressor. But if the defendant made a mistake and there was no aggressor, how can we say that the defendant was "right"?

Certainly, we cannot blame a defendant who, through no fault of his, lacked the necessary information. Because of the cognitive impairment, he was not a fully responsible agent, just as children or the insane, through no fault of theirs, are not fully responsible agents. That is why consent given by minors, the mentally ill, or ill-informed individuals is legally invalid. A reasonably mistaken person is perhaps the most sympathetic kind of a defendant. However, our understanding of his predicament does not change the fact that we exculpate him because of his objectively limited understanding of the situation, assuming that he would have behaved differently had he known the facts.

For those reasons, it is conceptually more accurate to analyze mistaken self-defense as excuse rather than justification. Although the perpetrator may have numerous grounds for mitigating his fault, both justificatory and excusatory, only the actual attack by the victim presents grounds for moral approval (or at least acceptance but not merely forgiveness) of the perpetrator's act. Accordingly, only actual aggression by the victim may be considered for the purposes of comparative criminal liability.

Provocation

The defense of provocation, or "heat of passion,"[140] represents another illustration of the impact the victim's behavior may have on the perpetrator's criminal liability. This defense mitigates what otherwise would be murder to manslaughter and is available to someone who killed in the heat of passion following a serious provocation. This partial defense is incorporated in all state laws as well as the MPC.

This defense has been the subject of ongoing academic debate as to why the law treats killing more leniently when it is provoked. Do we mitigate the defendant's fault because of his subjective state of mind ("extreme mental or emotional disturbance," using the words of the MPC[141]) or because the victim's own wrongful acts make the victim partially responsible for the suffered harm;[142] in other words, is this defense a partial excuse or a partial justification?[143] In this section, I suggest that provocation is largely (although not exclusively) a partial defense of justification and another example of an established criminal doctrine that reduces the perpetrator's liability because of the victim's conduct.

We need to start with a more general question, however. What does it mean to say *partial* justification? Normally, justified conduct is that which "the law does not condemn, [and] even welcomes."[144] It is "a good thing, or the right or sensible thing, or a permissible thing to do."[145] When conduct is justified, the message the law sends is clear: you did the right (or at least a permissible) thing; if ever in similar circumstances, you may do it again.[146] That message works well for *complete* defenses of justification, such as self-defense or necessity. But what is the message contained in a *partial* justification? May you do what you did again? The answer is certainly "no," since a partial defense only mitigates but does not completely eliminate the wrongfulness of a criminal act.

That answer has led some scholars to reject the very possibility of a partial justification. If certain conduct is wrongful, how can it be justified, even partially, asks Suzanne Uniacke.[147] In Uniacke's view, a partial defense can only be excusatory.[148] I find this position flawed. The fact that, despite a valid defense, we still condemn the defendant's act means only that his defense is partial; it does not determine the nature of the defense.

Much more persuasive is Douglas Husak in his analysis of defenses in the context of theories of punishment. It is usually accepted that "justifications and excuses are *desert-based* rationales for reducing the severity of the defendant's sentence."[149] A complete justification reduces the wrongfulness of an act, whereas a complete excuse reduces the blameworthiness of an actor, in both instances to such a degree[150] that the actor's behavior does not merit punishment.[151] That same logic applies to partial defenses, but the degree to which the wrongfulness of an act or the culpability of an actor is reduced does not eliminate liability altogether; instead, the liability is mitigated.[152] A partial justification, therefore, renders the *act less wrongful* and a partial excuse renders the *actor less blameworthy* compared to what they would have been in the absence of the mitigating factor.[153]

In light of that, is provocation a partial justification or a partial excuse? For the majority of scholars who have addressed the issue, it is the latter.[154] Joshua Dressler, who has authored a number of insightful writings about the defense of provocation and argued against its abolition, maintains that society places too high a value on human life to justify, even partially, an intentional killing of a mere wrongdoer.[155]

This conclusion appears rather doubtful. There are circumstances when the law reduces liability for homicide based on something done by the decedent prior to death. For example, assisted suicide is a lesser offense than murder under both the MPC and the codes or case law of most states.[156] The victim's consent to, or participation in, the homicide is a mitigating factor for the purposes of capital punishment both under the MPC and the laws of the majority of death penalty jurisdictions.[157] Mitigation based on the victim's conduct makes sense only if the rationale for such mitigation is justificatory; were it excusatory, the law would focus on the perpetrator's capacity instead. Therefore, the high value assigned to human life is not by itself a sufficient reason to deny partial justification to the defense of provocation.

Another of Dressler's arguments is more compelling. He observes that if the "heat of passion" defense is to be explained in justificatory terms, "it must also be recognized that the title of the defense is then a misnomer."[158] Indeed, "[u]nder a justificatory theory, it is not the defendant's mental state but victim's conduct, which primarily explains the rule. To be consistent, passion should not be required."[159]

It is true that the name "heat of passion" reflects only the subjective component of the defense—the defendant's temporary volitional impairment.[160]

However, its other name, the defense of provocation, focuses more on the objective picture of the crime: it is the provocation by the victim that is central to the defense. Anyway, as interesting as linguistic evidence can be, "what's in a name?"[161]

It is perhaps more important to acknowledge that a defense does not have to be based on a single underlying principle. A product of historical tradition, political compromise, and changing cultural norms, the law often combines elements of more than one rationale. A justification defense may include a subjective component. For example, to invoke a justification defense of necessity, the defendant has to prove, inter alia, that he (subjectively) believed his conduct to be necessary to avoid harm to himself or another and that the harm he caused is (objectively) lesser than the harm or evil he was able to avoid. The presence of a subjective component does not, however, strip necessity of its justificatory nature.

The same is true with respect to the partial defense of provocation. It certainly includes a subjective component (the defendant's state of reduced self-control). However, the only emotions that are taken into account are "anger, rage, resentment, or terror"[162] directed at the putative victim, that is, emotions *responsive* to an offense upon the defendant. The defense is available only to the extent the violent reaction of the defendant was commensurable with the provoking event. As one of the most respected treatises on criminal law points out,

> [t]he problem of provocation in the homicide cases cannot be considered effectively without keeping constantly in mind the relation of the retaliatory act to the provocative one. The foundation principle is that where the former is not unreasonably excessive and out of proportion to the latter, the basis of mitigation is established (if the latter was not altogether inadequate), but where it is unreasonably excessive and out of proportion no mitigation will be recognized.[163]

The requirement of proportionality is a natural component of justificatory defenses. One may use only such force in self-defense as is proportionate to the threat facing him; one may never use deadly force for the defense of mere property.[164] But excusatory defenses are fundamentally different. With one policy exception (most states do not permit the defense of duress in homicide cases, although the MPC does),[165] exculpatory defenses by and large ignore the harmfulness of the act and focus instead on the mental and emotional adequacy of the actor. Indeed, it would be neither logical nor fair to condition the availability of the defense of insanity, minority, or mistake on the amount of harm caused by a madman, infant, or someone whose perception was totally distorted. Even in those cases of duress, in which the defendant causes much more serious harm than the harm he was threatened with, the defense is still available. In fact, the defense of duress is relied upon *precisely* when the defendant has caused harm that is not less significant than the harm with which he was threatened. Otherwise he would have been eligible for the defense of necessity or would not have been prosecuted at all.[166] In short, the very fact that the *partial* defense of provocation requires proportionality while even *complete* defenses of insanity, minority, or mistake do not signals that provocation has a strong justificatory component.

Moreover, a number of penal codes, following the broader MPC version of the defense, require an objectively "reasonable explanation or excuse"[167] for the defendant's emotional disturbance. Why would the law require a reasonable explanation for the unreasonable behavior (killing)? Partly, as evidence of true loss of self-control. However, if the only rationale for the mitigating defense were excusatory, it should also be available to any defendant who can prove honest but unreasonable rage (just as, in a number of states, imperfect self-defense is available to a person who honestly but unreasonably believes that circumstances justify the killing).[168] The fact that the law asks not only how badly the actor was distressed but also *why* he was so badly distressed[169] implies that the rationale for the defense lies in the *source* of provocation, not merely the actor's disturbed state of mind.

Consider *People v. Spurlin*.[170] In that case, the defendant killed his wife after an intense argument over their mutual infidelities and then killed their sleeping nine-year-old son with a hammer blow to his head. Assuming that Spurlin was entitled to the defense of provocation for the killing of his wife, should he have been allowed to invoke the same defense for the killing of their child? If we believe in the excusatory "heat of passion" rationale, the answer should be yes. Indeed, what proves the lack of self-control better than a deadly attack directed at an innocent child?

Yet, many of us would probably feel uncomfortable with that answer. After all, the intentional killing of an innocent unoffending person is an absolute taboo in the Anglo-American legal tradition. In the famous case *Regina v. Dudley and Stephens*,[171] two starving men, after twenty days in a lifeboat and nine days without food, killed a boy to save their lives by feeding on his flesh.

A few days later, they were picked up and rescued by a passing ship. At the trial for murder, Dudley and Stephens raised necessity as their defense. Despite the court's empathy for "how terrible the [defendants'] temptation was; how awful the suffering,"[172] the court rejected their claim, saying that there is no defense to taking the life of another "when that other is neither attempting nor threatening [to take] yours, nor is guilty of any illegal act whatever towards you or anyone else."[173] Today as well, no American state recognizes necessity as a full or partial defense to murder.[174] Similarly, in the vast majority of states, duress does not exonerate[175] or mitigate[176] intentional killing of an innocent. Neither may a person defend himself against a deadly attack if, while doing so, he has to kill an innocent party.

Comparing necessity, duress, and self-defense with the "heat of passion," I cannot help but wonder: if all sorts of overwhelming emotions—such as despair, compassion, or fear of imminent death—do not reduce perpetrators' culpability for killing an innocent, why should rage provoked by someone else? If we deny mitigation to a man who shot his victim because of the fear induced by a third party,[177] how can we grant it to a man who bludgeoned a sleeping child to death because of the rage induced by a third party? And if we cannot grant it, we have to reject the excusatory rationale as the sole ground for the partial defense of provocation, as, in fact, do courts and legislatures of a number of states pursuant to the doctrine of "misdirected retaliation."[178]

The doctrine of misdirected retaliation denies mitigation from murder to manslaughter in cases in which the victim did nothing to provoke the attack. In most American jurisdictions, the defense of provocation requires that the homicide occur as a result of the victim's own provocation.[179] In contrast, if "one who has received adequate provocation is so enraged that he intentionally vents his wrath upon an innocent bystander, causing his death, he will be guilty of murder."[180]

This common-law view of provocation clearly derives from the justificatory principle. It assumes that even though the defendant acted under the "heat of passion," his guilt may be reduced only with respect to the victim who is *partially responsible* for the defendant's unhinged emotional state.[181] In some states, the law also authorizes mitigation if the defendant's "deadly force was directed at the provoker and hit the other by accident, or if as a reasonable mistake of fact he thought the provocative act had been perpetrated by the deceased."[182] As I discussed earlier in connection with self-defense, I find it more appropriate to treat cases of mistake (including a reasonable mistake) as excuse and not justification.[183]

Under the MPC, it does not matter who provoked the offender.[184] The commentaries to section 210.3(1)(b) provide that the offender's emotional distress does not have to arise from some "injury, affront, or other provocative act"[185] attributable to the deceased. Several states have provisions modeled after section 210.3(1)(b),[186] but this does not mean that they automatically decline the doctrine of misdirected retaliation. Quite often states adopt the text of an MPC provision but reject a position expressed in the commentary. For example, the MPC language regarding duress and necessity has been very influential among the states; however, the view (expressed in the commentaries) extending these defenses to prosecution for murder is followed in the case of necessity by none of the states and in the case of duress by very few.

Similarly, some states that describe provocation in terms of "extreme mental or emotional disturbance" at the same time, either by statute or by case law, reject the MPC view authorizing mitigation for the killing of a non-provoker.[187] In *Spurlin*, for instance, the court admitted that the California Penal Code is silent on the source of provocation. Nonetheless, citing common-law principles and interpretations of those principles adopted by several other jurisdictions, the court concluded that, for the provocation defense to be available, "the deceased must be the source of the defendant's rage or passion."[188]

The same rationale plays a role in the traditional common-law requirement that the provocative act occur in the presence of the provoked killer. Explaining his disapproval of a more relaxed standard, a judge wrote:

> It would, it seems to me, be extremely mischievous to let passion engendered by something one has heard, enter into and determine the nature of a crime committed while under its influence. *The innocent as well as the guilty, or those who had not as well as those who had given provocation, might be the sufferers.*[189]

In sum, the partial defense of provocation includes elements of both excusatory and justificatory rationales. The emphasis most states put on the objectively reasonable explanation of the defendant's rage indicates, however, that the source of provocation is crucial for mitigation. In other words, it is the provoked *act* that is less wrongful, not simply the provoked *actor* that is less culpable. Moreover, the doctrine of misdirected retaliation can be explained only in terms of partial justification. It is the behavior of the victim that partially justifies the offense. This does not mean that it is right to kill a provoker;

this only means that it is less wrong to kill a provoker than to kill an innocent victim. Therefore, the provocation defense, just like defenses of consent and self-defense, is at least partially predicated on the victim's conduct.

• • •

The foregoing review of the doctrines of consent, self-defense, and provocation reveals that the rule according to which the victim's conduct is deemed irrelevant to the perpetrator's liability has exceptions so broad that it can hardly be called a rule. In most cases of consent, self-defense, and provocation, the law reduces or completely eliminates the perpetrator's liability based on the acts of the victim that prompted the perpetrator's harmful act toward that victim. This inevitably raises a normative question: should not the law, as a coherent system of norms, apply the principle of victims' contributory responsibility across the board? Chapter 2 sets forth policy arguments in favor of treating the conduct of the victim as a factor affecting the criminal liability of the perpetrator.

2 WHY DOES CRIMINAL LAW NEED A GENERIC DEFENSE OF COMPARATIVE CRIMINAL LIABILITY?

FAIR AND EFFICIENT PUNISHMENT

The primary reason to consider the role of the victim in the committed offense is a sense that, at least in some circumstances, it affects the liability of the perpetrator and the punishment he should receive.[1] Conceptually, theories of punishment fall into two large groups, retributive and utilitarian. For a retributivist, punishment is justified because the offender deserves it; for a utilitarian, it is justified if it promotes some societal good.[2]

Retributivist Considerations

The dominant theory of punishment underlying Anglo-American criminal doctrine is retributivism, according to which punishment is justified by the desert of the offender. Although other goals, such as deterrence, incapacitation, and rehabilitation, may affect penal policies, it is widely recognized that "[j]uridical punishment can never be administered merely as a means of promoting another good either with regard to the criminal himself or to civil society, but must in all cases be imposed only because the individual on whom it is inflicted has committed a crime."[3] Otherwise, the state would be justified in punishing anyone, regardless of fault, as long as that brings about a net social gain.[4] The priority of the "just desert" principle is not only theoretical. Research on the psychology of justice shows that the community's principles of punishment are largely retributive[5] and that people explicitly name retributivism as the philosophy that should govern punishment in our society.[6]

In the retributive system of justice, a person may not be punished unless his wrongdoing was accompanied by a culpable mental state[7] with respect to the wrongdoing.[8] In addition, many scholars agree that "it's not culpability alone that counts in determining desert. . . . Rather, the amount of harm caused determines the seriousness of the wrong done, and the amount of wrong done does affect desert."[9]

The bond between harm and just desert, although not universally accepted, has strong support in both our law and morality.[10] We decide whether people deserve praise or punishment based, in part, on the end results of their actions. A sprinter who almost won the race does not deserve the same medal as the sprinter who, in fact, came first. Similarly, a driver who almost hit a pedestrian does not deserve the same punishment as a driver who did, in fact, hit and kill someone.

Many criminal law doctrines implicitly or explicitly draw on the moral significance of harm. Take the defense of necessity. The perpetrator who invokes this defense is guilty of violating a legal (and often moral) norm. Nonetheless, he may be completely absolved of criminal liability if his prima facie offense was committed in order to avoid a greater harm or evil.[11] If harm had no independent moral significance, the actor who made the right choice and, say, broke into his roommate's bedroom in search of a first-aid kit for a severely injured guest would not be justified in what he did.

The moral significance of harm makes the attribution of harm essential to the idea of just desert.[12] If the victim is completely innocent and there is no other independent intervening cause, it is clear that the perpetrator is responsible for *all* the harm. But what about a victim who was at least as instrumental as the offender in causing the resulting injury or loss? Consider, for example, the victim who was a willing participant in a fatal drag race, or the victim who killed himself while playing a game of Russian roulette.[13] Is it fair to say that, although there were two equally reckless participants, the defendant caused *all* the harm?

In *Commonwealth v. Atencio*,[14] three friends, Marshall, Atencio, and Britch, played Russian roulette:

> First, Marshall examined the gun, saw that it contained one cartridge, and after spinning it on his arm, pointed it at his head, and pulled the trigger. Nothing happened. He handed the gun to Atencio, who repeated the process, again without result. Atencio passed the gun to the deceased, who spun it, put it to his head, and then pulled the trigger. The cartridge exploded, and he fell over dead.[15]

Both Marshall and Atencio were convicted of manslaughter in the death of Britch. The appellate court recognized that Britch's voluntary participation in the game would bar a civil action.[16] In a criminal prosecution, however, Britch's contributory recklessness was ignored because of the state interest "that the deceased should not be killed by the wanton or reckless conduct of himself or others."[17] The problem with this argument is that it essentially sacrifices the principle of just desert for the benefit of net social gain. Under the court's logic, the state would be justified in punishing an innocent if that would deter undesirable social behavior. Hence, this outcome contradicts a cornerstone principle of criminal law, which allows courts to impose sanctions only when an actor is guilty of an offense.

Certainly, not all cases of the victim's negligent or even reckless behavior should reduce the offender's blameworthiness. The fact that a victim may not have behaved cautiously enough does not and should not diminish the criminal liability of a rapist or a thief. I will discuss these issues in Chapter 4. For now it is sufficient to acknowledge that, in principle, there are circumstances in which the requirements of fair and proportionate punishment mandate that the offender's liability be evaluated in light of the victim's own behavior.

Utilitarian Considerations

Whereas retributivism provides a nonconsequentialist basis for punishment, various utilitarian theories view punishment as a means to achieving societal goals—deterring the offender from committing future crime (specific deterrence), deterring others from crime (general deterrence), isolating and incapacitating the offender (incapacitation), and rehabilitating the offender (rehabilitation). Although rejecting the view that criminal justice should be governed by consequentialist considerations alone, I nevertheless recognize that they represent *a* value and therefore should be promoted to the extent that doing so does not interfere with the just desert principle.

In the utilitarian world, the main criterion for determining whether a certain measure is warranted is its efficiency, economic or noneconomic. Two distinct efficiency arguments may be made in favor of incorporating comparative responsibility in criminal law—one dealing with the reduction of costs of crime and the other dealing with the increase of moral authority of criminal law.

Reduction of the Costs of Crime. Crime imposes economic costs on society in terms of both losses and precautionary measures against it. One way to minimize those costs is to create incentives for potential victims to be more cautious.[18] Alon Harel has proposed a system of comparative fault under which crimes against careless victims will be punished less severely. As a result, criminals will be more inclined to commit crimes against careless victims because that will subject them to a lesser penalty.[19] Criminals' preference will, in turn, influence the behavior of potential victims. "Potential victims will be disposed to take better precautions given that criminals will be less likely to commit crimes directed at cautious victims."[20]

What is troublesome in Harel's refined theory is that he does not seem to differentiate between two kinds of victims—one guilty of attacking an innocent bystander and the other guilty of merely walking late at night. Moreover, it may well be that it is easier to influence people's everyday routine (e.g., going out late) than to prevent certain antisocial behavior. In that case, based on Harel's logic, the law should reflect that discrepancy by punishing a mugger or rapist of a late-night walker less severely than the victim who was defending himself against an unprovoked attack.

I agree with Harel that criminal law should adopt a regime of comparative liability. However, I am averse to his utilitarian reasoning, which subordinates moral considerations to efficiency. Accordingly, the theory of comparative criminal liability outlined in this book significantly differs from the one envisioned by Harel.

Increase of Moral Authority of Criminal Law. To be effective, criminal law must enjoy moral credibility. That may be achieved only if the distribution of criminal sanctions is seen as just.[21] This, in turn, requires that criminal law (1) be not overused (and therefore devalued) and (2) assign "liability and punishment in ways that the community perceives as consistent with the community's principles of appropriate liability and punishment."[22]

An excessive use of criminal sanctions may reduce the deterring effect of the law, since internalization of the rules of criminal law requires strong moral condemnation of the proscribed conduct by the law-abiding members of the community.[23] Consequently, the inflationary use of criminal law may cause the condemnation eventually to wear thin and vanish.[24]

To avoid that outcome, a German scholar, Bernd Schünemann, has advocated a restrictive approach to the interpretation of penal statutes, urging courts to reject criminal sanctions in certain circumstances when the victim neither deserves nor needs protection.[25] This rule of interpretation, known in German legal theory as *Viktimodogmatik*, was to be applied only to "relationship offenses," such as fraud, and not to violent crimes.[26] Decisions about when victims do not need or deserve protection were to be made based on the statistical findings of victimologists.[27]

Schünemann's work has made an important contribution toward a more realistic, contextualized vision of crime. At the same time, his proposal is limited in a few important respects. The first limitation is normative and relates to the fact that, for Schünemann, courts should pay attention to victims' conduct mainly because doing so would produce fewer criminal sanctions. Thus, if it turns out that *Viktimodogmatik* does not create the desired effect, the rule would have to be abandoned, even though it results in more fair verdicts.

The second limitation lies in the procedural nature of Schünemann's proposal. As a rule of interpretation, *Viktimodogmatik* leaves almost boundless discretion to each interpreter and is likely to lead to inconsistent verdicts. In contrast, conceptualizing the victim's conduct as a full or partial defense of justification makes it an integral part of the substantive criminal law, mandates courts to give it effect, and ensures more consistent application.

Another problem with Schünemann's proposal is that it affects only a small group of nonviolent offenses, in which the victim was not diligent enough to protect his own interests. It is not clear why the victim's fault should be given weight in this (and only this) context. Shouldn't the victim who initiated the game of Russian roulette be at least as responsible for his lot as a gullible victim who failed to double-check a fraudster's representations?

Finally, decisions about which victims do not need or deserve legal protection should not be based on victimological studies. Statistical information may be helpful in identifying particularly frequent or vulnerable victims in order to educate and protect them from danger. This information, however, may not determine the level of liability of a particular defendant. To serve justice in a specific case, the court may judge a defendant only for what he did to his victim, not for what a statistical defendant did to a statistical victim. Schünemann would need to agree with this principle in order to promote his goal of efficiency based on internalization of moral norms by the community. In general, although I do not see the reduction of criminal sanctions as the principal reason for adding the victim's conduct into the liability equation, I agree with Schünemann that such reduction is likely to follow and make the reformed criminal law more efficient and morally influential.

An alternative argument directed at improving the effectiveness of criminal law was made by Paul H. Robinson and John M. Darley. They advocated in favor of changing the foundation of desert-based liability—from moral philosophy to the community's shared principles of justice.[28] The authors suggested that such a system would enjoy high moral authority and that authority could be used for creating moral norms and ensuring compliance with them.[29] While not following Robinson and Darley in their utilitarian revision of the rationale for justice, I share their view that, by and large, it is good when the law does not clash with moral perceptions of the community.

The famous Kalven and Zeisel study of American juries has shown that public intuitions and jury verdicts do not follow the law regarding contributory fault of the victim. According to the study, jurors consistently acquit the offender or convict him of a lesser offense if the victim contributed to his own injury.[30] For example, jurors acquitted defendants charged with negligent automobile homicide where the "deceased driver may also have been negligent," where the "[v]ictim, who drank to excess, walked or staggered across the road," and where "[d]efendant traveled too fast, but woman (deceased) may have darted into path."[31]

Similarly, the Capital Jury Project, a multidisciplinary study of how capital jurors make their life or death sentencing decisions, has shown that the victim's role in the crime was one of the leading factors determining the outcome. The study reported that, at first glance, the raw numbers suggested that juries were more likely to give a death sentence when the victim was a woman rather than a man, a married person rather than single or divorced, and a parent rather than a childless victim.[32]

> Importantly, however, within each of these subcategories, the cases that resulted in a life sentence generally were still those in which the jurors perceived the victim as a risk-taker or as someone engaging in antisocial behavior. For example, although almost two-thirds of the cases with victims who were parents resulted in a death sentence (60% of the cases overall), if the parent victim was involved in high-risk behavior, only one-quarter (25%) of the cases resulted in a death sentence, while 83% of the cases in which the parent victim did not engage in such behavior resulted in death sentences.[33]

Changing the law to reduce the offender's liability because of the faulty conduct of the victim would certainly bring it closer to the lay perception of justice. At the same time, a law is not necessarily good simply because it mimics public opinion.[34] Public views on the allocation of responsibility for rape are well known for their unfairness to the victim. "She got herself raped," read one of the slogans at a demonstration protesting against guilty verdicts issued in a gang-rape case.[35] Numerous polls have pointed out that the public has redefined the crime of rape "in terms of its notions of assumption of risk."[36] Juries in rape cases do not limit their deliberations to the only legally relevant issue—consent of the victim. Instead, they "closely, and often harshly, scrutinize . . . the female complainant and [are] moved to be lenient with the defendant whenever there are suggestions of contributory behavior on her part."[37] The "contributory behavior" of the victim sufficient for the defendant's acquittal or conviction of a lesser offense has included drinking, wearing sexy clothes, flirting, or having a prior relationship with the defendant.[38]

In the Kalven and Zeisel study, for example, judges reported unwarranted acquittals where

- the assault happened at a beer-drinking party ("[t]he jury probably figured the girl asked for what she got");
- the victim had a few beers before "she entered a car with defendant and three other men and was driven to cemetery where act took place";
- the victim and defendant, who formerly had been married, spent a lot of time together with a view toward reconciliation (the jurors were of the opinion that if rape occurred "in a course of conduct that [victim] had accepted, she was in no position to complain of her leading him on"); and
- the victim, who was "drinking but not drunk," accepted a ride back home from a man she had just met at a dance hall; "rape occurred in lonely wooded area."[39]

One of the most extensive studies of citizen perceptions of rape found that 66 percent of the polled population believed that women's behavior or appearance provokes rape, and 34 percent believed that women should be held responsible for preventing their own rape.[40] According to a 1991 telephone survey of five hundred Americans, 38 percent of men and 37 percent of women believed that a woman is partly to blame for her own rape if she dresses seductively.[41] In a contemporaneous Florida case, a three-man, three-woman jury acquitted a man of abducting a woman at knifepoint and repeatedly raping her. The jury based its decision partly on the fact that the victim was wearing a lace miniskirt with no underwear. Explaining the jury verdict, the foreman said: "We felt she asked for it the way she was dressed."[42]

Should these public views be incorporated into law? If the law, as said by Robinson and Darley, ought to assign "liability and punishment according to the principles of justice that the community *intuitively uses to assign liability and blame*,"[43] we may end up with a "mini-skirt" defense to the crime of rape. Unlike Robinson and Darley, I do not see the community's beliefs as a self-sufficient foundation for justice. A rape victim is not, and should not be, responsible for rape even if the community believes otherwise.[44] However, Robinson and Darley are perceptive in paying close attention to public views. Both criminal law and community norms are parts of the same social discourse, and unless criminal law addresses existing discrepancies, it would be seen as divorced from real life, too abstract and irrelevant.

Moreover, as Robinson and Darley correctly point out, criminal law plays an important role in shaping the social consensus necessary for sustaining moral norms.[45] Discussing the dialogue between the law and public opinion, Robinson and Darley wrote:

> We have seen the process at work recently in enhancing prohibitory norms against sexual harassment, hate speech, drunk driving, and domestic violence. It has also been at work in diluting existing norms against homosexual conduct, fornication, and adultery. While it is difficult to untangle how much the criminal law reform followed and how much it led these shifts, it seems difficult to imagine that these changes could have occurred without the recognition and confirmation that comes through changes in criminal law legislation, enforcement, and adjudication.[46]

In contrast, by excluding an issue from consideration, the law fails to influence the social discourse. If people's everyday experience tells them that in some circumstances the victim is almost as guilty as the person on trial, yet the law completely denies that, jurors receive no guidance from the law.

When jurors blame the victim of rape, they do so, at least in part, because the law does not offer them a way to distinguish her "fault" from that of the victim of a drag race. As a result, jurors deliver unfair and legally indefensible verdicts, and the law misses an opportunity to shape new social consensus on sexual misconduct and women's rights. In addition, the law loses its moral authority in general: it is not likely that people in borderline situations would turn for guidance to a system of rules that they perceive as unjust. It is, therefore, crucial for maintaining the moral authority and efficiency of criminal law to provide a meaningful theory of comparative fault, one that directly addresses the community's perceptions and judgments and offers a workable method for evaluating the liability of offenders and victims.

CONSISTENCY OF CRIMINAL SANCTIONS

Let us start with a simple question: if in every single state the defense of provocation reduces the perpetrator's liability for killing an offending victim, why doesn't a similar defense apply to assault or battery? Indeed, only a couple of states allow for a lesser form of assault to be charged when the victim provoked the attack or the defendant acted in the heat of passion,[47] and only a few more states allow provocation to serve as a mitigating factor at sentencing once a defendant has been convicted of assault.[48]

Furthermore, the MPC provides that "simple assault is a misdemeanor unless committed in a fight or scuffle entered into by mutual consent, in which case it is a petty misdemeanor."[49] This language generally applies to an altercation, in which both parties were to some degree at fault and which did not result in serious injuries.[50] However, very few states have followed the MPC.[51] Some states, while adopting the general language of the provision, did not include the mitigation afforded by the MPC.[52] Other states explicitly rejected mutual combat as a defense.[53]

Take one more example. All states and the MPC criminalize intentional destruction of another person's property.[54] Section 3.10 of the MPC provides justification to "seizure or destruction of, damage to, intrusion on or interference with property of another"[55] if these actions would be protected by a defense or privilege recognized in the law of torts or property. Neither tort nor property law, however, recognizes the defense of provocation. Thus, under the MPC, provocation may not serve as a partial defense for destructive or intrusive actions against property of another.

In a few limited circumstances, provocation has been successfully raised as a defense to the charge of malicious destruction of property.[56] However, state penal codes carry no statutory provisions to that effect. Instead, the applicability of the defense is based on how some courts have interpreted the requirement of malice. In these decisions, most of which are quite old, courts have concluded that provocation defeats malice, thereby constituting a defense against malicious mischief or malicious destruction of property.[57] Other courts have opined that malice "is a chameleonic term, taking on different meanings according to the context in which it is used."[58] Yet these courts were also more likely to believe that provocation may negate malice only in the context of homicide.[59]

In recent years, only one jurisdiction has explicitly allowed provocation as a defense to malicious destruction of property.[60] In *Brown v. United States*, the District of Columbia appellate court reversed a conviction that stemmed from an incident in which the defendant smashed the front windows and door of her mother's house in an effort to get inside and take custody of her runaway son.[61] The appellate court concluded that the trial court erred in not allowing the defendant to introduce evidence of provocation:

> We cannot say that an ordinary, reasonable person, after searching for her son for ten days only to learn that he was staying with her own mother and that her own mother had not only failed to inform her of her son's whereabouts but also refused to return the boy to the custody of his own parent, could not have been so impassioned by these circumstances as to lose her self-control and, acting without reflection, destroy windows and a door in an attempt to get into her mother's house and retrieve her lost son.[62]

According to the court, since malice was an element of the offense and provocation negates malice, provocation was a proper defense.[63] Moreover, the court said in dicta that provocation should be available whenever an offense involves malice, for example, in cases of malicious disfigurement and malicious interference with a contract.[64] This approach, however, is atypical. In most instances, the defense of provocation is allowed only in the prosecution for homicide.

That brings about a rather absurd result. Criminal law grants a partial defense to a killer provoked by a victim. Yet, if the justifiably outraged actor, instead of shooting the victim, slapped him on his face (assault) or threw a valuable vase on the floor (destruction of property), in the majority of jurisdictions, there would be no similar mitigation. How can it be reasonably explained that offensive behavior of the victim may partially justify a more serious injury but not a less serious one? As a matter of both logic and public policy, this is an unsatisfactory outcome.

COHESIVENESS OF A CRIMINAL TRIAL

Although the victim's comparative fault is ignored at the liability stage of the trial, it comes back as a mitigating factor during the sentencing stage. For instance, the *Federal Sentencing Guidelines* provide that "[i]f the victim's wrongful conduct contributed significantly to provoking the offense behavior, the court may reduce the sentence below the guideline range to reflect the nature and circumstances of the offense."[65] The Model Sentencing and Corrections Act includes among mitigating factors a situation when "the defendant acted under strong provocation."[66] The MPC gives the court a discretionary authority to substitute probation for prison when "the victim of the defendant's criminal conduct induced or facilitated its commission."[67] Presently, twenty-three states and the federal government recognize the victim's participation in the crime or consent to the criminal conduct as a mitigating factor.[68]

The victim's participation in, or consent to, homicide is generally recognized as a mitigating factor for capital sentencing purposes.[69] The MPC explains:

> If a murder victim plays a role in bringing about his own death, either by participating in dangerous conduct (e.g., playing Russian roulette or joining in the commission of a violent felony), or by consenting to the homicidal act (e.g., in the context of a mercy killing), the judge or jury may wish to consider this conduct when sentencing the offender who is legally responsible for causing the death.[70]

Twenty-four of the thirty-two death penalty jurisdictions listing statutory mitigating factors include the victim's conduct as a relevant mitigating consideration under some circumstances.[71] Eighteen states[72] closely follow the language of the MPC, which allows mitigation when "[t]he victim was a participant in the defendant's homicidal conduct or consented to the homicidal act."[73] In three other jurisdictions, only the victim's consent to, but not participation in, the defendant's homicidal act qualifies as a statutory mitigating factor.[74] Four more states consider whether "the victim was a willing participant in the defendant's conduct"[75] or "[w]hether the victim of the offense induced or facilitated it"[76] or list factors similar to the MPC's.[77]

This discrepancy in how the role of the victim is evaluated at the liability stage and the sentencing stage of a trial is largely unwarranted. Admittedly, these two stages serve different purposes. The first one—the subject of penal codes and criminal trials—concerns the definition of culpable conduct and the adjudication of guilt. The second one concerns the consequences of conviction for the offender.[78] However, as has been correctly pointed out, "we are accustomed to thinking about the criminal law, and the procedures for enforcing it, as divided into two separate stages. Only rarely do we acknowledge that the conventional separation of these stages into compartments is highly misleading."[79]

There have been attempts to draw a conceptual distinction between the tasks performed at the two stages of a criminal trial. For example, Paul H. Robinson argued that penal codes and courts often confuse three primary functions of criminal law: announcing ex ante the rules of conduct (the rule articulation function), determining ex post whether an actor's violation is blameworthy and deserves condemnation as criminal (the liability assignment function), and deciding on the appropriate amount of punishment (the grading function).[80] Comparing the latter two, Robinson wrote:

> While the first step in the adjudication process, the liability function, requires a simple yes or no decision as to whether the minimum conditions for liability are satisfied, this second step, the grading function, requires judgments of degree. It must consider such factors as the relative harmfulness of the violation and the level of culpability of the actor.[81]

Recognizing three separate functions of criminal law—rule articulation, liability assignment, and grading—is, indeed, "a useful way in which to analyze and organize criminal law doctrine."[82] I am skeptical, however, about Robinson's attempt to pair each function with one specific stage of the criminal adjudication process. In my view, the grading function—the one requiring judgments of degree—goes through all stages of crime prevention, guilt adjudication, and penalty assignment.

For example, before a judge or jurors come to a simple yes or no decision in a case of involuntary homicide, they have to consider the *degree* of the defendant's fault. The difference between regular recklessness and recklessness manifesting extreme indifference to the value of human life translates into the difference between manslaughter and murder.[83] The magnitude of risk and the extent to which that risk was justifiable determines the choice between no liability, negligent homicide, and manslaughter.[84] The yes-or-no answer is a result of consideration of a number of questions involving "the relative harmfulness of the violation and the level of culpability of the actor,"[85] which means that the grading function is continuously invoked throughout the guilt adjudication stage.

My position finds support in one of the most important sections of the MPC, the one explaining its purposes.[86] Those purposes are combined into two separate subsections—the first deals with the definition and grading of offenses (i.e., the adjudication of guilt), whereas the second addresses the sentencing and treatment of offenders (i.e., the penalty). It is the *former* subsection that sets forth the goal to distinguish between serious and minor offenses. An official commentary explains that the provisions included in that subsection "not only serve to describe the conduct that the penal law makes criminal but also reflect a legislative grading of offenses, differentiating serious and minor derelictions and, within each class, offenses of greater or lesser gravity."[87] This language strongly suggests that various fault- and harm-related considerations should be reviewed at the guilt adjudication stage and should affect not only the defendant's punishment but also the offense or the grade of the offense of which he is convicted.

Should the same considerations be reviewed twice—at both stages of a criminal trial? Robinson persuasively argues that considerations relevant at the guilt adjudication stage should be revisited at the penalty stage.[88] For instance, excuse defenses serve the "assigning of liability" function by assuring that criminal liability is not imposed unless the actor had the capacity to avoid the violation.[89] If elements of a defense are present but, say, do not reach the required magnitude, the defense fails. To give an example, a failed duress defense may mean that, while some coercion was present, it was not strong enough to render the actor completely blameless for the violation. Does it follow, however, that the actor who fails to prove a duress defense is as blameworthy as one who committed the same offense with no coercion whatsoever? While the degree of mitigation may not be dramatic, most people would likely distinguish the two cases.[90]

The fact that there are numerous factors significant to both stages of a criminal trial raises several questions: Why are some of the sentencing factors also relevant to the adjudication of guilt, while other ones are not? Why does "extreme mental or emotional disturbance" or duress affect both the defendant's verdict and his punishment, whereas the defendant's young age or good criminal record is reviewed only at his sentencing?[91] Finally, how does the victim's participation in the criminal act fit into this picture?

Addressing a capital trial, the Supreme Court has defined the issue for the penalty stage as the determination of the defendant's "culpability," "responsibility," "blameworthiness," or "desert."[92] Unfortunately, not only are these terms often used interchangeably but also it is far from clear what exactly they encompass.[93] If they are used in the same sense as at the liability stage, then it is inexplicable why any factors relevant to the defendant's culpability, responsibility, blameworthiness, or desert are excluded from consideration at the liability stage. If, on the other hand, these terms have different meanings when used in connection with a penalty, what are they?

Kyron Huigens confronted this terminological ambiguity and compellingly showed that the word *culpability* has been invoked in connection with the penalty phase of a capital trial in two different meanings—as "fault in wrongdoing" and as "eligibility for punishment."[94] For example, a minor role of a defendant in the committed crime or the lack of intent to kill is a fault mitigator, whereas the offender's young age is an eligibility mitigator.

Fault mitigators differ from eligibility mitigators in several important respects. One is that fault is not only a necessary condition for punishment but also an affirmative, justifying reason to punish.[95] "Eligibility, in contrast, is only 'a necessary condition for punishment.' We do not suppose that a person's being possessed of ordinary capabilities is an affirmative, justifying reason to punish him."[96] Another significant difference is that fault is an aspect of wrongdoing, while eligibility is not. For example, the defendant's lack of intent to kill and his minor role as an accomplice are mitigators that can be translated into the opposite, as offense elements or aggravating factors. The matter of the perpetrator's age, on the other hand, is a mitigator that does not have an opposite pair.[97] Rules that govern eligibility for punishment are not correlated to criminal law's conduct rules.[98]

If we look from that perspective at the victim's conduct as a relevant mitigating consideration, it would be obvious that it is a fault mitigator like "extreme mental or emotional disturbance" or duress and not an eligibility mitigator like the defendant's young age or good criminal record. We not only *may*, but we *should* punish an offender who killed an innocent, unoffending victim. In the same way, we not only *may*, but we *should* acquit a defendant who killed an attacking victim in legitimate self-defense. The corresponding conduct rules prohibit killing of a nonaggressor and permit necessary self-defense.

Then, if the victim's conduct is a fault factor, why is it not considered at the stage at which all other fault is considered? How can we satisfy the requirement of just desert if we ignore the magnitude of the offender's fault when deciding whether he is guilty or innocent? The only logical solution to this problem is to consider fault (as opposed to eligibility) mitigators, including the conduct of the victim, at both stages of the criminal trial.

Pursuant to this proposal, all fault mitigators should be first assessed at the liability stage. If, although present, they do not reach the threshold required to eliminate or reduce the *liability* of the offender, they may be considered again at the penalty stage—in order to reduce the *penalty*. In fact, this approach is already followed in capital cases with respect to certain mitigators. For example, the "extreme mental or emotional disturbance" of the defendant is first considered at the guilt stage (as a factor reducing murder to manslaughter), and then, if the argument has not succeeded, again, for the purpose of sentencing. For the correct determination of the actor's responsibility, the conduct of the victim should be evaluated the same way, in both capital and appropriate noncapital cases.

One might ask: why does it matter at what stage of the trial a mitigator is considered as long as it reduces the defendant's sentence? There are several reasons why it matters. First, conviction of a crime is by itself a form of punishment, a social stigma and an obstacle to a successful life.[99] For that reason alone, a particular offense imputed to the defendant should reflect the amount of wrong done by him. If the perpetrator deserves to be convicted of a lesser offense, it is unfair to convict him of a more serious crime, regardless of the imposed sentence.[100]

Moreover, courts may, but do not have to, take the defendant's eligibility mitigators into account. Yet, courts *must* reduce the charged offense and/or punishment if the mitigator is fault-based, that is, constitutes a partial defense. Defendants are entitled to consideration of partial defenses, as a matter of justice, simply because fault is essential for determination of "just desert." In the words of Douglas Husak, "[t]o disregard such circumstances is no more defensible than to disregard a complete justification or excuse. Only a rejection of the principle of proportionality—that the severity of punishment should be proportionate to desert—would authorize the discretion to disregard a partial justification or excuse."[101]

In addition, the disconnect between the amount of fault presupposed by a particular offense and the actual amount of the defendant's fault may send a confusing message to the community and lead to inconsistent and unwarranted verdicts. In the absence of a cohesive theory of comparative responsibility, jurors who, as we know, do consider the fault of the victim often have to choose between all-or-nothing alternatives. Consequently, some offenders receive more severe verdicts than they deserve, while others, as a result of the jurors' exercise of the power of nullification, walk away unpunished.[102]

Notably, jurors recognize the difference between reducing the defendant's liability and reducing only his punishment. For example, as Kalven and Zeisel have shown, in almost 30 percent of all criminal trials included in their study, the judge would have decided the issue of guilt differently than the jury.[103] Yet at the penalty stage, the discrepancy between the judge's and the jury's decisions amounted only to 4 percent.[104] The jury was six-and-a-half times more likely than the judge to show leniency with respect to the determination of guilt and the proper charge; however, there was very little disagreement between the judge's and the jury's penalty decisions.[105] These findings suggest that the general public assigns importance to proper adjudication of one's guilt, not just to the punishment alone.

Finally, although sentencing guidelines often provide for mitigation of the offender's punishment due to the victim's faulty conduct, in reality this factor may not be used much. For instance, a survey of spousal homicide indicated that provoked wife defendants[106] had a lower risk of conviction than those who were not provoked. Yet, if convicted, they received no obvious break: eighty-four percent of them were sent to prison, and the survey found no statistically significant difference between provoked and unprovoked wife defendants in terms of the length of their sentences.[107]

The statistics of federal offenses also reveal that the victim's conduct does not play a major role at the sentencing phase. The *Federal Sentencing Guidelines* authorize courts to reduce the sentence below the recommended range if "the victim's wrongful conduct contributed significantly to provoking the offense behavior."[108] However, according to the *Sourcebook of Federal Sentencing Statistics*, in 2006, the victim's conduct was cited as a reason for mitigation in less than 0.4 percent of all federal cases in which the sentence to the defendant was reduced below the guidelines range.[109] This number seems somewhat low even considering that federal cases involve primarily "victimless" crimes and that the majority of all downward departures from the guidelines happen in drug-trafficking and immigration cases.[110] Interestingly, this statistic has not been noticeably affected by the recent Supreme Court decisions that took away the mandatory authority of the *Federal Sentencing Guidelines* and held them to be merely advisory.[111] Indeed, prior to those decisions, the victim's conduct was cited as a reason for the downward departure from the *Federal Sentencing Guidelines* in 0.2 percent of all mitigated federal sentences in 2001 and in 0.3 percent in each of 2000 and 1999.[112]

For all these considerations—maintaining fairness, accuracy, and consistency of verdicts; respecting prevalent community expectations; and ensuring cohesiveness between different stages of criminal adjudication—it is necessary to consider the victim's conduct as a fault mitigator at the liability, as well as the sentencing, stage of the trial.

DEVELOPMENT OF COMPARATIVE LIABILITY IN TORT LAW

The development of the theory of comparative fault in torts provides more support to the argument that the conduct of the victim is a relevant factor in the assessment of the perpetrator's criminal liability. Undoubtedly, criminal law and tort law differ in some significant respects—the former is public while the latter is private. The former punishes those who wrong society in order to impose "just deserts" upon the wrongdoer and deter others from engaging in similar behavior. The latter provides a remedy to individuals or entities harmed by other individuals or entities in order to make them whole.[113]

Nevertheless, criminal law and torts share a lot. First, they have a common origin—there was no distinction between torts and crimes in early English law.[114] This common ancestry is reflected in many core concepts essential to both theories. Requirements of harm,[115] violation of a social norm,[116] and causation[117] are among them. Moreover, as far as punishment is concerned, the "line between criminal law and tort law is blurred by the imposition in tort actions of punitive damages, which address the moral culpability of the tortfeasor,"[118] and by restitution statutes adopted in a substantial number of states. Restitution statutes provide for monetary compensation by an offender to the victim of a crime[119] and fundamentally rest on the tort principle that the wrongdoer should "restore" the victim to his status quo ante.[120] There is a good reason, therefore, to consider some arguments related to the development of the concepts of perpetrator liability and victim's fault in the law of torts.

The historical evolution of the concept of responsibility in torts was marked by a "progression away from the harsh and arbitrary common law rules of contributory negligence and joint and several liability toward the principle of comparative fault among all who contributed to the injury."[121] The rule of contributory negligence, for example, completely barred recovery to a plaintiff who was at fault, no matter how slightly compared to the defendant.[122] The rule grew out of the common-law doctrine of the unity of the cause of action, according to which an injury was a single event and could not be logically divided.[123]

Prior to the 1970s, the overwhelming majority of states adhered to the rule of contributory negligence. In the past thirty years, however, there has been a dramatic shift to comparative negligence, accomplished through judicial decisions and legislative enactments. At present, forty-six states employ one form or another of comparative negligence, which allows fault to be apportioned among all parties responsible for the injury or loss.[124]

It is instructive to review some of the reasons cited in state supreme courts' opinions in favor of changing the rule. Numerous decisions criticize the contributory negligence doctrine as harsh,[125] inequitable and unjust,[126] opposed to interests of justice and fair play,[127] and "draconian in operation."[128] One of the main arguments against the old rule is that its application produced an "all or nothing" result: the defendant was either liable for full damages or totally relieved of responsibility.[129] Even though the harshness of the rule was mitigated by various exceptions,[130] they still did not alleviate the general unfairness of the all-or-nothing approach.[131] In the words of a commentator, "[t]he stark impression left by this 'all or nothing' process simply defied reality and, hence, offended one's ordinary sense of justice."[132]

In addition, a number of courts rejected the contributory negligence rule because jurors rebelled at applying it,[133] thus violating their oaths to follow instructions[134] and detracting from public confidence in the law.[135] About a decade before the rapid spread and adoption of the comparative negligence standard, one commentator observed that there is "something basically wrong with a rule of law that is so contrary to the settled convictions of the lay community that laymen will almost always refuse to enforce it, even when solemnly told to do so by a judge whose instructions they have sworn to follow."[136]

All these arguments can be repeated almost verbatim with respect to the consideration of victims' fault in criminal law. Is it not unfair to assign all the responsibility for an injury to one party, the offender, and completely ignore the victim's contribution? Does not this practice defy reality and, hence, offend one's ordinary sense of justice? Social scientists for years have voiced these concerns. As one of them has pointed out, it is

> absurd that, whenever a crime occurs, the entire blame is placed on the offender without taking a dynamic view of the crime from every angle, and without considering, among other things, any precipitative or causative behavior by the victim that may have eventually affected the development or concept of the crime. Criminal responsibility has become one-directional.[137]

The argument that there may be a serious problem with a law that goes against community convictions is equally applicable to the victim's fault in criminal law, as the earlier discussion shows.[138] Serving on a jury may be the only formal point of contact with the system of criminal justice for many, if not most, citizens.[139] From this perspective alone, a law that consistently incites jurors to apply their power of nullification is troubling.[140]

Recent developments in tort law raise new questions applicable to criminal law doctrine as well. Adopted in 2000, the *Restatement (Third) of Torts: Apportionment of Liability* provides for apportionment of all personal injury claims "regardless of the basis for liability."[141] In other words, it allows for the apportionment of liability between negligent and intentional actors. The new rule reflects a powerful new trend. In the last decade, many state courts and legislatures addressed the issue of intentional / negligent comparative fault, including allocation of fault between a plaintiff and a defendant.[142]

The Restatement acknowledges that apportionment of liability between an intentional tortfeasor and a negligent victim presents special problems.[143] In its final draft, the Restatement took no position on that issue, reserving it for the developing "substantive law."[144] One of the reporters explained:

> [W]e originally did think that plaintiff's negligence should be a reduction to intentional torts. There is a growing and emerging body of case law that supports that . . . and of the cases where courts have faced this issue over the last 10 years or so, as courts have started to recognize this issue, they have more frequently than not recognized plaintiff's negligence as a defense to an intentional tort. Nevertheless, this is an emerging area.[145]

Traditionally, the harsh contributory fault rule did not apply to intentional torts.[146] When courts and legislatures adopted the comparative responsibility instead of the contributory fault doctrine, they largely ignored intentional torts.[147] Thus, the issue is still open, and courts[148] and commentators[149] provide arguments and propose solutions that may be helpful for deciding analogous questions in criminal law.

In the view of many courts and scholars, the main reason to use comparative fault in most types of intentional tort cases is simple: it is fair to do so.[150] It is widely believed that "persons are responsible for their acts to the extent their fault contributes to an injurious result."[151] Accordingly, to the extent the injurious result is attributable to an act of another, the offender should not bear responsibility for it. This logic is, to a large degree, applicable to both criminal and civil responsibility.

The Restatement reporter's Notes indicate that there are circumstances when the plaintiff's conduct may be a comparative defense against an intentional tort—for example, when the plaintiff's, as well as the defendant's, conduct was intentional or when the defendant honestly but unreasonably believed that his conduct was privileged.[152] In order to distinguish cases in which the plaintiff's failure to use reasonable care is relevant from those in which it should be ignored, the Restatement proposes that courts develop "substantive liability rules, often called 'no duty' rules, to cover certain types of plaintiff conduct, such as a claim that a victim of a sexual assault dressed provocatively, a claim involving domestic violence,"[153] or a claim by a "mugger that the victim was negligent for being out too late at night or for wearing too much jewelry."[154] Under those rules, "a plaintiff who starts a fight in a bar should be treated differently from a plaintiff who walks into a dangerous neighborhood and is assaulted."[155] The no-duty rules offer a workable model for distinguishing relevant and irrelevant faulty conduct of the victim in criminal cases as well. I discuss that further in Chapter 6.

Finally, the Restatement articulates criteria that may be considered for allocating responsibility among parties—fault and causation.[156] The fault factors in this computation include the character and nature of each person's risk-creating conduct, the circumstances surrounding the conduct, each person's abilities and disabilities, and each person's intent, awareness of, or indifference to the risks.[157]

To summarize, tort law and criminal law are based on many similar principles. In the past thirty years, tort law has experienced a significant change. It has abandoned the artificial all-or-nothing approach to liability and adopted a theory of comparative fault that recognizes that more than one person may be responsible for an injury or loss. Furthermore, in recent years, courts and academics have confronted the issue of comparative responsibility between an intentional tortfeasor and a faulty victim, developing rules and criteria that allow situations in which the victim's conduct reduced the defendant's liability to be distinguished from those in which it was irrelevant. That last development is particularly important because intentional torts, with their focus not only on the compensation of harm but also on punishment and deterrence, are particularly close to criminal law. Tort law, which in the past was the target of many of the same criticisms as criminal law today, has reformed itself, while criminal law continues to ignore the gap between its one-dimensional doctrine of responsibility and the more complex conception of responsibility shared by social sciences, moral philosophy, and the community. The comparative responsibility reform in torts alters both arguments and criteria for conducting a similar reform in criminal law.

• • •

In this chapter, I sought to provide generic reasons for why criminal law should systematically reduce the offender's liability when the harm or loss is attributable to the conduct of the victim. The main arguments are:

1. *Just desert.* Pursuant to this principle, the offender's punishment should reflect the amount of harm he caused. Accordingly, if the victim is responsible for a portion of the harm, the offender's criminal liability should be reduced.
2. *Efficiency.* The law should strive to be efficient. For that sake, it should develop in a dialogue with community perceptions of right and wrong and should not overuse criminal sanctions. Effectively, jurors have already incorporated comparative fault into criminal law. To maintain a fair and lawful system of criminal justice, a theory of comparative responsibility must be worked out to guide people in their decision-making.
3. *Consistency of criminal sanctions.* The law is a system in which various rules are interdependent. To be consistent, the law must treat similar states of affairs in a similar fashion. At this point, the law recognizes the victim's participation as a mitigating circumstance in a number of specific situations and, at the same time, refuses to recognize it as a general principle. That discrepancy leads to illogical, incoherent, and unfair decisions.
4. *Cohesiveness of a criminal trial.* The victim's fault or consent is a valid penalty mitigator in a number of circumstances. Since the victim's conduct is a "fault mitigator," it should be allowed as a defense at the guilt adjudication stage, rather than merely at the penalty stage.
5. *Development of comparative liability in tort law.* Tort and criminal law doctrines have significant similarities. Tort theory has recognized the principle of comparative responsibility and continues to broaden the scope of its application. The comparative responsibility reform that has occurred in tort law supplies guidelines for conducting a similar reform in criminal law.

Together, these arguments make a general claim that the victim's conduct *may* be a relevant consideration in determining the perpetrator's liability. The next few chapters, and particularly Chapters 4 and 6, propose a method for distinguishing situations in which the victim's conduct should be legally relevant from those in which it should be irrelevant, with the goal of developing a comprehensive theory of comparative responsibility in criminal law.

Part 2

TOWARD A UNIFYING THEORY OF COMPARATIVE CRIMINAL LIABILITY

3 WHAT HAPPENS TO VICTIMS' RIGHTS IN SITUATIONS OF CONSENT, SELF-DEFENSE, AND PROVOCATION?

IT IS GENERALLY recognized that the perpetrator's liability depends not only on an act of wrongdoing committed with certain culpability but also on a violation of some kind of a legal and moral norm. Most norms of criminal law are rights-based rather than duty-based;[1] namely, part of what makes the perpetrator's act offensive is a violation of a victim's right—the more serious the violation, the more serious the offense.

Conversely, a voluntary act (whether intentional, reckless, or negligent) that harms the victim but does not violate his rights is usually not subject to criminal liability. For example, I did not invite someone to my party. That could happen by mistake, even an unreasonable, negligent mistake, or on purpose. The uninvited person may be harmed—his reputation and social status may suffer, he may lose out on certain career opportunities presented at the party, or he may endure a monetary loss because of the purchases and other expenditures made in anticipation of the party. Despite all of those harms, tangible and intangible, subjective and objective, I am clearly not liable for them, because I have not violated any legal right of that person.

With this in mind, let us revisit the theories of consent, self-defense, and provocation. What is common to all of them? In all three theories, the victim did something that abridged his *right not to be harmed* and, therefore, completely or partially *justified* the actor by eliminating or mitigating the actor's responsibility for the harm. This suggests a unitary explanation to the three theories, an explanation that takes into account actions of both the perpetrator and the victim. Moreover, this suggests a general principle of criminal law, *the principle of conditionality of our rights*, that needs to be recognized across the board, and not just sporadically, in connection with a few historically defined defenses. The essence of this principle is that *the criminal liability of the perpetrator should be reduced to the extent the victim, by his own acts, has diminished his right not to be harmed by the perpetrator.* Defenses of consent, self-defense, and provocation illustrate how this principle works in the confrontational and nonconfrontational settings.

CONSENTING VICTIMS

In most instances, consent presents an easy case. By giving consent, a person voluntarily *waives* his right to a certain freedom that he otherwise would enjoy. For example, one may not limit my freedom of movement by locking me up in one's apartment, unless I agree to that confinement. By agreeing, I waive, for a certain period of time, my right to move freely. In addition, I assume the risk, whether I realize that or not, that I may not like being all alone in an unfamiliar apartment, that I may suddenly remember important business I have to attend to, or even that I may have a hard time getting out in the case of a fire.

In other words, I may be objectively hurt by my consent and I may subjectively regret it. Nevertheless, my rights have not been violated; therefore, the person who locked me in is guilty of no offense. As the famous maxim goes, "a person is not wronged by that to which he consents."[2] But how literally should we read this maxim? Does consent always have the power to change the moral and legal character of another person's actions? It certainly precludes a number of serious offenses, such as theft, rape, or kidnapping. At the same time, at least some cases of physical harm—such as consensual gladiatorial contests, deadly torture, or organ-harvesting killings—intuitively feel wrongful despite their voluntary nature. This incongruity raises two questions: one, why do we perceive consent to bodily harm so differently than consent to any other activity; and two, if we were to revise the current law of consent, where should we draw the line between permissible and impermissible bodily harm?

The answer to the first question lies in the different nature of the act in cases of theft, rape, or kidnapping, on the one hand; and cases of killing or maiming, on the other hand. In the first group of cases, the *act itself* does not violate a prohibitory norm. Having sex, transporting someone to a different location, or taking other people's property is not bad *per se*. It becomes bad *only* because of the absence of consent. In other words, in all those cases the role of consent is *inculpatory*—nonconsent is a part of the definition of the offense.[3] In contrast, killing or hurting another is bad *per se*. The fact that a person may be legally justified in, say, killing an aggressor in self-defense does not make the killing as morally neutral as borrowing a book; it is still regrettable. It is still regrettable that a dental patient has to suffer pain, even though the dentist is justified in causing it, whereas there is nothing regrettable in consensual sex or consensual change of ownership. To lose or reduce its inherent wrongfulness, the act of killing or hurting requires justification. The role of consent here is *exculpatory*; it may only serve as a defense.

In practical terms, it means that consent precludes even a prima facie case of rape or theft, regardless of whether the consensual act brings about more good than harm and regardless of whether the defendant is aware of the victim's consent. Significantly more is required for a successful defense. Why is that so? Mainly because we view a defense of justification as a limited license to commit an otherwise prohibited act in order to achieve a socially and morally desirable outcome. For instance, if a group of mountaineers caught by a snowstorm took refuge in a deserted cabin and consumed the owner's provisions, they would be justified under the defense of necessity.[4] This limited license is teleological in nature; it presumes an objectively preferable outcome and the good faith of the actors. If, say, the mountaineers simply decided to have a party in the cabin, we would not grant them the defense of necessity even if, unknowingly, they in fact saved their lives by hiding from the upcoming snowstorm. In order to be justified, the mountaineers must establish three elements: (1) the basis for the defense (actual necessity), (2) an objectively preferable outcome (a positive balance of harms and evils), and (3) the subjective awareness of the justifying circumstances and intent directed at achieving this preferable outcome.[5]

Applying the same logic to the defense of consent, we, therefore, should only grant complete justification to the perpetrator who, in addition to having valid consent of the victim (the basis for the defense), also achieved a better balance of harms and evils, was aware of the victim's consent, and was motivated by the desire to achieve a better result. The first issue that needs to be addressed, therefore, is what is *valid consent*? Even more generally, what is the meaning of *consent*? Does this term refer to one's willingness to agree to a certain proposal (factual attitudinal consent) or one's expression of acquiescence by words or conduct (factual expressive consent)?[6] It appears that the answer to this question depends, once again, on the function of consent in a particular offense: if nonconsent plays the inculpatory role, then either attitudinal or expressive consent should suffice as a predicate for a legally valid consent and preclude the offense. For example, the charge of rape would be unwarranted if a legally competent person voluntarily expressed his willingness to engage in a sexual act, regardless of how closely that willingness reflected his true feelings. That charge would be equally unwarranted if a legally competent person wholeheartedly welcomed the sexual intimacy yet never outwardly expressed his feelings.[7] In contrast, when consent plays the exculpatory role, only expressive acquiescence may provide the basis for legally valid consent. This stricter requirement is necessitated by the last element of the defense: the perpetrator must be aware of the victim's consent, and it is impossible to be "aware" of someone's state of mind, unless that person has somehow expressed his preferences.

To be legally valid, factual consent must be rational and voluntary, that is, freely given and informed.[8] Consent obtained by duress or fraud regarding the nature of the perpetrator's act is void ab initio,[9] and so is consent given by a person who cannot understand the nature of that to which he consents. Certain groups of people (e.g., children, mentally ill, intoxicated) in most instances are deemed incapable of granting valid consent.[10] In addition, there is a strong argument that courts should require higher levels of rationality and voluntariness of the victim's decision as the amount of inflicted or risked harm increases.[11] For example, a simple "Sure, why not?" may be sufficient to constitute consent for piercing one's ears but not for cutting them off. Particularly dangerous or irreparable decisions (e.g., consensual homicide) may even be presumed involuntary until proven otherwise.[12]

Legally valid consent is all that is needed to exculpate the perpetrator of an offense that lists nonconsent as an element. For a successful defense, on the other hand, the perpetrator also has to prove that, by his prima facie illegal act, he managed to avoid a greater harm. This requirement raises a complicated question of law and policy. Traditionally, criminal harm is understood as wrongful interference with the victim's essential welfare interests;[13] the interference is deemed wrongful if it violates the victim's rights. Thus, in theory, consent—being a waiver of rights—should equally preclude criminal wrongdoing in cases of assisted suicide, consensual cannibalistic killing, and sadomasochistic beating. Under the current law, however, the outcome is completely opposite: in all three cases, the defendants are guilty, and in the first two cases, guilty of the same offense, murder. And yet many of us would probably perceive a meaningful difference between these three fact patterns, a difference that is not accounted for by either the current legal rule or the traditional doctrine. What is this difference, and how should the statute and the doctrine be revised to reflect accurately the perpetrator's culpability?

In recent years, a number of scholars have suggested that the concept of criminal harm should not be limited to violation of one's autonomy.[14] In their view, gladiatorial contests and similar acts are impermissible because they violate the participants' dignity, and dignity is so essential to our humanity that in cases of a conflict between autonomy and dignity, the former ought to yield.[15] Accordingly, consent may not serve as a defense to the violation of dignity.

Meir Dan-Cohen, for example, argues that the reason society should outlaw slavery, even in the hypothetical case of voluntary "happy slaves,"[16] is because slavery represents a "paradigm of injustice," which by its very terms denies people's equal moral worth and thus treats them with disrespect.[17] Similarly, R. A. Duff finds voluntary gladiatorial contests unacceptable because of the "dehumanization or degradation perpetrated by the gladiators on each other, and by the spectators on the gladiators and on themselves."[18]

I share the view that certain degrading behavior may be wrongful even when it does not violate the victim's rights. Society may be concerned about human dignity in various circumstances, including those in which a prohibitory norm does not originate in a rights violation. Consider experiments conducted in the 1980s that involved the use of fresh cadavers as "crash dummies."[19] When those experiments became known, they caused public outrage. But why? We usually do not feel offended by autopsies or postmortem organ donation. Perhaps, as Joel Feinberg suggested, the answer has something to do with the perceived symbolism of the different uses:

> In the air bag experiments cadavers were violently smashed to bits, whereas dissections are done in laboratories by white-robed medical technicians in spotless antiseptic rooms, radiating the newly acquired symbolic respectability of professional medicine.[20]

Or perhaps the difference is not merely symbolic, and violently smashing cadavers to bits is, in fact, disrespectful—disrespectful of our only recently shared humanity? An act of autopsy or removal of an organ for transplantation is not qualitatively different from a regular surgery. Extracting a kidney, inter vivo or postmortem, does not reduce one's moral status to that of a thing. Smashing a body in an industrial experiment or using human remains to manufacture soap does have this effect. In other words, even when an act of indignity is committed on an unconscious or dead body or when the victim does not perceive an assault on his dignity as such, a wrongful act has been done.

Furthermore, violation of dignity does not require malicious intent of the perpetrator. Regardless of how respectfully Armin Meiwes treated Bernd Brandes, cannibalism *by its very terms* denies people equal moral worth and, thus, assaults the victim's dignity. The concept of dignity, therefore, does not reflect the subjective state of mind of the perpetrator or the victim but instead has an "objective," normative meaning. What is at stake here is people's moral dignity, or dignity of personhood, as opposed to social dignity, or dignity of rank. Social dignity is nonessential; in a society that permits social mobility, it can be gained and lost. Moral dignity, by contrast, is an essential characteristic of all human beings.[21] It is so important for our collective humanity that we extend it to all those who satisfy "the minimum requirements of personhood,"[22] and even beyond that, to those who closely miss them.

And yet, as important as moral dignity is, its violation should not be criminalized lightly. Whenever the state prohibits consensual behavior, for the sake of dignity or any other reason, it suppresses individual liberty and autonomy—partly paternalistically, but mostly for the benefit of society at large. In the words of Joel Feinberg,

> When B requests that A do something for (or to) him that is directly harmful or dangerous to B's interests, or when the idea originates with A and he solicits and receives B's permission to do that thing, then (in either case) B can be said to have consented to A's action. If nevertheless the criminal law prohibits A from acting in such cases, it invades B's liberty (by preventing him from getting what he wanted from A) or his autonomy (by depriving his voluntary consent of its effect).[23]

Therefore, the threat to society should be serious enough to warrant use of criminal sanctions.[24] For instance, the careless attitude to human dignity exhibited by *Fear Factor*, a television reality show, has raised concerns of a number of its viewers. One journalist commented: "Do we really need to see people buried under 400 rats, each biting the exposed body parts of the desperate contestants? No. And it doesn't get any more palatable when someone yells out, 'Keep your butt cheeks clenched!'"[25]

It is understandable that those pictures may disturb some members of the public, yet the nature and magnitude of the personal and societal harm brought about by the show would not justify a criminal ban—it is simply "not the law's business,"[26] at least, not the criminal law's business. Anthony Duff has accurately observed that not punishing someone's conduct does not mean approving it; instead, that can mean the lack of standing to judge or condemn such conduct.[27] We do not have to approve of radical cosmetic surgery, religious flagellation, or sadomasochistic brutality; however, society may be better served by not prosecuting those consensual activities.

In other words, not any violation of human dignity deserves criminal punishment, but only such that affects society at large. To avoid overcriminalization yet capture the most egregious cases, I suggest that disregard of one's dignity should be criminalized only if it is combined with a setback to an interest protected by criminal law. To that end, the criminal doctrine should explicitly include dignity violation in the concept of wrongdoing.[28] Criminal harm then would retain its current meaning as a wrongful setback to an important welfare interest, but "wrongful" would mean either (1) such as violates the victim's autonomy or (2) such as violates the victim's dignity.[29] The two kinds of criminal harm comprise the same evil—objectification of another human being. That evil may be brought about by an injury to a vital human interest, combined with either a rights violation (e.g., theft) or disregard of the victim's dignity (e.g., consensual deadly torture). The absolute majority of criminal offenses, being nonconsensual, include both kinds of harm.

As for the consensual physical harm, it should be punishable only when an important welfare interest normally protected by criminal law is set back in a way that denies the victim his equal moral worth. For example, by killing Brandes, Meiwes did not violate the former's right to life.[30] However, he not only defeated the most essential interest of Brandes (his interest in continued living) but also used Brandes as an object, a means of obtaining the desired cannibalistic experience, and thus disregarded his dignity. In contrast, consensual mercy killing destroys the patient's interest in continued living but, when warranted by the patient's condition and motivated by compassion, respects and preserves his dignity. Such killing, therefore, should not be subject to criminal sanctions. Unfortunately, the current law does not recognize this difference. In *Michigan v. Kevorkian*, for example, the state prosecuted Dr. Kevorkian for administering a lethal injection to a former racecar driver who, as a result of advanced Lou Gehrig's disease, was no longer able to move, eat, or breathe on his own.[31] Even the patient's family had accepted his choice to escape the suffering and indignity of the slow demise. But not the trial court or the appellate court: Dr. Kevorkian was convicted of second-degree murder, and his conviction was affirmed.[32]

The proposed revision of the concept of criminal harm has two normative consequences. One is that consent should always be at least a partial defense, since it defeats at least one aspect of harm, namely, violation of rights. A partial justification does not make a wrongful act right; it makes it less wrongful compared to an identical but nonconsensual act. Consider *United States v. Holmes*, a famous mid-nineteenth-century case in which a ship's crew and thirty-two passengers were cast adrift on a lifeboat after a shipwreck on the high seas.[33] The boat was grossly overcrowded, and it soon became apparent that it would sink unless some lives were sacrificed. The first mate ordered the crew to throw overboard all male passengers whose wives were not on the boat. Holmes was one of the crewmembers who followed the order. By the time a rescue ship arrived, sixteen passengers were jettisoned, fourteen men and two women, although the circumstances surrounding the death of the women were not quite certain. The *Holmes* court observed:

> It was a matter of doubt whether these women (two sisters of Frank Askin . . .) had been thrown over, or whether their sacrifice was an act of self-devotion and affection to their brother. When Holmes seized him, his sisters entreated for his life, and said that if he was thrown over they wished to be thrown over too; that "they wished to die the death of their brother."[34]

Holmes was convicted of manslaughter. The court pointed out that, while normally people do not have a duty to save each other by sacrificing their own lives, in this case such a duty existed—the duty of the crew to the passengers.

Now, suppose that the lifeboat carried no crewmembers, and the passengers did not forcibly throw selected people overboard but instead asked for volunteers. Suppose further that the sisters Askin, along with their brother, offered their lives in order to save others. Would it be wrong for their fellow passengers to accept this sacrifice and throw them overboard? I think that, even if it were, it would certainly be less wrong than drowning those who have not volunteered. It would be less wrong because it was the Askins' choice to give up their lives. The actor who threw them over did not violate their rights. Accordingly, he brought about less harm than in the nonconsensual offense and, thus, deserves a lesser punishment.

Moreover, there is a strong argument that the perpetrator in this case deserves not merely partial but complete justification. As suggested above, a consensual act should be punished only if it both sets back an important welfare interest of the victim and infringes upon the victim's dignity. In the modified *Holmes* case, the perpetrator destroyed the victims' interests in continued living, but he did not disregard their dignity. Instead, he assisted them in carrying out their noble decision to save numerous human lives, which otherwise would have been lost.

The second normative consequence of the proposed revision of the doctrine of criminal harm is that consent alone does not suffice to justify the victim's death or injury. To qualify for a full justification, the perpetrator has to establish that his harmful act has produced an overall positive "balance of evils." That harmful act may advance interests of people other than the victim (as in the modified *Holmes* story), provided, however, the perpetrator did not wrongfully interfere with the victim's well-being, that is, he did not significantly set back the victim's interests and, at the same time, disregard the victim's dignity. Naturally, the more serious (disabling and irreversible) is the harm to the victim, the more serious must be the reason for the injurious action. A sadomasochistic beating, which leaves no permanent damage, should be justified by the mere fact that its participants desired it. Even those who believe that such beating offends the victim's dignity would probably agree that it does not significantly affect the victim's long-term interests. On the other hand, only extraordinary circumstances might be able to justify consensual deadly torture.

In addition, for complete justification, the perpetrator would have to establish that not only did he act with the victim's consent and achieved a positive balance of harms and evils, but he also intended that outcome while causing harm. This subjective requirement, common to other justification defenses, is mandated by the fact that consent of the victim creates a very weak content-independent reason for action: it does not impose on the perpetrator an *obligation* to act but merely provides the perpetrator with an *option*. For example, I may request (and simultaneously consent to) a surgery. If my doctor does not believe I need one or is reluctant to perform it himself, he is under no duty to do so. As a free moral agent, the perpetrator needs a good-faith belief in the justifiability of interfering with another person's physical well-being in order to be justified.

In short, one's acquiescence or even affirmative request is not a sufficient condition for the defense of consent. When a child breaks a rule, we demand:

"Why did you do that?" This is a question about a moral reason for action and effectively about the availability of a defense. What we want to know is whether the child had a good reason for violating the rule of conduct. We are unlikely to accept "Because so-and-so told me to" as a valid reason or defense. The classic parental reply to that would be: "And what if he told you to jump off the Brooklyn Bridge?" By this reply, we in fact say: "You are a free moral agent. Why, being a free moral agent, did you choose to break the rule (cause harm)?"

One could argue that when the perpetrator, acting in the best interests of the victim, produces a measurably positive outcome, the victim's consent is nonessential. Indeed, sometimes the law justifies a benevolent intervention that overrides another person's autonomy. For example, it is permissible to use force against a person in order to stop his suicidal attempt. At least in part, this rule reflects societal perception of suicide as inherently irrational. Whether this perception is accurate and the rule is morally sustainable may be debated. It is clear, however, that the scope of this rule is very narrow. It is impermissible to force-feed a competent, free individual who wishes to starve himself to death. It is impermissible to perform a surgery on an unwilling patient, even if that surgery is beneficial for the patient's health. And it is certainly impermissible to perform involuntary euthanasia on any conscious human being in any circumstances.

Consider *Gilbert v. State*, in which the court convicted a seventy-five-year-old man of first-degree murder for shooting his wife to death.[35] Roswell and Emily Gilbert had been married for fifty-one years. For the last few years of her life, Emily suffered from osteoporosis and Alzheimer's disease, and her condition rapidly deteriorated. Testifying at his trial, Roswell Gilbert said: "There she was in pain and all this confusion and I guess if I got cold as icewater that's what had happened. I thought to myself, I've got to do it . . . I've got to end her suffering."[36]

As dramatic and sad as this case is, the appellate court was right to affirm the defendant's conviction. Roswell Gilbert was motivated by compassion and the desire to protect his wife from suffering, and in fact he did everything in his power to make her death as painless as possible.[37] But even if her condition were so desperate that Roswell objectively benefited Emily by cutting short her agony, he should not be entitled to justification. Unauthorized homicide of an autonomous human being is, and should be, murder. No one has the right to decide for another person that his life is not worth living; or, citing the words of the *Gilbert* opinion, "'[g]ood faith' is not a legal defense to first degree murder."[38]

To summarize, for a complete defense of justification, the perpetrator's reasons for the consensual injurious act, both objectively and subjectively, must (1) be overall benevolent and (2) not significantly injure both the victim's welfare interests and dignity. These normative requirements make sense theoretically as well as practically. From the theoretical perspective, they place consent squarely within the family of justification defenses. All of them, from self-defense to necessity, seek to overcome the deontological constraint against intentional infliction of harm. These defenses may be granted to a person who chose a certain course of action *despite* its negative effects (as opposed to *for the sake of* its negative effects) and either succeeded in producing a morally preferable outcome or at least did his best to produce it.[39] From the practical perspective, these requirements leave room for balancing the harms and benefits caused by the perpetrator. This is an important difference from the current law, which is absolute in what it allows and disallows.

The proposed rule would strike a good balance between private and public interests. On the one hand, by giving legal weight to self-regarding decisions of the victim, the law would show respect to the autonomy of the victim as well as the perpetrator. On the other hand, by protecting the victim's dignity from most egregious abuse, the law would guard our collective interest in preserving humanity. Overall, adopting a rule based on a uniform principle common to other justification defenses would lead to more fair, consistent, and morally sustainable verdicts.

AGGRESSORS AND DEFENDERS IN CASES OF SELF-DEFENSE

The Case of Innocent Aggressors: Justification or Excuse?

In a case of self-defense, the aggressor (and ultimate victim) does something similar to the consenting victim. By attacking an unoffending person, the victim-aggressor *gives up* his right to bodily integrity and possibly even to life. Most philosophical explanations of self-defense implicitly or explicitly draw on the idea of the aggressor's forfeiture of rights[40]—"at the moment a homicidal aggressor puts another life in jeopardy, his own life is forfeit to his threatened victim."[41] Without a foundation of this kind, it is difficult to explain why the defendant is justified in killing a deadly aggressor, that is, why the life of one person is preferable to the life of another.

The concept of forfeiture has an intuitive appeal when we think of the paradigmatic case of a culpable aggressor attacking an innocent victim. But what if both the victim and the aggressor are innocent? An aggressor may be innocent because his aggression was not voluntary (the so-called innocent threat)[42] or because of an affirmative defense of excuse (duress, insanity, or infancy)[43] or sometimes even justification.[44] The last statement requires certain elaboration because usually innocent aggressors are defined as those who attack nonculpably yet without justification.[45] This qualification is understandable: the traditional criminal law doctrine presumes that only one side in a conflict may be justified. As George Fletcher phrased it, the "determination that the conduct is justified presupposes a judgment about the superior social interest in the conflict."[46] Accordingly, if an attack is justified, the victim has no right to resist it. But is this conclusion always true?

Consider the following hypothetical: a group of people is captured by criminals. The criminals are about to kill everyone, but then they have a change of heart and offer their victims a deal: if Jack rapes Jill, the criminals will let everyone go. Otherwise, no one's life will be spared. Realizing that this is the only way to rescue several lives, including Jill's own, Jack reluctantly agrees. Jill, on the other hand, vehemently protests that she would rather die than be violated. When Jack attempts to overpower her, Jill fights back and seriously injures Jack.

In this hypothetical, both Jack and Jill are justified. Jack is justified under the defense of necessity (the balance of evils).[47] Sexual intercourse compelled by force involves both harm and evil. Yet, judging from the objective perspective, those harm and evil are still lesser than the harm and evil associated with the murder of several innocent people; thus, Jack deserves justification. But Jill is justified as well. A person is allowed to use any necessary force, including deadly force, to resist forcible rape.[48] Yet, although both Jack and Jill have valid defenses, Jill is "more right" than Jack: if she kills Jack in self-defense, she will be justified, but Jack will not be justified if he kills Jill while trying to rape her or in response to her use of defensive force. Interestingly, as between Jack and Jill, the law treats an innocent aggressor no differently than a culpable one: Jill may use the same force against Jack as against a villainous rapist. Moreover, the law treats an "innocent threat," a person who has committed no criminal act at all, the very same way.

Take the case of Mrs. Cogdon, who, in a somnambulistic state, killed her daughter Pat with an axe.[49] Engulfed in a dream, in which she attempted to protect her daughter from violent intenders, Mrs. Cogdon "left her bed, fetched an axe from the woodheap, entered Pat's room, and struck her two accurate forceful blows on the head with the blade of the axe, thus killing her."[50] Mrs. Cogdon was charged with murder but acquitted because the act of killing was deemed to be involuntary and thus "was not, in law, regarded as her act at all."[51] But what if before the first fatal blow fell, Pat woke up and tried to defend herself—would she be justified if, after all other attempts failed, she shot her mother to death? The answer is yes. Yet how can we say that Mrs. Cogdon, who reportedly adored her daughter, has forfeited her right to life without even waking up? Even if she did, shouldn't that be determined by the state, at a trial, and not by a private actor? And isn't forfeiture of the right to life too harsh a penalty for an unsuccessful homicidal attempt?

One way out of this conundrum is to regard the hypothetical killing of Mrs. Cogdon or Jack not as justifiable but rather as excusable homicide, that is, to claim not that Pat was right in killing her mother or Jill was right in killing Jack, but that both Pat and Jill were wrong yet we understand their predicament and forgive them. This position has been cleverly advocated by Lawrence A. Alexander:

> We can sympathize with and excuse a person who uses deadly force to fend off innocent aggressors, but we cannot say that it is right for him to do so. Attack by innocent aggressors is better characterized as a case of duress that excuses homicide, not a case of Wrong that justifies it.[52]

At first glance, Alexander's proposal seems attractive. It allows us to distinguish between killings of villainous and innocent aggressors. However, it also leads to two major conceptual problems. The first one deals with innocent bystanders, the second one with the defense of another.

If we are willing to excuse the intentional killing of an innocent aggressor, it must be because we focus entirely on the emotional upheaval of the attacked. But, from that perspective, there is no difference between an innocent aggressor and an innocent bystander. By that logic, we have to excuse intentional killing of an innocent bystander too. In fact, we have to excuse intentional killing of *any number of innocent bystanders* if such sacrifice appears to the perpetrator necessary for his personal survival. For instance, we have to exculpate a man who, in order to save his own life, obeyed a terrorist's order and planted a bomb in a daycare center. It is unlikely that many of us would find this solution morally acceptable. As Lord Salmon has put it, "Is there any limit to the number of people you may kill to save your own life and that of your family?"[53]

The other problem is the following: one of the differences between justification and excuse is that excuse is always personal, whereas justification is universal (anyone is licensed to act this way).[54] Therefore, a person may not benefit from someone else's excuse but may benefit from someone else's justification.[55] The defense of another extends to a third party the justification of self-defense available to the attacked person. If we view Pat's defensive killing of her mother as merely excusable, that would mean that no one else would be able to save Pat's life by killing Mrs. Cogdon. That outcome does not seem right.

Moreover, the excusatory interpretation of self-defense destroys the very basis for the defense of another. Traditionally, a third-party defender is said to "stand in the shoes" of the person in danger.[56] If the attacked person were merely excused in his self-defense, the third party would be entitled neither to that excuse (excuse is always personal) nor to the justification based on the extension of self-defense (why should he, if the victim of the attack is not?). One way to put up with a third party's intervention would be by also granting him a personal excuse. Then the law would consider the defender's actions wrong but would excuse his violent reaction to the witnessed attack. A major problem with this proposition is that it makes it absolutely irrelevant on whose side the third party intervenes, the attacker or the attacked. The defense of another, thus, loses any moral ground.

Alexander deals with this dead-end outcome by suggesting that "third parties may intervene only pursuant to a lesser evils calculus"[57]; thus, according to Alexander, when an innocent victim is outnumbered by innocent aggressors, a third party may intervene only on the side of the aggressors.[58] For example, if two people attack me because they mistakenly but reasonably believe that I am about to attack them, they are innocent aggressors. I may use any necessary force to defend myself. However, if a bystander who has been watching the entire incident and knows that the two aggressors are wrong decides to intervene, he would be able to do so only on the side of the aggressors. Could that be right? Or, say, I am attacked by a group of violent maniacs who clearly qualify for the defense of insanity. Does Alexander suggest that a Good Samaritan may only help *them* to finish *me*? I share Alexander's intuition that "[t]his conclusion will leave some readers very unhappy."[59]

Self-Defense as a Theory of Justification

This analysis brings us back to the starting point—self-defense (other than mistaken self-defense) requires some kind of a justificatory, and not merely excusatory, explanation as to why an aggressor's claim to life is inferior to a nonaggressor's. Those who reject the theory of forfeiture often favor its alternative, the theory of specification. Pursuant to the specification theory, individuals do not lose rights; their rights are limited from the outset. For example, a person does not have a right not to be killed. Instead, he has the right not to be killed wrongly or unjustly (pursuant to the moral version of specification) or except in certain circumstances (pursuant to factual specification), and in this limited form his right not to be killed is absolute.

This perspective is appealing but misguided. It is appealing because, at least on its face, it avoids the moral objection against "punishing" innocent aggressors by taking away their rights. Under the specification theory, innocent aggressors, like everyone else, simply lack certain rights. Lacking rights is obviously regrettable, but not as regrettable as losing them, particularly without fault. This psychological phenomenon has been described in the economic literature as the "endowment effect": people would rather not have an entitlement at all than lose it.[60]

The appeal of the specification theory, however, is quite illusory: in essence, it denies people the most basic human rights and social freedoms. Under this theory, for instance, Jill has never had a right "not to be raped." She only had a limited right "not to be raped, unless such rape is beneficial to society." It is doubtful that incorporating this and similar propositions into law would result in a morally superior legal and social discourse.

Moreover, if we followed the view that people's rights are limited from the outset, we would not be able to explain why Jill had a right to defend herself against rape or why someone whose property was justifiably taken for public or private use is entitled to compensation.[61] Recall the hypothetical in which a group of mountaineers caught by a snowstorm took refuge in a vacant cabin and consumed the owner's provisions. Under the specification theory, the cabin owner never had a right that his property not be taken in this kind of emergency; therefore, the mountaineers do not owe him any compensation. That outcome would not only be blatantly unfair but would also contradict a significant body of law.[62]

A better theory is the one under which the owner of the cabin has unabridged property rights and the mountaineers, Jack, and Jill have unabridged rights to physical inviolability. Those rights, however, are not absolute. People may lose them by their own acts (e.g., consent or unprovoked aggression). In addition, rights may be overridden although the right-holders did nothing to lose or reduce them.[63] For example, when Jack raped Jill, he overrode her right not to be raped in order to preserve equally or more important rights of a group of people. From the perspective of punishment, he overrode Jill's right nonwrongfully; from the perspective of Jill's autonomy, however, it was a wrongful act.[64] At all moments of Jack's attack, Jill retained the right that he not do that to her. By disregarding Jill's right, Jack breached his duty to Jill and lost his own right to physical inviolability. That allowed Jill to fight back the same way she would be allowed to resist a villainous aggressor.

So, where does this take us? Between the two major theories of rights—forfeiture and specification—the former provides a more sustainable, both morally and logically, justification for self-defense, with two caveats. First, I find its name rather unfortunate.[65] "Forfeiture" is a loaded term strongly associated with punishment. It is possible to forfeit a right nonculpably (e.g., a person may lose parental rights if he becomes insane). Usually, however, forfeiture presupposes fault. For the purposes of comparative criminal liability, it is, therefore, more accurate to talk about loss or reduction of rights by both culpable and nonculpable aggressors rather than forfeiture.

The other caveat is perhaps more important. I suggest that we distinguish between aggressors who *chose* to change their moral status vis-à-vis the perpetrator and aggressors who lacked that capacity. The second group includes "innocent threats," as well as aggressors covered by defenses of mistake, extreme infancy, and insanity (but *not* necessity or duress). We ought to hold that only the aggressors who have the capacity to choose a course of action may be said to have lost or reduced their rights; otherwise we will end up with an absurd conclusion that a person may lose rights while acting in sleep or delusion. When aggressors lack this capacity, the justification for the perpetrator's use of defensive force should be based on the "overriding" of rights of the innocent aggressors, not on their loss of rights.

Compare, for example, cases of self-defense against a villainous aggressor and against an innocent aggressor like Mrs. Cogdon. In both instances, the attacked person is justified in causing harm to the aggressor to the extent necessary to protect himself from the harm the aggressor would otherwise inflict. But in the first case, the aggressor did something to deserve that harm, whereas in the second case, the unfortunate Mrs. Cogdon just happened to be at the wrong place at the wrong time. As between Mrs. Cogdon and Pat, the law prefers a nonprovoking and nonoffending victim Pat; thus, Mrs. Cogdon's right of physical inviolability is "overridden" by a more stringent competing right of Pat.[66] What makes Pat's right to use force more stringent is that her harmful actions are responsive to the threat not attributable to her, and a responsive act does not bear the same moral weight as an independent act.

One may—and probably should—feel qualms that sometimes rights depend on pure luck or lack thereof. Yet, justly or not, this is certainly true for many other areas of life as well: say Matt Murphy happened to be at the right place at the right time to catch Barry Bonds's record-breaking home run ball and, thus, secure property rights in it.[67] In contrast, Andrew Speaker happened to be at the wrong place at the wrong time to catch a dangerous form of tuberculosis. As a result, he was confined in a hospital, his liberty rights temporarily overridden by considerations of public health.[68]

Self-Defense, Rights, and Compensation

Although the law authorizes use of force against innocent and culpable aggressors alike, when the aggressor is injured, his right to compensation largely depends on his innocent or culpable status. For example, all states have adopted Crime Victim Compensation Statutes, which provide for payment of compensation to victims of crimes or their dependents. These statutes, however, bar recovery to victims who by their own conduct (e.g., provocation) contributed to their injuries. Similarly, many European public compensation schemes bar or limit recovery when the victim is partly at fault. For example, in Germany, "[c]ompensation can be refused if the victim has been (jointly) responsible for the injury"; in Greece, compensation may be reduced "if it is considered that the victim's behaviour contributed to the occurrence or level of loss incurred"; and in the Netherlands, "[p]ayment may be refused on grounds of co-responsibility of the victim."[69] As Markus Dubber pointed out, to "find that a person is compensable as a victim is to find that she is innocent; to find her not innocent is tantamount to declaring her noncompensable."[70]

An innocent threat like Mrs. Cogdon is both an aggressor and a victim. Should she be entitled to compensation even though Pat would have been justified in causing her injury? The statutes do not address this issue specifically. However, under most of them, as well as under the Uniform Victims of Crime Act (UVCA), the focus is not on the offender but on the victim. This is not surprising: a person may be hurt by someone who, technically speaking, is not an "offender" (e.g., minor, incompetent, insane). The principal question for the victim's recovery is whether the victim himself is responsible for his injury.

When the victim is fully responsible, courts usually reject his claim for compensation. However, when the victim's responsibility is only partial, the court may first consider the victim's capacity and only then decide whether he deserves any reward. In *In Re Beach*, for instance, the victim, a young boy, sustained injuries in a fight with another boy, a fight the victim himself instigated. The court did not automatically deny him recovery. Instead, it opined that "the victim's age and corresponding capacity can be considered in our contributory misconduct analysis, and, if we choose to do so, we believe we can reduce an award . . . and thereby enter the applicant's youth and character into the equation."[71] By analogy, there seems to be a strong argument that if Mrs. Cogdon were killed or injured by Pat's self-defense, the court should take into account Mrs. Cogdon's complete, if temporary, lack of capacity and allow her compensation. She should be entitled to compensation the same way the cabin owner whose rights were overridden under the private necessity should be compensated by the mountaineers and the same way a person confined in the quarantine for public health reasons should be compensated by the state.

What is the relationship between compensation (i.e., being innocent), punishment (i.e., being guilty), and the right to fight back? Here are some examples. If Jack raped Jill in order to save the lives of all hostages and she objected but did not fight back, he would most likely be justified. If the stranded mountaineers broke into a deserted cabin, they would be justified. If Pat shot Mrs. Cogdon in self-defense, Pat would be justified. In all three cases, the victims did nothing to lose their rights; these rights were overridden by some more stringent rights of others. In all three cases, the victim should be entitled to compensation. But only in the first case would the victim be justified if she fought back. Why is that?

I believe that this is so because only in the first case has the perpetrator lost his right to physical inviolability by breaching his duty to Jill. In the second case, the mountaineers certainly breached their duty to the cabin owner. Just as Jack, they committed a justified, nonpunishable wrongdoing with respect to their victim. However, unlike Jack, they are protected from the owner's use of force by the comparative magnitudes of their interests: the law authorizes only limited use of force for protection of property. Under the MPC, for instance, the "use of force to prevent or terminate trespass is not justifiable . . . if the actor knows that the exclusion of the trespasser will expose him to substantial danger of serious bodily harm."[72] Accordingly, the cabin owner would not be justified if he forcibly expelled the mountaineers into the deadly snowstorm.

As for the modified case of Mrs. Cogdon, in which Pat wakes up before her mother had a chance to bludgeon her to death, the reason Pat did not lose her right to physical inviolability is that, unlike Jack, she was not the initial aggressor. Her attempt to fend off Mrs. Cogdon's attack was entirely responsive, necessary, and proportionate. Compare Pat's predicament with George Fletcher's well-known hypothetical:

> Imagine that your companion in an elevator goes berserk and attacks you with a knife. There is no escape: the only way to avoid serious bodily harm or even death is to kill him. The assailant acts purposively in the sense that his means further his aggressive end. He does act in a frenzy or in a fit, yet it is clear that his conduct is non-responsible. If he were brought to trial for his attack, he would have a valid defence of insanity.[73]

There is little disagreement that if Pat found herself confronted by a psychotic aggressor with an axe, she would be justified in killing him, whereas he would not be justified in killing her in response to her use of force.[74] But are the attackers in these two stories all that different? Mrs. Cogdon killed Pat while acting in a dream in which she sought to protect her daughter from violent intruders. "She dreamt that 'the war was all around the house,' that the soldiers were in Pat's room, and that one soldier was on the bed attacking Pat."[75] From what we know about psychosis, Fletcher's aggressor could be acting under a delusion that a wild bear was about to attack him and he had to fight for his life.[76]

I am not trying to say that there is no difference between defenses of excuse and justification. Nor am I making a rather obvious point that sometimes the legal line between voluntary and involuntary conduct is blurred. Instead, these examples are meant to demonstrate the different considerations underlying theories of punishment, compensation, and self-defense. From the perspective of punishment, if a person is innocent (even an innocent *aggressor*), he may not be punished. From the perspective of self-defense, if a person is an aggressor (even an *innocent* aggressor), the target of his attack may kill or injure him in order to save his own life. From the perspective of compensation, if a person is an innocent aggressor, his right to compensation depends on his capacity.

Jack in the "Jack and Jill" hypothetical is an example of an aggressor who acted under the valid claim of necessity. If Jack acted as he did, but merely because the criminals threatened to rape *him* unless he raped Jill, his legal defense would be duress (necessity would not be available to him because Jack would not be able to establish that, by raping Jill, he avoided a more serious harm or evil). In both instances, even if innocent in the eyes of the law, Jack would nevertheless lose his right to physical inviolability against Jill by consciously selecting her as an involuntary target of his purposefully harmful act, thus violating her rights and denying her equal moral worth. Therefore, if Jill fought back and injured Jack, he should not be entitled to compensation.

In contrast, innocent aggressors who substantially lacked either cognitive or volitional capacity, that is, those who committed no voluntary act or culpable omission and those covered by the defenses of insanity, extreme infancy, or reasonable mistake deserve different treatment. Unlike Jack in both the "necessity" and the "duress" hypotheticals, these actors do not channel the harm or select their victims. They, quite literally, bear no responsibility for their actions. Accordingly, they should be entitled to compensation.

PROVOKING VICTIMS AND PROVOKED PERPETRATORS

Provocation and the Loss of Rights

In most cases of provocation, we see a variation of the same theme as in cases of self-defense: a perpetrator reacts, or rather overreacts, to an offensive attack on his rights by killing the offender. The violated right of the perpetrator, however, is less significant than the right to life—it is either the right to physical integrity and liberty or an important proprietary right. Traditionally, the "paradigms of misbehavior"[77] that warranted the reduction of the perpetrator's liability in cases of homicide have been (1) an aggravated assault or battery, (2) mutual combat, (3) commission of a serious crime (chiefly violent or sexual assault) against a close relative of the defendant, (4) illegal arrest, and (5) adultery.[78] Because the violated right of the perpetrator is not as essential as the right he violates, the perpetrator is not completely exonerated of his offense. Instead, his liability is reduced from murder to manslaughter.

In his analysis of provocation, Joshua Dressler finds the proposition that a provoking victim "forfeits his right to life (or, incoherently, forfeits part of his life), or that a private aggrieved individual may unilaterally determine that another human being 'sort of' deserves death or that his life does not count as much as another's—morally objectionable."[79] Let us take Dressler's concerns one by one.

True, the traditional theory of forfeiture may not work in all circumstances of provocation, just as it does not work in all cases of self-defense. One type of case that does not fit into the model is mistaken provocation, in which the defendant strikes someone who has not violated any of his rights. That could happen by reason of the defendant's misinterpretation of either the victim's actions or his own rights. Just like cases of mistaken self-defense, these cases should be viewed only through the prism of the excusatory rationale; in other words, if the defendant's fault be mitigated, that should happen for reasons other than the conduct of the victim. As for the more conventional cases of provocation, such as aggravated assault or battery, some version of loss of rights or assumption of risk seems much more acceptable.

Dressler's rejection of the forfeiture theory appears to be based on the erroneous assumption that this theory regards killing of a wrongdoer as morally insignificant.[80] However, neither this nor other theories of justification imply that. Even when we completely acquit a person for killing an aggressor in self-defense, we do not praise him. Dressler himself has maintained for many years that a prima facie criminal act may be justified when it is merely "permissible" or "tolerable," not necessarily commendable.[81] This is particularly true when we deal with provocation cases: unlike complete justification, partial justification does not eliminate liability; instead, the liability is reduced. I argued earlier in this chapter that sometimes even a completely justified act may be wrongful. As for a provoked act, it is *always* wrongful. It is a wrongful act that, due to certain mitigating circumstances, is simply less wrongful than that required by the charged offense.

Of course, normally, the rights the offender risks or loses should be on a comparable scale with the rights he attacks. Only to that extent is the defendant justified in his responsive strike. This is one reason why provocation is merely a partial justification. And, like any partial justification, provocation does not make the defendant's strike permissible; it only reduces the wrongfulness of the strike relative to what it would have been had the victim not lost some of his rights by violating the rights of the defendant.[82]

Dressler's second concern is that, by saying that provoked killing is partially justifiable, we are giving individuals the license to kill. I wonder whether, in making this claim, Dressler does not overlook the difference between a backward-looking defense and a forward-looking authorization of an otherwise prohibited act. That difference was highlighted in *Public Committee Against Torture in Israel v. State of Israel*.[83] The Supreme Court of Israel rejected the proposition that, in exceptional situations, the General Security Service (GSS) may use physical means in an interrogation of suspected terrorists. At the same time, the court did not foreclose the possibility that if criminal charges are brought against GSS interrogators, they may be able to raise the defense of necessity. The court thus drew the line between "potential liability of GSS investigators" and inferring "the authority to, in advance, establish permanent directives setting out the physical interrogation means that may be used under conditions of 'necessity.'"[84] Similarly, there is a meaningful difference between authorizing an individual to "unilaterally determine that another human being 'sort of' deserves death'"[85] and objectively and retroactively considering the degree to which the defendant's actions were justified.

Provocation and Its Triggers: The Case of Adultery

One of the most contentious issues in connection with the defense of provocation, which warrants a separate discussion, is whether discovery of an adultery should provide any, even partial, justification for the defendant's violent assault directed at his spouse or the spouse's paramour. To address this question, it is helpful to look at the law of adultery in historical perspective.

In his *Commentaries on the Laws of England*, William Blackstone described adultery as a public crime that is also a civil injury of which "surely there can be no greater."[86] The origin of the offense lay in property notions of the wife. Under the common law, "the very being or legal existence of the woman [was] suspended during the marriage, or at least [was] incorporated and consolidated into that of the husband: under whose wing, protection and *cover*, she performe[d] every thing."[87] In return for the support and protection, the wife owed her husband "consortium" of legal obligations that included services, society, and sexual intercourse.[88] Since adultery interfered with the husband's exclusive entitlements, it was perceived as "the highest possible invasion of property,"[89] similar to theft. In fact, civil actions for adultery evolved from actions for enticing away a servant from a master and thus depriving the master of the quasi-proprietary interest in his services. Given that under the early common law the status of wives was comparable to that of servants, husbands could use the action of trespass against another for the deprivation of their wives' services.[90]

The legal consequences of adultery were quite severe. In 1650, the Puritans of the Commonwealth enacted a statute that made adultery a capital offense punishable by death, and although this statute was nullified after the Restoration, the Puritans in the American colonies made adultery with a married woman a capital offense. Later, when the laws in most colonies were relaxed, death was replaced with a fine for men and flogging for women. Sometimes, adulterers were punished by life-long shaming. Like the heroine of the classic Hawthorne novel *The Scarlet Letter*, they could be forced to wear the embroidered letter "A" (for adultery) on their garments or have the letter burned into their foreheads.[91]

Perception of adultery as a serious offense has determined its role as a legal defense for the deceived husband who discovered the adultery and killed the unfaithful wife or her lover. "[A] man cannot receive a higher provocation," wrote Judge Holt in 1707.[92] He thought it to be an anomaly of law that a husband who caught his wife in an act with another man and killed the offender was not entitled to complete justification:

> [W]hen a man is taken in adultery . . . with another man's wife, if the husband shall stab the adulterer, or knock out his brains, this is bare manslaughter: for jealousy is the rage of a male, and adultery is the highest invasion of property. . . . If a thief comes to rob another, it is lawful to kill him. And if a man comes to rob a man's posterity and his family, yet to kill him is manslaughter. So is the law though it may seem hard, that the killing in the one case should not be as justifiable as the other.[93]

Some sixty years later, Blackstone, while also classifying such a killing as manslaughter, nevertheless graded it as "the lowest degree of it" and maintained that if "the court directed the burning in the hand," it should be "gently inflicted, because there could not be a greater provocation."[94]

This sentiment has been shared by many, and until recently spousal infidelity uniformly provided grounds for mitigation from murder to manslaughter. Moreover, a few American states, by a statute or court decision, regarded killing in these circumstances as justifiable homicide.[95] For example, in Georgia, a person could be justified if he killed his spouse's lover (but not the spouse) in order to prevent the beginning or the completion of an adulterous act.[96] The rule originated in *Biggs v. State*, in which the court interpreted the justifiable homicide statute to include killing by a husband of his wife's paramour:

> In what has society a deeper concern than in the protection of female purity, and the marriage relation? The wife cannot surrender herself to another. It is treason against the conjugal rights. Dirty dollars will not compensate for a breach of the nuptial vow. And if the wife is too weak to save herself, is it not the privilege of the jury to say whether the strong arm of the husband may not interpose, to shield and defend her from pollution?[97]

Under that rule, the lover could "lawfully defend himself against the husband's violence by flight only, or at least by means short of deadly";[98] in other words, the lover was treated the same way an aggressor is treated under the law of self-defense.[99] The Georgian law was repealed in 1977, when the state supreme court concluded:

> In this day of no-fault, on-demand divorce, when adultery is merely a misdemeanor, and when there is a debate raging in the country about whether capital punishment even for the most heinous crime is proper, any idea that a spouse is ever justified in taking the life of another—adulterous spouse *or* illicit lover—to prevent adultery is uncivilized.[100]

Today, killing of an adulterer or an adulteress is no longer justifiable by the law of any state. However, it is an open secret that juries regularly exercise the power of nullification and follow the "unwritten law," by which a spouse has the right to avenge the wrong done to his marriage by killing the wrongdoer.[101] When asked to decide such a case, jurors often ignore the judge's instructions and either acquit the defendant or find him guilty of a lesser offense even when formal grounds for such mitigation are lacking.

Kalven and Zeisel's study provides numerous examples of this practice.[102] In one case, a woman was seriously injured when her lover's wife attacked her with a knife. The defendant wife claimed that the victim was taking her husband away with the illicit relationship. In his summary of the case, the judge noted that the jury "believed defendant and under 'unwritten law' found defendant guilty of lesser offense of assault with a weapon and fixed a fine of 1-cent and costs."[103] He also commented on the jury's failure to go all the way to an acquittal: "The jury thought the prosecuting witness deserved 'a whipping' but that defendant went too far."[104]

In another case, the wife went to the home of her husband's mistress, broke in, and, in a struggle, injured her with an iron pipe, fracturing the woman's skull. While there were ambiguities as to who was the initial aggressor, the judge's comment indicates that the defendant's acquittal was caused by nonevidentiary considerations on the part of the jury: "This is a case in which the jury was not interested in the finer distinctions of criminal law."[105] These and other responses to Kalven and Zeisel's questionnaire show that the judges have no illusions about the impact of their instructions on the jury in comparison to the "unwritten law." According to the study, one judge remarked about the difference in the verdict he would have reached in a homicide case (capital murder) and the one the jury actually delivered (second-degree murder): "Perhaps the so-called unwritten law."[106]

Although courts strongly criticize the "unwritten law," they too have found a way to avoid harsh verdicts by relying on legal fiction, such as the rebuttable presumption of temporary insanity. In *Hamilton v. State*, for example, the defendant appeared at the police station immediately after shooting his wife's lover and said: "I have killed Calvin Martin. I didn't want to kill that man, a number of people may think it was a long time, I love my wife and children and I told Calvin over a year ago if he didn't leave my wife alone I was going to kill him."[107] The defendant was charged with murder, convicted of first-degree manslaughter, and sentenced to ten years in prison. He appealed, seeking acquittal on the ground of "temporary insanity as a result of months of brooding"[108] over the affair between his wife and the victim. The appellate court opined:

> The unwritten law, as it is so called, which authorizes a man to take the law into his own hands and take the life of a person allegedly having illicit relations with his wife, does not exist in Oklahoma, but we can perceive where a man of good moral character such as that possessed by the defendant, highly respected in his community, having regard for his duties as a husband and the virtue of women, upon learning of the immorality of his wife, might be shocked, or such knowledge might prey upon his mind and cause temporary insanity. In fact it would appear that such would be the most likely consequence of obtaining such information.[109]

The court confirmed the conviction but found the sentence excessive and shortened the term of imprisonment from ten to four years.[110]

The common theme running from cases and commentaries of colonial times into the modern application of the "unwritten law" is that the victim has wronged the defendant and, at least in part, deserves the harm befallen on him. Yet, at the same time, major social transformations—from the woman's role in the family and society to the public attitude toward marriage and sex—have clearly affected the perception of adultery as a serious wrong. Public opinion polls suggest that while Americans (90 percent of women and 85 percent of men, according to a recent Pew survey)[111] believe that adultery is morally wrong, many of them do not feel it should be criminalized.[112]

The law, to a large degree, has followed the social change. In the past forty years, more than half of all states have decriminalized adultery. Today, only twenty-four states have criminal adultery laws,[113] and only four of them classify the offense as a felony.[114] These laws are hardly ever enforced, and when enforced, the penalties are usually minor. Moreover, according to a cross-section of legal authorities, sociologists, and cultural observers, the reason these laws even remain on the books is that they have been "so infrequently invoked, there's been little pressure on anyone to decriminalize adultery."[115]

Interestingly, while the legal status of adultery as an offense has been steadily declining, the role of adultery as a defense in homicide and assault cases has remained practically unchanged. In the absolute majority of states, spousal infidelity can still trigger mitigation from murder to manslaughter. In some of those states, only witnessing the adulterous act gives legal grounds for mitigation, whereas in other states, simply learning about the adultery from the unfaithful spouse or a third party may be sufficient for a successful defense.[116]

Only one state, Maryland, has explicitly excluded spousal infidelity from the list of events providing legal basis for provocation. Maryland Penal Code reads: "The discovery of one's spouse engaged in sexual intercourse with another person does not constitute legally adequate provocation for the purpose of mitigating a killing from the crime of murder to voluntary manslaughter even though the killing was provoked by that discovery."[117] The law was adopted in response to several trials in which the defendant successfully avoided a murder conviction by claiming that he had killed his wife because he was provoked by the discovery of her infidelity.

> The case that opened the eyes of Maryland residents and led to the passage of the revised law occurred in August 1995:
>
> Rosedale resident Brian Nalls, 26, said his wife, Kimberly, admitted to cheating on him. When she said she was going to leave him that afternoon, the construction worker responded by pulling out a 12-gauge shotgun. He shot the

> 25-year-old mother as she stood in the kitchen. She died within minutes. He then called 911, confessed to the crime and surrendered to police.
>
> Although there was no evidence of infidelity presented at his January 1996 trial, Nalls was convicted of manslaughter and sentenced to 10 years. He was acquitted of second-degree and first-degree murder.[118]

Ten years after the adoption of the Maryland law, no other state has followed suit. Considering the strong public sentiment about the immorality of adultery evident in polls as well as the longevity of the "unwritten law," this is hardly surprising. Moreover, given that many states have adopted the MPC or similar version of provocation which does not list specific situational triggers but instead mitigates murder to manslaughter in cases of "extreme mental or emotional disturbance for which there is a reasonable explanation or excuse," the question becomes partly factual (was the defendant really suffering such extreme mental or emotional disturbance?) and partly legal (should witnessing, suspecting, or learning of adultery constitute reasonable explanation or excuse for extreme mental or emotional disturbance?).

Assuming both questions are answered affirmatively, that is, we agree that discovery of an adultery can cause extreme hurt and outrage and that the defendant has in fact experienced them, should that be sufficient for a successful defense of provocation? As we saw earlier, provocation is based, in part, on the justificatory rationale. That calls back the question posed in the beginning of this section: should adultery ever justify homicide, if only in part? I believe that it should not. Under the principle of conditionality of rights, a provoker may lose certain rights, and thus diminish the wrongfulness of the perpetrator's act, only when the provoker attacks a welfare interest of the perpetrator protected by law. Historically, when the wife and other family members legally remained in a quasi-proprietary relationship with the head of the household, the justificatory rationale of provocation in cases of adultery was logically cohesive.

Since then, both the legal and the lay meanings of familial relationships have undergone dramatic changes. Today, the law recognizes emotional ties within a family as well as certain duties of care and rescue. However, the proprietary basis of the familial rights and duties has long since vanished. Perhaps, conceptually, marital infidelity could be viewed now along the lines of detrimental reliance or a breach of trust. If any legal recourse is to be provided, the remedy for adultery should lie outside criminal law. And de facto, if not de jure, that is where it is. De facto, criminal law no longer protects one's entitlement to marital faithfulness. Even under torts, these expectations are not generally recognized as a legal right. Only eight states allow alienation-of-affection lawsuits. These lawsuits are rarely filed and, when filed, are usually disposed of at an early stage.[119] All these developments indicate that spousal infidelity should no longer provide a justificatory basis for the defense of provocation.

Does this automatically mean that discovery of adultery should never serve as a mitigating factor? No, it does not. Whether that discovery should be regarded a "reasonable excuse" is a totally separate issue. In general, excuse is considered reasonable if a reasonable person in the defendant's situation would not be able to avoid criminal violation.

Consider the paradigmatic excuse defense of duress. Duress may be claimed by the defendant who committed an offense because he was coerced to do so by the use of, or threat to use, unlawful force against himself or another, which *a person of reasonable firmness in his situation* would have been unable to resist.[120] The defense of duress is a limited concession to human weakness, namely, human fear of death or serious bodily harm. This concession, however, is truly limited: in the predominant majority of jurisdictions, this defense is unavailable in prosecutions for murder (and sometimes other serious offenses) even when the most stringent requirements of the imminent and inescapable lethal threat are satisfied.[121]

If we were to grant a similar limited concession to the feelings of hurt and wrath aroused by discovery of marital infidelity, it might make sense to restrict the scope of this excusatory defense in a similar fashion. The defense then would partially excuse (unlike duress, the "heat of passion" is only a partial defense) the defendant's violent outburst of emotions in circumstances when even a reasonable person would have trouble controlling himself, provided, however, that the victim has suffered no serious physical harm.

Thus, a husband who found his wife in bed with another man and killed either of them would not be able to claim "heat of passion," just as he would not be able to claim duress for homicide committed under compulsion. However, if he merely threw his wife's paramour down a flight of stairs (prima facie assault and battery) and then made the paramour's Armani suit, Gucci shoes, and Rolex watch follow their owner (prima facie criminal mischief), he would be entitled to instructions on the excusatory mitigation under the "heat of passion."

The foregoing discussion of adultery in the context of provocation may shed some light on the frustrating inconsistency of decisions in many provocation cases. Perhaps those decisions are inconsistent because the current law of provocation shelters under its roof two conceptually different defenses. The first, "true" provocation, is a mix of partial justification and partial excuse. Its justificatory capacity stems from the responsive character of the perpetrator's attack on the provoker who was the initial aggressor and violated some important legal rights of the perpetrator. This defense should be available to the perpetrator who killed, injured, or caused other harm to the provoker in response to assault, kidnapping, property damage, and similar wrongful acts.

The other defense, which, for the sake of clarity, may be called the "heat of passion," is purely excusatory. It applies in the circumstances when the perpetrator does not have a legal right that the victim not act in a certain way but has some moral claim or legitimate expectation that the events that caused his loss of control not happen. Those events may include witnessing adultery or being the target of offensive taunting or verbal abuse. To the extent the perpetrator's response to those events was not grossly disproportionate to the victim's misconduct, the perpetrator should be able to claim partial excuse. Understandably, when the perpetrator has no legal or moral right that certain unpleasant things not happen yet he loses control and causes serious harm to the victim, his reaction may be deemed unreasonable and disproportionate by law. Limiting the magnitude of offenses that may be mitigated under the "heat of passion" theory may be a good policy solution in cases which by definition include only *completely wrongful* acts by the defendant.

Conceptually separating "true" provocation from the "heat of passion" should help to avoid traditional confusion about the nature of available mitigation. By definition, only "true" provocation by the victim may reduce the wrongfulness of the perpetrator's act. Accordingly, any victim who suffered harm as a result of an offense committed in the "heat of passion" should be entitled to compensation. Conversely, compensation may be awarded only to those "true" provokers who lacked full capacity at the time of the offense.

• • •

The analysis of the theories of consent, self-defense, and provocation reveals a common principle underlying all three defenses and perhaps criminal law in general—*the principle of conditionality of our rights.* By that principle, a person may lose some rights because of his own conduct. If that happens, the perpetrator ought not to be held accountable for violating the rights that have been lost. Chapter 4 discusses under what circumstances people may lose their rights, voluntarily and involuntarily.

4 THE PRINCIPLE OF CONDITIONALITY OF RIGHTS

HOW CAN VICTIMS LOSE OR REDUCE THEIR RIGHTS?

The right not to be harmed is a fundamental human right and, as such, may very rarely, if ever, be lost completely; however, it may be reduced. That certainly does not mean that it may suddenly drop from 100 percent to 70 percent. What it means is that the right not to be harmed constitutes a cluster of distinguishable rights, including the right not to be attacked; not to be attacked with deadly weapons; and not to be physically hurt, seriously injured, maimed, tortured, raped, or killed. A person's actions may trigger the loss of some of those specific rights and, in this sense, reduce the overall right not to be harmed.

Accordingly, a person who with the owner's consent destroyed a valuable piece of property has violated no rights of the owner and is usually guilty of no offense. And a person who while acting in self-defense applied more force than reasonably necessary is responsible only for that "extra" force because the aggressor has lost his right not to be attacked at all but retained a right not to be attacked with a disproportionate amount of force.[1]

These examples, illustrating the principle of conditionality of rights, prompt a vital question: how can people lose their rights to life, liberty, or property? Some scholars believe that victims are to be blamed for any misfortune that happens to them. For instance, a criminologist, Heinrich Applebaum, has argued that unless the police start cracking down on the victims of criminal acts, the crime rate in this country will continue to rise.[2] In his view, the people who are responsible for crime are the victims: "They walk down a street after dark, or they display jewelry in their store window, or they have their cash registers right out where everyone can see them. They seem to think that they can do this in the United States and get away with it."[3] Therefore, Applebaum's solution to the problem was to hold victims responsible:

> I say throw the book at anybody who's been robbed. They knew what they were getting into when they decided to be robbed, and they should pay the penalty for it. Once a person has been a victim of crime and realizes he can't get away with it, the chances of his becoming a victim again will be slim.[4]

Comparable views have been expressed by legal practitioners and academics alike. For example, a lawyer representing Mike Tyson at a rape trial contended in a typical assumption of risk argument that, because Tyson's propensity for violence was common knowledge, "to date him was to consent to sex."[5] Alon Harel, on the other hand, explained his position by considerations of economic efficiency and argued that "protection of careless victims is a particularly costly enterprise and consequently we may have to sacrifice some of the protection granted to careless victims."[6] To the extent that conclusion felt uncomfortable, Harel advised "not to think primarily of the controversial rape cases," to focus instead on numerous morally acceptable situations, and to expand the principle in accordance with our moral beliefs.[7]

Not thinking about an uncomfortable issue is not an option, however, if we are to build the principle of comparative liability into the structure of criminal law. Moreover, Harel's suggestion to expand the comparative liability principle "in accordance with our moral beliefs" does not offer much guidance as to what exactly should be done. In a diverse society like ours, moral beliefs differ considerably, and their formation is often affected by developments in criminal law.

In contrast, the conditionality of rights principle provides both the methodology and specific answers to the question of how the victim's conduct may reduce the perpetrator's criminal liability. Pursuant to this principle, there are two relevant questions: (1) what rights did the parties possess prior to the prima facie criminal encounter; and (2) has the victim lost or reduced his rights, voluntarily or involuntarily? Both questions include legal as well as factual considerations. The answer to the first one depends, in part, on whether the law recognizes particular rights under particular circumstances. The second question involves two inquiries: one, is the right in question alienable (voluntarily and involuntarily); and two, has the victim in fact (voluntarily or involuntarily) lost or reduced it?

Voluntary Reduction of Rights

Consent and Alienability of Rights Naturally, if the victim does not possess the relevant right or the right is deemed inalienable, he may not lose or reduce it. For example, I have no property rights in my neighbor's car. Therefore, I cannot effectively consent to its use or sale. Conversely, I have property rights in my own car, and I can give valid consent to my friend's using it. The law recognizes the alienability of my property rights in my car. This does not necessarily mean that my consent alone would make the use of the car lawful: my friend may have no driver's license, or he may be intoxicated; nevertheless, the resulting unlawfulness of the action to which I have given consent does not make my property rights in my car inalienable. It is some other rule not directly related to the rule governing my rights in my car that makes my friend's driving unlawful.

Although the law generally permits people to alienate their rights, we often read about the inalienability of our right to life.[8] What this statement usually means is that consent of the victim is not a defense to homicide. But does one necessarily follow from the other? The fact that, under certain circumstances, an actor may be held responsible for consensual homicide should not automatically mean that the victim's right to life is inalienable. It can mean, just like in the car example, that there is some *other* rule that makes the killer's conduct unlawful. Judith Jarvis Thomson takes a similar view:

> Suppose I am terminally ill, and want to be able to provide for my children. Here is a rich man, who likes to kill. I say "For so and so much, to be given to my children, you may kill me now." Suppose, then, that he accepts my offer, and kills me. No doubt he does not act *well*. Perhaps he does what is impermissible for him to do. But I think it arguable that he violates—even that he infringes—no right of mine, and that if he does act impermissibly, it is nothing to do with my rights that makes this so.[9]

The implicit reason the killer in Thomson's hypothetical does not interfere with his victim's right not to be killed is that the victim has successfully waived it. The killer, therefore, may not be punished for violation of the victim's rights. However, as I argued in Chapter 3, the victim's consent to physical harm may function only as a defense of justification. To be fully justified, a person has to establish that he harmed the victim in order to achieve a better balance of harms and evils. Here, the perpetrator intentionally harms both the victim's interest in continued living and the victim's dignity (like Meiwes, he uses the victim as means for obtaining a desired experience) simply because he "likes to kill." Accordingly, he may be only partially justified, and his act remains wrongful and criminal.

We, thus, may, and should, do both: recognize the alienability of people's personal rights and punish wrongful harm, even when it is consensual. This approach eliminates the arbitrary labeling of some people's rights as inalienable and supplies a more satisfactory justification for criminal sanctions. Pursuant to it, the perpetrator deserves punishment for something he actually did, for *his* wrongdoing, and not the victim's inability to deliver valid consent.

Provided the individual's right is alienable, he may waive it by consent. To be valid, consent has to be freely given and rational.[10] From time to time, courts deny the validity of factual consent, concluding that it does not satisfy those requirements. In *People v. Samuels*,[11] for example, the defendant was convicted of aggravated assault for whipping an apparently willing victim in the course of production of a pornographic movie. The case was complicated by the fact that the victim could not be located to confirm his consent.[12] The court, however, dismissed the very possibility of such consent, saying: "It is a matter of common knowledge that a normal person in full possession of his mental faculties does not freely consent to the use, upon himself, of force likely to produce great bodily injury."[13] The *Samuels* court's argument is a perfect example of circular reasoning: a person who consents to X is insane because one has to be insane to consent to X. After the victim's insanity is thus established, the conviction follows automatically because consent of an insane person is invalid.

It is easy to ridicule this logic. Yet, there are situations when almost anyone would wonder whether the victim was rational. For example, how rational was Brandes when he consented to being killed and eaten by Meiwes? His consent to cutting off his penis some time before his death was hardly valid: by that time, Brandes had downed twenty sleeping pills and half a bottle of Schnapps.[14] But when he agreed to the killing, Brandes was not intoxicated. He was informed of every detail of the plan and gave it his full approval, as the video made by Meiwes shows. Brandes was a mature man and an educated professional. He was not clinically insane, although he apparently suffered from a "strong desire for self-destruction."[15]

This story once again raises a question regarding the level of rationality and competency that should be required for effective consent to bodily harm of different proportions (e.g., rough sex on the one hand and a radical surgery on the other). The Brandes example also reveals the empirical fallacy of the a priori assumption that anyone who consents to pain or injury is crazy: Brandes was not. This is a disturbing thought but, unless we want the character of our society to change dramatically, we may not characterize people's decisions as irrational merely because we disagree with them.

Another argument commonly used by courts to strike the validity of the victim's consent is that, under certain circumstances, people do not act entirely voluntarily, even when they are not subject to formal duress or coercion. For example, in *R. v. Carriere*, a Canadian court explained its concern about the voluntariness of consensual fights:

> [T]he "consent" in many of these "fair fights" with fists is often more apparent than real. Challengers are, most often, those who feel assured that they can overwhelm opponents. Those who accept the challenge often do so, not because they wish to fight, or truly consent to it, but because they fear being branded as cowards by their peers.[16]

Similar issues have been raised in connection with the voluntariness of consent in the sadomasochistic context. Lord Templeman in *R. v. Brown* classified consent of the masochists in the group as "dubious or worthless," suggesting that these individuals were younger than the men on the sadist side and psychologically vulnerable.[17] Even more serious questions about the rationality and voluntariness of consent arise in connection with assisted suicide and mercy killings. Those who attempt suicide often suffer from constant physical pain, depression, or other mental disorders. Courts have been duly suspicious of the claims that a sick individual has voluntarily requested death. Such a claim may require a very high standard of proof. Yet, at the same time, it is hard to agree with Justice O'Connor's conclusion that "the risk that a dying patient's request for assistance in ending his or her life might not be truly voluntary justifies the prohibitions on assisted suicide."[18]

Distinguished from the concerns about the validity of consent in specific circumstances is a truly paternalistic argument that people are inherently incapable of rational and voluntary choices and, thus, should not be trusted to make important decisions about their lives.[19] For instance, H.L.A. Hart took this position and rejected John Stuart Mill's vision of liberty, citing numerous factors that "diminish the significance to be attached to an apparently free choice or to consent."[20] Hart wrote:

> Choices may be made or consent given without adequate reflection or appreciation of the consequences; or in pursuit of merely transitory desires; or in various predicaments when the judgment is likely to be clouded; or under inner psychological compulsion; or under pressure by others of a kind too subtle to be susceptible of proof in a law court.[21]

Few would disagree that people can make "bad" decisions (no matter how we define this term) and that their choices are seldom, if ever, free from various influences. Moreover, as Robin West persuasively argued in her critique of Richard Posner's rationalistic vision of the world, people are often driven by self-destructive forces, desires for failure or humiliation, and the ultimate yearning for authority.[22] In many instances, people's consent is socially predetermined, and choices people make are not in their best interest. According to West, for example, women often define themselves as "giving selves" and picture relationships as consensual in order not to be violated.[23]

These are all potent arguments in support of the claim that people's freedom of choice is not absolute and, under certain circumstances, people may not take full advantage of it. However, limited as it is, this freedom has enormous personal and public value. We associate personal fulfillment and political freedom with people's ability to control their lives and make social and political choices. The very concept of responsibility would lose sense if we take away people's right to make their own mistakes and deal with the consequences. Finally, the fact that people's choices may be imperfect does not mean that "Big Brother" is more likely to make better choices for them. As Paul Roberts correctly pointed out:

> Paternalism at its best entails well-meaning and justified interference with autonomous choice. But if in practice things do not work out for the best—if, for example, one's leaders are incompetent, corrupt, stupid, or evil—paternalism is the royal road to totalitarianism, since it invites government to substitute for its citizens' expressed preferences that which the state judges they "really" (objectively) want or need. This is a recipe for tyranny.[24]

To sum up, laws that serve to ensure that people's harmful self-regarding decisions are rational and voluntary—that is, truly reflect their preferences—promote the values of liberty and autonomy. Such laws should be balanced to require higher proof of rationality and voluntariness as the amount of harm increases. At the same time, laws that deny people the power to make self-regarding decisions that hurt no one but themselves significantly encroach upon individual autonomy and, in the absence of serious public harm, are unacceptable in a free, democratic society.

Assumption of Risk Assumption of risk is considered to be a form of consent. Specifically, it constitutes express or implied consent to undertake a certain risk of harm.[25] Implied consent is given by, or may be imputed to, the victim when he undertakes a substantial risk of harm—whether recklessly, negligently, or even nonculpably (e.g., in a situation when the dangerous conduct may be justified or excused by the circumstances).[26] For example, if I convince my visibly inebriated friend to drive me home, I should be deemed to have assumed the risk of a car accident and possible injuries. I might have chosen that risk recklessly (I thought it would be fun to watch my drunken friend's driving), negligently (I unreasonably believed my friend to be sober), or nonculpably (I became suddenly ill, and no other transportation was available).[27]

The requirements for a valid assumption of risk are essentially the same as for consent in general. In order to be effective, assumption of risk must be informed, voluntary, and given for the particular, or substantially the same, conduct of the actor.[28] In the words of the *Restatement (Second) of Torts*, "consent to a fight with fists is not consent to an act of a very different character, such as biting off a finger, stabbing with a knife, or using brass knuckles."[29] Similar criteria applied to a criminal case would explain why consent to date Mike Tyson may not be viewed as consent to sexual assault by Mike Tyson.

At the same time, assumption of risk is distinguishable from consent in some significant respects. Discussing the difference between the two concepts in the law of torts, John Mansfield wrote:

> Consent is the right term to use when the plaintiff was willing that a certain event occur, probably some conduct on the part of the defendant, because he desired an invasion of a normally protected interest. Ordinarily he will believe that the invasion is substantially certain to follow the event, and the term consent focuses on his belief in the certainty of the invasion. Assumption of risk is the right term to use when the plaintiff was willing that a certain event occur, but he neither desired an invasion of a normally protected interest nor did he suppose that such an invasion was substantially certain to result. The focus is on the uncertainty of the result from the plaintiff's point of view.[30]

In other words, for Mansfield, the difference between consent and assumption of risk lies in how the victim subjectively perceives the probability and desirability of a right infringement. In the case of consent, this probability is very high and the right infringement is desirable; in the case of an assumption of risk, the probability of a right infringement is much more remote and the right infringement is undesirable. I wonder whether this observation is necessarily correct. Consent does not always presume higher certainty or desirability of the authorized conduct. I may reluctantly agree to let a friend borrow my roller blades for the weekend, although I am practically certain that she will not take advantage of my consent: not only is she aware of how much I resent people who borrow my things, but also her foot is four sizes larger than mine.

In contrast, assumption of risk may include a very high degree of certainty that a particular result will follow. For example, I may desire to enhance my appearance by means of a cosmetic surgery. I may be aware that most patients who have gone through this surgery have developed certain unpleasant side effects. I agree to the surgery and assume the risk that I will also suffer those side effects. I obviously hope that I will be an exception, but based on the available statistics and my doctor's opinion, I am practically certain that the risk of those side effects will materialize. Thus, neither the objective probability nor the victim's subjective belief regarding the probability of a right infringement marks the difference between consent and assumption of risk. What is this difference then and is it even significant for the voluntary reduction of rights?

Heidi Hurd has expressed concern that if we treat assumption of risk as a form of consent, then a victim "could be thought to have assumed the risks of a defendant's wrongdoing whenever she knew of those risks and voluntarily encountered them."[31] As a result,

> [w]e should then find that a woman who wore a low-cut red dress to a rough bar reduced her rights against rape if she knew that in dressing provocatively she might incite the unwanted attentions of a drunken aggressor. And we should find that the jogger who entered Central Park at dusk knowing of the risk of being mugged was complicit in his own mugging; his voluntary assumption of a known risk properly reduces the penalty imposed on the predictable assailant. And we should find that the woman who ran to the store for a jug of orange juice on New Year's Eve voluntarily reduced her rights against being struck by a drunk driver, for she knowingly and voluntarily invited

> those risks when she ventured onto the roads on that treacherous night. And we should find that a person who knowingly left her keys in her car invited its theft, thus reducing the penalty justifiably imposed on the car thief.[32]

To avoid this unfortunate outcome, Hurd suggested that the victim should be deemed to have reduced his rights only when the victim consents either to another's physical *contact* with his person or property or, alternatively, to another's wrongful *conduct* under circumstances in which the victim appreciates its risks and wrongfulness. In the first case, consent is "morally magical" because it eliminates wrongdoing altogether (e.g., consensual sex is not wrong). In the second case, wrongdoing is not eliminated but the victim should be thought complicit in the wrong done to him as a result of that conduct (e.g., a person who was hurt while playing Russian roulette is complicit in his injury).

I am not persuaded this contact-conduct distinction is helpful. It is not clear to me, for instance, why we should put consent to physical contact into a separate category. What if A, an adult woman, consents to someone watching her take a shower, or taking nude pictures of her, or posting those pictures on the Internet? There is no physical contact involved in any of these situations. However, A's consent seems to be equally "morally magical" in that it completely eliminates wrongdoing. On the other hand, I do not think that consent to killing, torture, or live cannibalism, which, according to Hurd, fits into the first category, is always "morally magical." I doubt that Brandes's consent to all those acts completely eliminates their wrongfulness. As discussed earlier, the concept of wrongfulness should not be limited to the violation of rights alone.

Moreover, this contact-conduct distinction is not necessary in order to "accurately parse between those who drag race and those who leave their keys in vehicles stolen by drag racers."[33] To lose a right voluntarily, the victim has to authorize particular conduct of the defendant. A person assumes the risk that this particular conduct may cause him harm; however, he does not assume the risk of *different* conduct—in the same way a person who explicitly consents to particular conduct does not automatically consent to different conduct. Accordingly, a drag racer assumes the risk that he and his competitors will be driving at a very high speed on the road that is not suited for such races. He does not assume the risk, however, that a losing competitor will pull out a gun and shoot him. The drag racer has consented only to the race and not to the shooting.

When a person leaves his keys in the ignition, he may mean nothing by that act and authorize nothing. Or, alternatively, he may mean that, based on an earlier communication, his friend should feel free to borrow the car for a few hours. In the second example, the conduct, which the car owner has authorized, is his friend's limited use of the car; nothing more, nothing less. In either case, he clearly did not authorize a thief to take his car.

Perhaps a more important distinction between consent and its constructive form, assumption of risk, lies in how these two concepts relate to unlawful acts. A person may, expressly or tacitly, *consent* to unlawful conduct of another; in that case, he becomes a coauthor of his injury. These are, for instance, cases of consensual deadly torture or drag racing. However, a person may not be deemed to have *assumed the risk* of unlawful conduct by another. That is so because people who violate the law have no right to force others to accommodate their criminal behavior by acting in a certain way or refraining from action. "In civilized society men must be able to assume that others will do them no intended injury—that others will commit no intentioned aggressions upon them."[34] A different rule would reward unlawful behavior at the cost of lawful behavior, which would be both unfair and inefficient.[35] In addition, such a rule would contradict the internal logic of criminal law. Consider, for instance, the law of complicity.

To be accountable for a wrongful act of another independent actor, one does not have *to do* much. The most trivial of assistance or encouragement is sufficient to result in accomplice liability. In *State v. Helmenstein*, for example, while a few teenagers were discussing prospective burglary of a convenience store, a sister of one of them "expressed a desire for some bananas."[36] The court opined that this "clearly would make her an accomplice."[37] In the famous (or rather infamous) British case of *Wilcox v. Jeffery*, the defendant's role was even less prominent: he was present at a London concert of the celebrated American saxophonist Coleman Hawkins and later published an article about it. The court found him guilty of aiding and abetting Hawkins's violation of a law prohibiting foreigners to take "employment paid or unpaid while in the United Kingdom."[38] Lord Goddard summarized the facts relevant to Wilcox's conviction:

> The appellant attended that concert as a spectator. He paid for his ticket. Mr. Hawkins went on the stage and delighted the audience by playing the saxophone. The appellant did not get up and protest in the name of the musicians of

> England that Mr. Hawkins ought not to be here competing with them and taking the bread out of their mouths or the wind out of their instruments. It is not found that he actually applauded, but he was there having paid to go in, and, no doubt, enjoying the performance, and then, lo and behold out comes his magazine with a most laudatory description, fully illustrated, of this concert.[39]

In contrast with the minimal requirements of actus reus, the level of the mens rea necessary to establish complicity is very high. The rule adopted in the majority of states is that unless one has the *purpose* to promote or facilitate the conduct constituting the offense committed by another, he is not an accomplice.[40] True, in many jurisdictions "a person encouraging or facilitating the commission of a crime [may] be held criminally liable not only for that crime, but for any other offense that was a 'natural and probable consequence' of the crime aided and abetted."[41] The natural-and-probable-consequences doctrine, however, has been subject to severe criticism. A number of courts and the MPC have rejected it, maintaining that when the conduct of the principal is "not within the conscious objective of the accomplice,"[42] the accomplice is not liable for it. In other words—consistently with other criminal law doctrines—a person may be responsible for more-severe-than-anticipated consequences of a wrongful act, but if that act was committed by someone else, he may be responsible only for the consequences of the act that he *purposefully* supported.

The analogy of the law of complicity with the doctrines of consent and assumption of risk is rather lucid: to put a stamp of approval on the conduct of the perpetrator, the victim must purposefully support *that conduct*. Drag-racers or Russian roulette players participate in a joint enterprise and thus purposefully support each other's high-risk conduct.[43] A terminally ill patient purposefully supports his friend's act of giving him a lethal injection. But a woman wearing a low-cut red dress does not purposefully support the act of rape. She may be aware of the provocative qualities of low-cut red dresses, and she may be reckless or negligent in her choice of clothes and companions. Nevertheless, she should not be deemed to have assumed the risk of rape, because to be at least in part accountable for an act of another, one must have the *purpose* to promote or facilitate that conduct.

Another way to come to the same conclusion is by looking at the material elements of an offense. Under the MPC, material elements include criminal conduct, its result, and attendant circumstances that satisfy the definition of the offense and negate any defense of justification or excuse.[44] To reduce one's rights voluntarily, a person does not have to act purposefully with respect to the result or attendant circumstances; however, he must purposefully engage in or authorize the conduct that results in social harm. For example, a person may negligently perceive his drunken friend as sober (attendant circumstance) and he may negligently disregard the risk of being injured (result), but as long as he purposefully persuaded his drunken friend to drive him home (conduct), he may be said to have assumed the risk of harm. In contrast, if a person authorized his friend to give him a lethal injection (conduct) in order to kill him (result) but a friend chose to stab him to death (same result but different conduct), the killer would not be able to claim that the deceased has voluntarily waived his right to life.

The question that naturally arises from this discussion is how close should that "other" conduct be to the authorized act in order to be covered by the victim's consent or assumption of risk? I can see two sets of scenarios in which the victim's consent is extended to the "other" conduct: one, when the "other" conduct is incident to the authorized act; and two, when it is inadvertent, that is, involuntary (a reflex) or voluntary but either nonculpable or, at worst, negligent (if the "other conduct" is negligent, the perpetrator may still be held responsible for an offense for which negligence suffices to establish culpability).[45]

Some actions are necessarily incidental to the authorized conduct, and some consequences are incidental too. By letting a friend borrow my car parked in my driveway, I also license him to enter my property without committing trespass. But by inviting a friend for a drink, I do not authorize him to assault me—simply because one act does not *require* the other. Obviously, nothing is black-and-white in the real world, and often the determination of what is "incidental" would not be as much a categorical matter as a matter of degree. Yet the distinction is still helpful. It allows us to see why a sportsman who consents to a boxing match takes a chance that he may be severely beaten, yet he does not assume the risk of being stabbed. And why a woman who consents to a kiss takes a chance that she may contract her partner's herpes, yet she does not assume the risk of being raped.

The second situation, in which the victim voluntarily reduces his right not to be harmed without authorizing the specific harmful conduct, is a case of a mishap. Take the 1988 prosecution of Joseph Porto charged with second-degree murder for the strangulation death of his girlfriend, Kathleen Holland.

At his trial, Porto took the witness stand and tearfully confessed. According to his testimony,

> Holland had begged him to wrap a rope around her neck to produce a state of near suffocation, called sexual asphyxia, that is said to heighten erotic pleasure. In his excitement, he said, he pulled too hard. Nassau County Prosecutor Kenneth Littman derided the new story as the "oops defense." But the jury found Porto guilty on only the lesser charge of criminally negligent homicide, a crime punishable by no more than four years in prison.[46]

Porto told the court that he had smothered Holland till his "hands got tired," then used his high school graduation tassel to do even a better job. Kathleen Holland did not authorize Porto to choke her so hard. But, provided Porto's story was true, the jury delivered a fair verdict. When people engage in dangerous activities involving other people, they assume the risk of a misunderstanding, mistake of judgment or imperfect performance by others. Being merely clumsy or slow or dim is not yet a crime. Only when the perpetrator is grossly negligent should he be held liable, and even then, only for an offense for which negligence satisfies the required level of culpability. Porto's conduct was beyond merely clumsy, slow, or dim. Based on his own testimony, he surpassed the level of ordinary, civil negligence; thus, the jury's verdict was appropriate.

Of special interest are cases in which the scope of the victim's consent matches the scope of the parties' actions and the defendant is not the direct cause of the harm to the victim. Examples include cases of death resulting from a fatal round of Russian roulette or a drag race, that is, cases in which we can speak about the victim's explicit consent to, or disregard of, substantial risk. Consider *Commonwealth v. Peak*.[47] In that case, three buddies, John Young, George Ramsey, and Charles Peak, "after discussions in two barrooms, agreed to race their cars."[48] Young lost control of his car and was killed in an accident. There were no other casualties.[49] Ramsey and Peak were found guilty of involuntary manslaughter of Young.[50] The court opined:

> Defendants by participating in the unlawful racing initiated a series of events resulting in the death of Young. Under these circumstances, decedent's own unlawful conduct does not absolve defendants from their guilt. The acts of defendants were contributing and substantial factors in bringing about the death of Young.[51]

It seems fair that the victim's own recklessness should not completely absolve the defendants of their guilt. The question is: their guilt for what? Ramsey and Peak are certainly guilty of violating the law prohibiting speeding contests, but are they guilty of killing Young? Wasn't it Young himself who agreed to participate in the race? Wasn't it his own lack of judgment or poor driving skills that cost him his life? Some courts, after struggling with these questions, have found no liability because the defendants' conduct was not the direct cause of the victim's death.[52]

Juries often acquit defendants in similar circumstances, regardless of what the law says. For example, in a drag race case reported by Kalven and Zeisel, the jury acquitted the defendant of all homicide charges, and the judge explained: "Because the jury did not follow the charge of the court, they saw some evidence of contributory negligence on part of the person assaulted."[53] In another case, a woman was charged with negligent homicide for accidentally killing a friend. The two had been drinking and playing with a .22 caliber revolver, firing it at random and playfully snapping it at each other. On one of those rounds, when the defendant was holding the gun, it went off and killed the victim. The jury disregarded the judge's instruction and acquitted the defendant.[54]

But is the all-or-nothing verdict appropriate in these circumstances? Perhaps a more realistic and fair approach would be to apportion responsibility among those who have contributed to the criminal outcome, specifically, to hold Ramsey and Peak liable for the death of Young but reduce their level of liability. For instance, if negligent homicide is a felony of the third degree,[55] Ramsey's and Peak's participation in a dangerous activity that resulted in homicide could bring them the conviction of a misdemeanor. In fact, the MPC already has a provision that may be used for that purpose. Section 211.2 prohibits reckless conduct that "places or may place another person in danger of death or serious bodily injury."[56] Convicting Ramsey and Peak under that section would reflect the level of their fault better than either finding them guilty of homicide by twisting the concept of proximate causation or relieving them of any responsibility.

To recap, the victim may reduce his right not to be harmed either by explicit consent or by assumption of risk. In both instances, the victim must be informed, act voluntarily, and either purposefully authorize certain harmful self-regarding conduct or purposefully engage in a risky activity. To the extent the harmful actions (1) are within the limits of, or substantially the same as, or incidental to the authorized conduct or (2) vary from the authorized conduct through no fault of the perpetrator or because of the perpetrator's negligence, the perpetrator's liability for the harm to the victim should be reduced or eliminated. Yet the perpetrator should be fully responsible for his harmful unauthorized actions committed recklessly or intentionally.

Involuntary Reduction of Rights

In an involuntary case, the criterion for determining whether a victim has lost any of his rights is embedded in the very concept of conditional rights. By the doctrine of social duty, "each one is required to use his own rights, as not to injure the rights of others."[57] Quoting a famous saying often attributed to Justice Holmes, "the right to swing my fist ends where the other man's nose begins."

The corollary of having a right is that someone owes the right-holder a duty.[58] If I have a right to life, you may not kill me. If you try to kill me, you violate your duty to me and thus lose moral parity with me. That loss of moral parity reduces your right to inviolability and allows me to disregard it *to the extent necessary to protect my right* to life. This is a case of complete justification. Overstepping these boundaries in cases of imperfect self-defense (either by exceeding the level of force reasonably necessary for the defense or by not following other requirements of a valid exercise of self-defense) or provocation results only in partial justification of the perpetrator. In contrast, in cases of mistaken self-defense and provocation, when the defendant strikes someone who has not violated any of his rights, the conduct of the victim provides offenders with no justification at all (although it may provide them with an excuse).

The *conditionality of rights* approach offers a practical and logical algorithm for distinguishing relevant and irrelevant elements of the victim's conduct. For example, it makes it clear that a woman may not reduce her right not to be raped by wearing sexy clothes, having a drink with the offender, being involved in a prior relationship with him, or even agreeing to some intimacy. She does not reduce her rights simply because the offender has no corresponding right that she not do any of these things. The inherent limitation on the victim's *involuntary* reduction of rights, therefore, can be stated as follows: *The offender's liability may be mitigated by the conduct of the victim only if the offender has the right that the victim does not engage in such conduct.* If that language were explicitly included in jury instructions, jurors would have much better guidance as to what factors may or may not weigh on the determination of the perpetrator's guilt.

Naturally, the victim may lose or reduce his right only if the right is forfeitable. Assuming all rights are alienable voluntarily, are they necessarily forfeitable as well? There is a reason to believe that they are not. For example, an argument can be made that no matter what a person does, he may not involuntarily lose his right not to be tortured, either by the state or by an individual. International and national statutes and court decisions have unanimously maintained that the right to be free from torture is a basic human right, not merely a revocable privilege. In line with this, the Universal Declaration of Human Rights states: "No one shall be subjected to torture or to cruel, inhuman or degrading treatment or punishment."[59] Unlike some other provisions of the Declaration, this one does not contain any qualifiers. A person may not be tortured even if the torture is inflicted nonarbitrarily and for a good cause.[60] Similarly, in *Public Committee Against Torture in Israel v. State of Israel*, the Israeli Supreme Court, confronted with a "ticking bomb" argument, held that interrogation must be "free of torture, free of cruel, inhuman treatment of the subject and free of any degrading handling whatsoever."[61] The court stressed that, under both international and Israeli laws, "[t]hese prohibitions are 'absolute.' There are no exceptions to them and there is no room for balancing."[62]

Of course, the language of the Universal Declaration of Human Rights and the Israeli Supreme Court's decision may be explained without relying on the theory of rights. In fact, it may be explained by the already familiar consideration of dignity: in order to preserve dignity, we, as society, choose to criminalize involuntary torture, even though the victim may have lost his right not to be tortured.

This is a plausible argument, and it has the beauty of symmetry and consistency with the explanation of the ban on voluntary torture. However, I do not believe that there ought to be complete symmetry between the theories of voluntary and involuntary alienability of rights. The law that recognizes people's rights to interact voluntarily confirms our deeply embedded, systematic expectations of liberty; such a law reflects the default rule. In contrast, the law that allows people to disregard other people's rights is an exception. Naturally, an exception must be much more narrowly crafted than a rule; therefore, it is reasonable to suppose that some rights are not forfeitable even though they are alienable. For example, I may donate a kidney voluntarily. But assuming I choose not to, I should never lose the right to retain my kidneys—not even if, through my fault, someone suffered a kidney failure and required immediate organ transplantation. All this, of course, does not preclude the possibility that the ban on involuntary torture is mandated by several reasons, including the high value of certain rights for personhood and our collective interest in preserving human dignity.

Even though courts have not explicitly articulated their rationale, they have consistently denied the perpetrator full or partial justification in cases of torture. In *Sensobaugh v. State*, for example, a husband found his wife with another man "under circumstances justifying the conclusion that they were about to have criminal relations."[63] The husband pulled out a gun but informed the other man that he did not intend to kill him; instead he "tied the [man], and while tied, cut off his penis with a razor."[64] At the time of the trial, Texas law viewed the killing of a paramour discovered fragrante delicte as justifiable homicide. The court, however, refused to give the defendant any benefit of that law and declared him guilty of aggravated assault. The appellate court affirmed the conviction and punishment (not exceedingly harsh though: a fine of $300 and two-months' imprisonment), opining: "Doubtless, if serious bodily injury had been inflicted by the appellant in an attempt to kill the injured party, his immunity would be secure under the statute, but the record negatives such an intent and makes it plain that his intent was not to kill but to torture and maim the paramour."[65]

What other rights may not be lost involuntarily? Should the right not to be raped be one of them? Douglas Husak, for instance, sees "no reason to exempt rape from the class of offenses for which victim fault can mitigate the liability of perpetrators."[66] One situation Husak has in mind is when "a woman agrees to have sex with a man, allows him to penetrate her, but changes her mind and asks him to stop in the midst of sexual intercourse."[67] Husak suggests that in these circumstances the perpetrator's liability might be mitigated. I cannot agree with this view for a number of reasons.

To lose a right involuntarily, the victim must somehow assault an important right of the perpetrator. In other words, post-penetration rape might be fully or partially justified if the perpetrator had a right that his sexual partner continued the intercourse as long as the perpetrator desired. I do not believe such a right exists. By consenting to undergo a root canal procedure or to attend a friend's poetry reading, one does not acquire an obligation to go through the painful experience until the very end. Moreover, one does not assume the risk that the dentist will continue drilling despite the patient's desperate objections. It seems obvious that the same should be true for sexual contact, no matter what is the reason for the request to stop it—pain, psychological discomfort, or anything else.

Courts refuse to order specific performance even of commercial contracts for personal services because "to do so would . . . run contrary to the Thirteenth Amendment's prohibition against involuntary servitude."[68] To the extent values of liberty and personal autonomy are worth anything, frustrated sexual expectations may give rise to a grudge, but not to a legal (or moral) right to proceed with the unwanted intimacy.

One could argue that mitigation of the defendant's liability in cases of post-penetration rape would be consistent with the philosophy of the MPC, which reduces rape from a felony of the first degree to a felony of the second degree if the victim was a "voluntary social companion of the actor upon the occasion of the crime" or had "previously permitted him sexual liberties."[69] I will not add anything new by saying that the Sexual Offenses section of the MPC can hardly serve as a model for sexual crimes legislation and should have been revised long ago.[70]

Even if the victim violated a legitimate right of the perpetrator, should her misconduct partially justify rape? Suppose a woman slaps a man on the face, he loses control, and, in a state of rage, rapes her. I do not think that in this case the defendant should be granted mitigation. Rape is no different from physical torture, which is not subject to the defense of provocation (in part, of course, because both acts are not completely impulsive; they take time and deliberation and, thus, go against the requirement that the perpetrator have no opportunity to cool off).

Perhaps, for the sake of clarity, statutes should explicitly say that rape may not be "provoked." Some statutes already do that for purposes of penalty mitigation. For example, the Federal Sentencing Guidelines authorize a sentence reduction in the case of wrongful conduct by the victim. The statute, however, makes this mitigation unavailable for sexual offenses.[71] Similarly, Alaska denies penalty mitigation based on the victim's provocation in sexual assault cases.[72]

Finally, to be justified under the theory of self-defense, the rape must be immediately necessary to prevent the victim from causing serious harm to the perpetrator. I suppose a case of "raping in self-defense" would look like that: a woman attacks a man with a knife. The man is not armed. To prevent the woman from stabbing him, he has only one choice: to rape her. I may be lacking in imagination, but I have trouble visualizing this scenario.

. . .

The foregoing analysis of the law and its rationales strongly suggests that the principle of *conditionality of rights* is a general principle of criminal law. Pursuant to this principle, one may lose his rights not to be harmed either voluntarily, by consent or assumption of risk, or involuntarily, by an attack on some rights of others. When the victim loses a right and suffers certain harm, this harm should not be imputed to the perpetrator.

People do not lose their rights involuntarily unless they have violated a duty to the perpetrator. Since people do not owe criminals a duty to lock their cars, or not walk down a street after dark, or dress conservatively, they do not lose their rights not to be offended by failing to take precautions against a possible offense. Quoting Fletcher, "this is what it means to be a free person, and the criminal law protects this freedom by not censuring those who expose themselves, perhaps with less than due care, to risks of criminal aggression."[73]

Yet, before this general principle may be implemented into the body of criminal law, it needs to be defined with more precision. What does it mean to say that a person has a "right"? Are these rights moral or legal? Do people have the right not to be subjected to a risk of harm, not only the right not to be harmed? And if they do, what does this right entail? These and other related questions are discussed in the remainder of this chapter.

WHAT DO "RIGHTS" MEAN?

The Place of the Principle of Conditionality of Rights in a Larger Theory of Rights

To have a right means to have a certain moral or legal status that defines the scope of freedoms and obligations between the right-holder and others. People can terminate or suspend their rights and thereby change these freedoms and obligations. The principle of conditionality of rights explains how, under certain circumstances, the victim's conduct can bring about that change. To define the meaning and boundaries of this principle with higher precision, it may be helpful to place it within the context of various rights-based relationships.

In his influential work, Wesley Newcomb Hohfeld pointed out that the word *right* may have several different meanings.[74] To highlight distinctions among them, he put each meaning in a correlative pair and came up with four concepts: right (in the strict sense), privilege, power, and immunity. Pursuant to Hohfeld's typology, a right is a claim by one person against another. The correlative of a right is a duty or, using Judith Jarvis Thomson's term, a behavioral constraint.[75] If X has a right to life, others have a duty not to kill him.[76] If they kill him, they breach their duty to X. In contrast, a privilege is merely one's freedom from the right or claim of another; its correlative is not a duty but a "no right." If Y unlawfully attacks X, X may use force in self-defense. X acts under a privilege, and Y has *no right* that X not act that way. On the other hand, Y does not have a duty to stay put and let X kill him. Y may quite lawfully run away.[77]

A power, according to Hohfeld, is one's ability to change an existing legal arrangement and, as a result, change the legal and moral rights of others. The correlative of power is liability. If Y extends to X an offer to purchase X's car, X acquires the power to accept the offer and, by doing so, unilaterally change his legal relations with Y, namely, impose on Y a liability to buy X's car.

Finally, immunity is freedom from the power of others regarding a certain legal relationship; it is correlative of disability. Until and unless X agrees to sell Y his car, X is immune in his property rights as against Y and everyone else "who has not by virtue of special operative facts acquired a power to alienate X's property."[78]

If we were to define the principle of conditionality of rights in Hohfeld's terms, it would be characterized as the victims' *power* to change the balance of rights (in the broad sense) between themselves and the perpetrators. For example, normally X may not hit Y. Y has immunity (and X has disability) with regard to Y's personal inviolability. We may also say that Y has a right not to be assaulted, and X has a duty not to assault him. However, Y possesses the power to change this state of events: if Y attacks X first, X will acquire the privilege of self-defense, and, to the extent necessary to X's defense, Y will not have the right that X not exercise this privilege. Alternatively, Y may consent to a boxing match with X and thereby change the whole spectrum of rights-based moral and legal relationships between X and Y. By consenting, Y also exercises his power to change X's and Y's moral and legal status vis-à-vis each other. The principle of conditionality of rights is, therefore, an example of *victim-specific* powers.[79]

More precisely, quoting Alon Harel, it is an example of "victim-specific powers which can be triggered exclusively by the victim's action rather than powers to change the circumstances in a way which indirectly results in the reduction of rights possessed by the victim."[80] In other words, the principle of conditionality of rights describes only those cases in which (1) the *victim's action* (2) *directly* changes the balance of rights between the victim and the perpetrator. The first limitation naturally stems from the proposition that a person may lose a right *only* by his own voluntary action. In all other instances (e.g., cases of necessity or innocent threats such as Mrs. Cogdon), the victim does not *lose* rights; however, as discussed earlier, his rights may be *overridden* by more stringent rights of others. The second limitation may be illustrated by the following hypothetical provided by Harel:

> Assume that John bought a fire extinguisher and placed it in his living room. Assume that Suzanne's house is burning, and consequently Suzanne, in a desperate attempt to save her house, breaks into John's house, takes the fire extinguisher, and uses it to save her belongings. Under these circumstances, Suzanne would most likely be acquitted on the ground that her act was necessary to prevent a much greater harm than was committed by her.[81]

True, if John had not bought the extinguisher and placed it in his house, Suzanne would have no reason to break in; however, can we say that, by buying the extinguisher and placing it in his home, John has diminished his right to be free from burglary and theft? Of course not; that would be silly. This case does not fall under the principle of conditionality of rights. The reason it does not is that the justification for Suzanne's break-in lies not in John's *actions* but in a certain *state of events* (the presence of a fire extinguisher in John's home) created by John's actions. If this state of events were created by someone else's actions, the result would be the same. For example, if the fire extinguisher had been purchased by John's worst enemy and, unbeknownst to John, placed in John's house, or if it had fallen from the sky, Suzanne would still have the right to break into John's home. Harel is correct in his conclusion that "[w]hat is characteristic of cases covered by the principle of conditionality of rights is not merely the fact that the victim can reduce or extinguish the duties owed to him but that it is the victim's action that has such a power rather than a state of affairs that can be brought about by the victim's action."[82]

Characterization of the principle of conditionality of rights as a victim-specific power has met criticism in the thought-provoking work of Íñigo Ortiz de Urbina Gimeno. In his view, the term *power* should apply only to legally permissible actions. He writes:

> The legal system is not indifferent to whether people wrongfully attack others or not, it positively seeks people not to act in that manner at all. The legal system does not grant attackers the power to diminish their rights through their wrongful conduct, it forbids them to act that way.[83]

It is certainly true that any legal system bans and punishes wrongful attacks, yet it also allows people to fend off such attacks privately by fighting back if necessary. There is no contradiction between these two policies. Moreover, as discussed in Chapter 3, sometimes interpersonal rights and liabilities differ from the rights and liabilities of an individual as against the state. Ortiz de Urbina Gimeno seems to have overlooked this difference and, as a result, misinterpreted the meaning of power in the interpersonal context. In the Hohfeldian sense, an attacker (X) has a power with respect to his target (Y): X has the power to relieve Y of the moral and legal constraint that, in the absence of an attack, forbids Y to hurt X. This new balance of rights may not be in X's interests; however, "power" does not necessarily mean something good. If I wear a valuable pin on my lapel, I have the power to lose it. Clearly, I would prefer not to exercise this power, in part because its exercise may diminish my property rights in the pin. In the same sense, X would prefer not to convey to Y the privilege of self-defense because that would diminish the scope of X's own rights; yet, from the objective perspective, this is exactly what X does by attacking Y.

One more layer of explanation may be needed to describe the principle of conditionality of rights: the principle addresses only those cases in which the victim's actions directly affect the rights or privileges of the *perpetrator* or someone on whose behalf the perpetrator is entitled to act. This explanation is prompted by Douglas Husak's critique. Husak supposed that in some countries, women have no legal right to dress provocatively. He then inquired, would the principle of conditionality of rights mean that "an Afghani woman who broke the law by wearing a miniskirt in public provides a partial defense for Afghani rapists?"[84]

Husak's question was largely rhetorical, and it did not take him long to concede that, properly understood, the principle of conditionality of rights does not eliminate or mitigate the perpetrator's liability because of *any* illegal act by the victim; instead, it requires "the *offender* to have the right that the victim not behave as she does."[85] That concession, however, enabled Husak to raise a more compelling challenge: if the right that the victim not act as he did is personal to the perpetrator, how would the principle of conditionality of rights account for the defense of others? Quoting Husak,

> When defendants kill in justified self-defense, of course, the faulty conduct of the victim clearly violates the rights of the perpetrator. When defendants kill in justified defense *of others*, however, the faulty conduct of the victim violates the rights of the person who is attacked, not those of the perpetrator.[86]

This issue certainly needs to be addressed, and the most natural way to address it is by considering the reasons for which the law authorizes use of force in protection of a third party. Under the common law, the right to defend others applied only to the defender's family members and close associates.[87] The restriction was the product of the defense's heritage: just like the law of adultery discussed in Chapter 3, the defense of others evolved from the right to protect one's property, particularly one's household (including wife, children, servants, etc.).[88] Today, the prevailing rule is much broader. Pursuant to it, one is justified in using reasonable force in defense of any third party, even a stranger, if he reasonably believes that the third party is in imminent danger of unlawful bodily harm from his adversary and that the use of force is necessary to avoid this danger.[89]

The rationale for the rule has changed too—the defense of others is viewed nowadays as a derivative privilege, an extension of the attacked person's self-defense,[90] a form of subrogation of rights: "One asserting the justification of defense of another steps into the position of the person defended. Defense of another takes its form and content from defense of self."[91] Clearly, this subrogation is possible only when the person whose rights are at risk is identifiable, either individually or at least as a part of an endangered group. For example, A would be justified in his use of force against B if B is about to throw a grenade into a classroom full of students. A would be justified even though it may be impossible to identify particular individuals on whose behalf A used force. Still, we know that there were *some* endangered people in that room whose rights would be violated if A did not act as he did.

Victimless crimes are different. By definition, they do not violate rights of any identifiable victims. Accordingly, none of those crimes, including the hypothetical offense of wearing a miniskirt, allows a private citizen to assert a personal right that has been violated and the protection of which might be fully or partially justified. In addition to that, even if the Afghani man had a right to interfere on behalf of the Afghani community and, say, put the Afghani woman under citizen's arrest, he still should not be able to use rape as a form of law enforcement: the fact that use of force may be justified under the circumstances does not imply that *any* use of force is justifiable. I will return to this question later in the chapter.

Rights: Moral or Legal?

The principle of conditionality of rights normatively describes a situation in which the parties' balance of rights as against each other has shifted. But what kind of rights are those—moral or legal? One can make a reasonable argument that these rights should be moral. After all, the principle of conditionality of rights is a principle of comparative responsibility, and responsibility is largely a moral concept. So perhaps Husak is right when he says that "since the question itself is moral, only a moral judgment can answer it."[92] We can think of a number of examples, particularly in the area of provocation, in which the victim acts immorally but legally with respect to the perpetrator (e.g., taunts or insults him), and we intuitively feel that if, in these circumstances, the perpetrator overreacts and assaults the victim, his punishment should be reduced. Kenneth W. Simons writes: "It would be plausible, on a partial justification rationale, to mitigate in the case of a victim who subjected the defendant to intense and protracted emotional abuse, even if that abuse is not otherwise criminal or tortuous."[93] I share Simons's intuition that emotional abuse should provide a basis for mitigation, yet I would reduce the perpetrator's liability through partial excuse[94] and retain full or partial justification only for violation of legal rights.

My choice is mandated by practical as well as theoretical considerations. Suppose the reduction of the perpetrator's liability were based on moral, instead of legal, rights—how would we decide what moral rights people possess? One possibility is to turn to conventional morality and search for a "broad and deep consensus that behavior is immoral before allowing victim fault to reduce liability."[95] This proposal, however, does not strike me as very realistic. How shall we do the searching—by polls? Shall we make participation in these polls mandatory, under the penalty of law, in order to ensure that the consensus is in fact "broad and deep"? How often shall we conduct these polls? And would not the very questions asked reveal inevitable social and cultural biases? In other words, how can we legitimately define the scope of the overwhelmingly recognized moral and immoral conduct?

Several decades ago, Judge Hand raised similar concerns in his famous immigration decisions when he pointed out the difficulty of determining what constitutes a "good moral character" or "the generally accepted moral conventions current at the time."[96] He found the task "impossible of assured execution; people differ as much about moral conduct as they do about beauty,"[97] and he discarded the idea of using poll data: "Even though we could take a poll, it would not be enough merely to count heads, without any appraisal of the voters."[98]

Moreover, even if we could obtain reliable data, should we always follow majoritarian moral beliefs? Polls suggest that at least in some states, the majority of the population may favor the "miniskirt defense" to rape. Suppose that the legislatures in those states enacted such a defense—would it be a good and fair law? A few years ago, the U.S. Supreme Court addressed a similar issue when, in *Lawrence v. Texas*,[99] it reviewed the constitutionality of state antisodomy laws. The Court admitted that for centuries homosexual conduct was condemned as immoral, and for many people it is still completely unacceptable.[100] Yet these considerations were held not to be sufficient to justify criminal prosecution.[101] The Court opined that the real question before it was "whether the majority may use the power of the State to enforce these views on the whole society through operation of the criminal law."[102] The Court answered that question in the negative, invalidated antisodomy laws, and reversed its earlier conflicting decision, *Bowers v. Hardwick*, holding: "*Bowers* was not correct when it was decided, and it is not correct today."[103] It is noteworthy that at the time the Court decided *Bowers*, twenty-four states and the District of Columbia criminalized consensual sodomy.[104]

But rejecting conventional morality as the basis for penal sanctions does not necessarily preclude another morality based theory of criminal liability, namely, critical morality. Unlike the positive, or conventional, morality ("the morality actually accepted and shared by a given social group"), critical morality involves "general moral principles used in the criticism of actual social institutions including positive morality."[105] Critical morality, in other words, can mean one of two things: either it is the "true" morality, which is objective and independent of the conventional morality, or it is what Ronald Dworkin calls a "moral position"–subjective moral convictions of society members that are not, however, "prejudices, rationalizations, matters of personal aversion or taste, arbitrary stands, and the like."[106]

Well, who would not want the law to be grounded in "true" morality? The only difficulty is in the practical implementation of this project. How would we go about it? How would we determine, define, and incorporate some (all?) moral rights of the parties into a legal defense? How would we notify the community of what the "true" morality entails, that is, what behavior is permissible? Husak, for instance, seems to believe that by agreeing to sexual penetration, a woman diminishes her right not to be forced to have sexual intercourse against her will.[107] I believe otherwise.[108] "True" morality, by definition, should have the correct answer, but neither Husak, nor I, nor the rest of the community can claim the privilege of its superior knowledge.

To be fair, critical morality is more commonly understood not as the objective truth that exists independently of the moral receptors of the beholders but rather as some rational moral position of a person or a group of people that is based on general moral principles and is free from "prejudice, mere emotional reaction, rationalization and parroting."[109] So understood critical morality, however, has its own shortcomings. One is that it requires a group of experts (presumably, a legislature) to sift various "arguments and positions, trying to determine which are prejudices or rationalizations, which presuppose general principles or theories vast parts of the population could not be supposed to accept, and so on."[110] Dworkin admits that it may be difficult even for an ideal legislator to perform the task: to the extent "he shares the popular views he is less likely to find them wanting."[111] Moreover, the legislator's decision will depend on his personal understanding of what our shared morality requires, "for whatever criteria we urge him to apply, he can apply them only as he understands them."[112] Finally, "[n]o legislator can afford to ignore the public's outrage."[113] In other words, this objective arbiter of other people's morality is as influenced by his own ideology, education, and political interests as anyone else. Why, then, quoting Judge Hand, should we trust the "judgment of some ethical elite, even if any criterion were available to select them,"[114] to decide what people's views amount to mere prejudices, rationalizations, and personal aversions and not to "moral positions"?

Were we to put "critical morality" in the foundation of the legal defense of comparative liability, judges and jurors would have no better guidance than their own understanding of moral norms. Consequently, conventional (or even personal, idiosyncratic), and not critical, morality would determine the perpetrator's culpability. Considering the variety of opinions on many moral issues in any society, and particularly in a multicultural society like ours, that would lead to inconsistent, unpredictable, and unfair criminal adjudication.

Because of these concerns, my proposal is deliberately curtailed. I advocate an affirmative defense that would completely or partially justify the perpetrator if, among other things, the victim has violated the perpetrator's legal rights. These rights should be legal and not merely moral because the scope of protected interests must be clearly and legitimately defined and communicated to the community.[115] This is required by the very principle of legality considered to be the first principle of American criminal law jurisprudence.[116]

In addition, using moral instead of legal rights to determine *legal* liability is a dangerous step back to the overwhelmingly criticized and rejected doctrine of "moral wrong." Pursuant to that doctrine, a person would lose a right to invoke a defense (mistake of fact) if he acted immorally, although not illegally, and his act produced a criminal result.[117] The classic case illustrating the doctrine is *Regina v. Prince*,[118] in which the defendant was prosecuted for "unlawfully tak[ing] or caus[ing] to be taken any unmarried girl, being under the age of sixteen years, out of the possession and against the will of her father or mother."[119] The defendant believed the girl to be eighteen years old, whereas in fact she was only fourteen. The court convicted the defendant, denying him the defense of a mistake of fact because, even if the circumstances had been as he believed them to be (i.e., the girl had been eighteen), his act would still have been immoral: it is immoral to take away a young woman from her parents without their consent.

The *Prince* decision has been criticized for equating moral and legal duties and coming close to giving the jury discretion to create new crimes.[120] In essence, the doctrine of "moral wrong" unjustifiably denies an individual a legal right (defense of reasonable mistake) because of his legal but immoral act. Were we to put moral rights in the foundation of the principle of conditionality of rights, we would end up with a similarly problematic outcome: the victim would lose a legal right (e.g., not to be assaulted) simply because he did something immoral (e.g., broke a promise).

For these reasons, it is preferable, in my view, to be somewhat underinclusive and limit the application of the principle of conditionality of rights to legal rights only. This seems to be a sensible solution from both theoretical and practical perspectives. As a practical matter, the defendant may be entitled to mitigation (based on the excusatory rationale) if the court finds that the victim's immoral but legal behavior was such that a reasonable person would be likely to lose his temper. Just like the defense of duress, this defense should be available to the perpetrator who acted under significant emotional pressure and, presumably, *not* the way he or any reasonable person would have acted but for that volitional impairment. Consequently, for the sake of conceptual clarity, this mitigation should be characterized as excusatory and not justificatory. The same is desirable as a policy matter, because by maintaining that a person whose behavior was absolutely legal, even if mean and malicious, may not be *justifiably* assaulted, this rule promotes respect for the law.

The defense of comparative liability should, therefore, take into account only legal rights of the victim and the perpetrator, but should it take into account *any* legal rights? Certainly rights that are no longer enforced and remain on the books only should not affect the perpetrator's liability. For example, spousal infidelity is not, in reality, a subject of today's criminal law; accordingly, adultery should not provide justification for the perpetrator's aggression. But assuming a personal or property right is widely recognized, should an attack on this right always give rise to the defense of comparative liability? For Aya Gruber, the answer is no. She would allow the defense only if the victim's conduct was both unlawful and "shocking to the conscience."[121] So, if the defendant overreacted and punched the victim upon discovering him picking flowers from the defendant's front lawn, the defendant would not be entitled to mitigation under Gruber's proposal.[122] And if the victim, while talking on his cell phone, got into a car accident with a speeding defendant, the victim's fault would be disregarded: his conduct could be unlawful, but it was hardly shocking. These outcomes seem as arbitrary and lopsided as decisions mandated by the current law. It is hard to see why the defense of comparative liability should not be available to the defendant whenever the victim violates *any* of the defendant's presently recognized legal rights. Naturally, the magnitude of that right would affect the extent to which the defendant should be shielded from criminal punishment. I will return to this issue in Chapter 6.

Rights Against Risk

How would the principle of conditionality of rights work in cases of attempts, endangerment, and other instances of risk-creation in which the actor does not actually bring about the relevant social harm? Kenneth Simons asks, for instance: "If a speeding driver almost strikes the victim, but misses, should it really matter whether the victim was jaywalking?"[123] Well, *if* we are willing to prosecute a driver who *almost* struck a pedestrian, I do not quite see why we should deny the driver a defense. If the victim's right to physical inviolability was recklessly endangered, and we view this endangerment as wrongdoing serious enough to justify criminal punishment,[124] it certainly matters to what extent it was the defendant's fault. Should we also refuse to consider the victim's conduct even if the victim intentionally threw himself in front of the defendant's car in an unsuccessful attempt to commit suicide? There is nothing idiosyncratic in my position. We know numerous examples of attempted crimes when the conduct of the victim makes all the difference for the liability of the perpetrator. A defendant charged with an attempted murder for shooting at the victim may be fully exonerated if he acted in self-defense or may be found guilty of a lesser offense if the victim provoked him.[125]

The principle of conditionality of rights applies to inchoate offenses the same way as to the completed offenses: if the victim does something that reduces his right not to be hurt, the subsequent attempt to infringe on that right by the perpetrator may be completely or partially justified. Of course, if there is no identifiable victim and the perpetrator is guilty of risk-creation with respect to the general public (e.g., an attempted terrorist act), the principle of conditionality of rights does not warrant a defense. But how should the law deal with a mixed case? Say, the perpetrator strikes against an aggressor or provoker but at the same time recklessly endangers the lives of a group of innocent bystanders (e.g., by throwing a hand grenade, which fortuitously fails to explode, at a particular person in a crowded marketplace). Pursuant to the principle of conditionality of rights, the victim's aggressive or provocative conduct should reduce or eliminate the perpetrator's liability for his actions with respect to that one person but not the rest of the endangered group. This conclusion is consistent with the MPC rule that denies justification to an actor who, in the course of legitimate use of force against an aggressor, "recklessly or negligently injures or *creates a risk of injury* to innocent persons."[126]

In the context of inchoate offenses, the reduction of right by the victim may also be voluntary and involuntary. In a typical voluntary case, the victim consents to certain harm—or assumes the risk of it—and the perpetrator inflicts or attempts to inflict that harm. For example, if A, following B's request, gives B what he believes to be a lethal injection but what in fact turns out to be a harmless vitamin, we may have reasons to prosecute A for attempted homicide; however, in charging A with a particular offense, it would be unfair not to give weight to B's consent. Similarly, if a group of people playing Russian roulette is arrested before anyone has been hurt, these people may be prosecuted under the theory of reckless endangerment, but it would be unfair not to reflect the voluntary character of their wrongdoing in the magnitude of the imputed offense.

Alternatively, in a typical involuntary case, the victim attacks certain rights of other people. In order to prevent the right violation, the perpetrator uses force against the victim. For example, the victim, in a state of rage, shoots randomly into the open windows of an apartment building. In an attempt to immobilize the assailant, a tenant throws at him a heavy chair. If the chair hits and injures the assailant, the tenant will be guilty of no offense; if the chair misses the assailant, the tenant will be guilty of no attempted offense either.

These examples are fairly straightforward. Yet there is a doctrinal question that needs to be addressed with more specificity: *why* is it permissible for the tenant in the previous hypothetical to use force? Do people have a right that others not jeopardize their important welfare interests? Under one academic view, the answer is no.[127] People only have a right not to be harmed, and mere risk does not constitute harm. So, if a pilot on my flight to Boston is severely drunk, yet he successfully lands the plane and I never find out that my life was in jeopardy, my rights have not been violated.

A contrasting view is that people have the right against risk imposition.[128] On one account, this right is grounded in everyone's interest in autonomy; "autonomy is exercised through choice, and choice requires a variety of options to choose from."[129] Those options must be not only numerous but also "worthwhile." By imposing risk, one diminishes other people's worthwhile options and thus diminishes these people's autonomy.[130] Pursuant to a somewhat different theory, the right against risk imposition is a derivative of people's legitimate interest in their welfare. Claire Finkelstein explains:

> Exposure to a risk of developing cancer, for example, diminishes a person's welfare because he now belongs to a class in which the relative frequency of developing cancer is greater than the relevant class of persons to which he belonged prior to that exposure. And a person has a legitimate interest in being in the class of persons with a lower chance of developing cancer, since to be in the class of persons with a higher chance of developing cancer is to be doing substantially less well in life.[131]

I share the intuition of those who believe that people have a right not to have their important interests endangered by others, and I find the "autonomy" and the "welfare" arguments quite plausible. My own hypothesis is consistent with both of them, yet it seeks to illuminate a different aspect of what is wrong with risk imposition: in most circumstances, risk has a negative value. People purchase insurance, hedge transactions, take safer if less convenient routes, avoid tasty food that may negatively impact their health, and generally make various efforts in order to minimize risks. When they choose to undertake a risk, they expect some remuneration for doing so (e.g., a higher return on a riskier investment). By imposing undisclosed, nonconsensual, "uncompensated" risk on the victim, the perpetrator in fact misappropriates the victim's leverage and thereby harms the victim. For example, by turning a "safe flight" into an "unsafe flight," the drunken pilot expropriates the value differential between the two flights in his own favor.

Consider an analogy: suppose I ordered foie gras in an expensive French restaurant but was served chicken liver instead. Few would disagree that I was wronged. I had been promised foie gras, and I paid for the privilege of having foie gras; yet my rights were disregarded. I was wronged even if I never touched the appetizer or never noticed the difference between foie gras and chicken liver. In the same sense, I was wronged when the pilot on my flight to Boston was drunk. I was denied what I paid for: the right to be transported by well-trained, capable, and responsible crew, not merely making it to Boston. The fact that I was not aware of the right violation is irrelevant. Just like in the foie gras story or Finkelstein's quote above, the harm is objective, not just epistemic. It consists of being denied an entitlement.

Saying that people are harmed by nonconsensual risk imposition certainly does not imply that any nonconsensual risk imposition deserves punishment. We may choose not to criminalize accidental risk creation even when it is unreasonable as long as it does not result in actual harm, but we should, nevertheless, recognize that the victim exposed to that risk has suffered a rights violation. That would explain why an endangered person or a third party would be justified in using force to eliminate the risk, or, to be more precise, why *under certain circumstances* an endangered person or a third party would be justified in using force to eliminate the risk. What are those circumstances?

Let us start with a rather uncontroversial example: if I see a man who is throwing bricks down the roof trying to hit children playing in the courtyard, I will be justified in using force to stop him. I most likely will be justified even if the man does some work on the roof and drops those bricks accidentally (negligently or even innocently) as long as he creates a significant risk of harm. In contrast, if the man is mean and malicious and wants to hurt the children, but they are playing 500 yards away, the risk will be too remote to provide me with good justification. Similarly, I will have a very limited right to use force if the only object on the ground the man can possibly hurt is an old tricycle. Finally, I will have no justification argument at all if the man working on the roof does not increase the risk of harm beyond the possibility that is inherently present whenever someone works on the roof.

As these examples indicate, the magnitude of the risk and the magnitude of the endangered interest may determine the scope of one's rights against the risk creator. What about the risk creator's culpability—does it affect the rights of those who are subjected to the risk? I believe this question should be divided into two: one, do people have rights only against culpable risk creators; and two, does the risk creator's culpability affect the wrongfulness of the risk creation? I would answer no to the first question and yes to the second one. A risk creator who seriously albeit nonculpably endangers a significant interest of another violates that person's rights. For example, if a pedestrian crosses a street, and a speeding driver runs the red light and barely misses him, the driver violates the pedestrian's rights, even though he may be justified in his dangerous driving (say, he is transporting a sick child to an emergency room). Just like in the Jack and Jill hypothetical discussed in Chapter 3, this driver's conduct is justifiable but wrongful with respect to the pedestrian. In the pedestrian's case, unlike in Jill's, the harm consists of mere endangerment, yet in both cases, the harm involves violation of rights.

As for the second part of the question, namely, whether the level of one's culpability affects the wrongfulness of the risk creation, consider the following example:

> Each Sunday morning I go for a drive in the country just for pleasure and thereby impose a one in a million risk of death on Jones, who lives near the road. That is clearly permissible. But suppose that I were to get an equal amount of pleasure from playing Russian roulette on Jones, with a bullet in one of a million chambers. Many people would find that impermissible.[132]

We certainly perceive an intentional act of risk creation as more wrongful than mere foresight of risk. Moreover, "[w]e think it morally bad to impose a risk of death on another for the sheer pleasure of doing so, however many chambers in one's gun."[133] Similarly, we view a risk created negligently or innocently as less wrongful than a risk created purposefully or with reckless disregard for the interests of others.

All these factors—the magnitude of risk and affected rights, and the degree of the risk creator's culpability—determine the balance of rights as between the parties. When there is a high risk of intentional violation by one person of an important interest of another, the latter's right to use force against the source of that risk is most compelling, and the risk creator's conduct should significantly reduce or eliminate criminal liability of the perpetrator for the harm suffered by the risk creator. The law of self-defense incorporates these considerations. a person is permitted to use any amount of force to protect himself against imminent threat of death or grave injury. In contrast, when the risk of harm is low, the risk creator is merely negligent, and the endangered interest is not as significant as the risk creator's right of personal inviolability, the reduction of the perpetrator's liability may be negligible. For example, a driver prosecuted for severely beating another driver should receive very little mitigation (if at all) even if he can prove by convincing evidence that the victim was driving negligently and nearly scratched the defendant's new car. In sum, the principle of conditionality of rights applies to inchoate offenses the same way it applies to completed offenses: if there is an identifiable victim, the conduct of that victim should be considered for the determination of the perpetrator's liability.

• • •

The principle of conditionality of rights described in this chapter supplies a foundation for the argument that the perpetrator's liability may be properly evaluated only in the context of victim-perpetrator interaction and provides a basis for distinguishing situations in which the victim's conduct should mitigate the perpetrator's liability from those in which it is irrelevant. The victim's conduct should mitigate the perpetrator's liability only when the victim has waived his rights voluntarily, by consent or assumption of risk, or lost them involuntarily, by attacking or threatening some legally recognized rights of others. In any of these cases, the victim exercises his power to change the balance of legal relationships between him and the perpetrator.

In some instances, society may choose not to recognize the victim's loss of rights (e.g., involuntary torture or rape) or proscribe certain actions even in the absence of a right violation (e.g., voluntary slavery). These instances, however, are quite limited. As a rule, when two cases differ only by the magnitude of the victim's rights violation, the defendant guilty of a lesser violation should be entitled to a lesser punishment.

Now that the boundaries and meaning of the principle of conditionality of rights are outlined in some detail, we can turn from the description of this principle to its specific implementation as a defense of comparative criminal liability. Among the questions that need to be addressed in this regard are the following: Assuming the victim by his own conduct has reduced his right not to be harmed, how long should this reduction be in effect? What should be the minimal set of elements necessary to establish the defense of comparative criminal liability? How should this defense function? Chapters 5 and 6 take on these questions.

Part 3

INCORPORATING THE PRINCIPLE OF CONDITIONALITY OF RIGHTS INTO CRIMINAL LAW

5 HOW LONG DO VICTIMS' RIGHTS REMAIN LIMITED?

THE QUESTION OF TIMING is crucial for the defense of comparative liability. For how long did I give up my freedom of movement by consenting to staying locked up in my friend's apartment? What is the chronological window during which people may legitimately act in self-defense? Over what period of time does a provoker reduce his right not to be harmed by the person he has assaulted?

In most cases, the period of time during which the victim's rights remain limited is determined by the nature of his actions. If a person is negligent or reckless, his right not to get harmed may be limited for as long as his negligence or recklessness creates the risk of harm to himself or others. If the victim encroaches on another's right to life, his own right to life may be reduced for the time necessary for the target of his attack to defend himself. If a person has provoked another, he may be at risk of an aggressive response for as long as it takes a reasonable person to cool off. Despite the more or less clear conceptual framework, many questions remain intensely debated.

In this chapter I discuss three legal settings in which the issues of timing have been particularly contentious—living wills, post-penetration rape, and nonconfrontational killings. The first two involve issues of voluntary reduction or loss of rights, whereas the last one prompts a question of involuntary reduction or loss of rights by the victim.

VOLUNTARY REDUCTION OF RIGHTS

Living Wills

Suppose a person has waived certain rights by issuing valid consent, should that consent remain valid until the action to which he consented is completed? This question literally acquires life-and-death dimensions when it comes up in connection with decisions recorded in living wills. Living wills are documents used to express people's treatment preferences in advance of an incapacitating illness. Today, they are recognized in all but a few states.[1] Standard forms of living wills either do not specify the period of their validity or explicitly provide for unlimited duration. Like wills of property, they become operative at some indefinite time in the future; thus, the problem of remote consent is built into their structure. In the words of Kenney Hegland, the "root problem, the unsolvable problem, is that living wills are written long before they come into play: We are asked to decide *now* what we want *then,* and we don't have much of a clue. The stuff of a Greek tragedy."[2]

Half a century ago, long before the passage of any advance health care directive legislation, Yale Kamisar expressed similar concern, wondering how remote consent can be deemed informed:

> Is this much different from holding a man to a prior statement of intent that if such and such an employment opportunity would present itself he would accept it, or if such and such a young woman were to come along he would marry her? Need one marshal authority for the proposition that many an "iffy" inclination is disregarded when the actual facts are at hand?

Indeed, a young man signs a living will requesting to be allowed to die should he ever be in a certain medical condition. Many years later, he suffers a stroke and finds himself in that exact condition, no longer capable of signing a new consent form. In the intervening decades, many things have changed, starting with the man himself and ending with the medical prospects and methods of care for bedridden patients. Should his living will still be respected? A physician made the following disturbing observation about one's transformation:

> The 21-year-old who wants to be shot rather than suffer the imagined ignominy of a nursing home is only too grateful to accept the nursing home and warm meals when he turns 85. A living will or a frank conversation with one's physician even at age 55 would rarely reflect what one's wishes would be at age 70.[3]

The incongruity between preferences of a younger man and his older version is inevitable: our values, perception of time, aversion to risk, and many other characteristics change as we age. Accordingly, "the self that has to decide to buy or not to buy disability insurance is not the future disabled self, and the two selves have different preferences."[4] The conflict of interests between those "successive selves, 'time sharing' the same body and consciousness,"[5] becomes particularly acute when the earlier and the later selves lose continuity and with it, arguably, common personhood.

Take the case of Margo, described by Ronald Dworkin.[6] Margo was a fifty-four-year-old Alzheimer's sufferer. Unlike many others in her condition, Margo did not experience pain or fear. She attended an arts class for Alzheimer's victims where day after day she painted essentially the same picture. She pretended to be reading mysteries but her place in the book jumped randomly, and dozens of pages were dog-eared at any given moment. Anyway, she was content. Perhaps even more than content. According to a medical student who visited her daily, "despite her illness, or maybe somehow because of it,"[7] Margo was one of the happiest people he had ever met. In particular, the student reported her pleasure at eating peanut-butter-and-jelly sandwiches. At the same time, he wondered: "When a person can no longer accumulate new memories as the old rapidly fade, what remains? Who is Margo?"[8]

Suppose, while still competent, Margo executed a living will which requested that, should she ever develop Alzheimer's, no medical treatment be provided for any life threatening condition.[9] If, at the age of fifty-five, Margo is diagnosed with cancer, what should we do about her living will? Should we respect Margo's wishes expressed years ago by a "different" Margo? Should we let her die although "she seems perfectly happy with her dog-eared mysteries, the single painting she repaints, and her peanut-butter-and-jelly sandwiches"?[10]

As tantalizing as these questions are, I would answer them affirmatively, siding with those who, like Joel Feinberg, have maintained that "[i]n virtue of the extended temporal bounds of *de jure* sovereignty, . . . a competent autonomous person may consent for his future as well as his present self."[11] Prospective autonomy is well established in various areas of law, including the law of medical consent. If a competent person agrees to undergo a surgery, his consent remains valid while he is under general anesthesia the next day. It remains valid even if his surgery takes place in a week or a month. "Unless there were some material reasons to think that the patient had altered his or her decision, the initial, competently made instruction would govern."[12]

A number of scholars have remarked that the continuous ability to withdraw or modify one's consent is essential for the validity of the indefinite continuous waiver of rights.[13] The current law also incorporates this view: most advance directive statutes, as well as Oregon's and Washington's Death with Dignity Acts, permit revocation of the living will by act or statement regardless of the drafter's mental or physical condition.[14] Naturally, the more remote was the patient's consent, the more proof should be required to establish that he, in fact, had an opportunity to repeal it but chose not to utilize it.

Post-Penetration Rape

Another area in which the issue of the duration of consent has recently become the focus of judicial, legislative, and academic attention is the law of rape. Suppose, in the middle of consensual intercourse, one partner tells the other to stop. Would the other partner be guilty of rape if he disregarded this request? Traditionally, the answer was no.[15] One court opined:

> The essence of the crime of rape is the outrage to the person and feelings of the female resulting from the nonconsensual violation of her womanhood. When a female willingly consents to an act of sexual intercourse, the penetration by the male cannot constitute a violation of her womanhood nor cause outrage to her person and feelings. If she withdraws consent during the act of sexual intercourse and the male forcibly continues the act without interruption, the female may certainly feel outrage because of the force applied or because the male ignores her wishes, but the sense of outrage to her person and feelings could hardly be of the same magnitude as that resulting from an initial nonconsensual violation of her womanhood.[16]

In recent years, a number of courts criticized that reasoning as based on archaic and outmoded social conventions and ruled that a defendant is guilty of forcible rape if, "during apparently consensual intercourse, the victim expresses an objection and attempts to stop the act and the defendant forcibly continues despite the objection."[17] These decisions reflect the same notion of continuous consent as the one we already saw in connection with living wills, namely, that continuous consent is good only as long as the consent-giver may revoke or modify it.

After a few state courts considered the issue, an important legislative development took place. In 2003, the Illinois legislature passed a revoked-consent statute. The statute provides: "A person who initially consents to sexual penetration or sexual conduct is not deemed to have consented to any sexual penetration or sexual conduct that occurs after he or she withdraws consent during the course of that sexual penetration or sexual conduct."[18] So far, this is the only revoked-consent statute in the United States.

The central question for those courts that recognize the offense of post-penetration rape is how quickly a reasonable person should obey his partner's request to stop. In *In Re John Z.*, the defendant argued that the act of sexual intercourse arouses a male's primal urge to reproduce; it is therefore "unreasonable for a female and the law to expect a male to cease having sexual intercourse immediately upon her withdrawal of consent. It is only natural, fair and just that a male be given a reasonable amount of time in which to quell his primal urge."[19] The court rejected the "primal urge" defense and opined that the defendant's failure to withdraw for four or five minutes after the victim's first request was not reasonable.[20] Similarly, the appellate court in *State v. Bunyard* held that "[w]hen consent is withdrawn, continuing sexual intercourse for five to ten minutes is not reasonable and constitutes rape."[21] The Supreme Court of Kansas, however, opined that it is up to the jury to determine whether the time between withdrawal of consent and the interruption of intercourse was reasonable.[22] "A reasonable time depends upon the circumstances of each case and is judged by an objective reasonable person standard to be applied by the trier of fact on a case-by-case basis."[23]

These judicial and legislative developments are in accord with the theory of rape. What makes rape wrongful is not merely use of force. Intercourse with an unconscious person or intercourse coerced by threat of injury does not require physical compulsion. Yet it is now widely recognized that such intercourse constitutes rape because of the lack or coerced nature of the victim's consent. By the same token, intercourse continued after revocation of consent should be viewed as rape. It seems ludicrous to maintain that the perpetrator who, for a substantial period of time, ignored the victim's pleas to stop should be granted mitigation simply because at some point in the past the victim did not object to intimacy.

INVOLUNTARY REDUCTION OF RIGHTS: NONCONFRONTATIONAL KILLINGS OF ABUSERS

As for the involuntary reduction of rights, the issue of timing is particularly critical and controversial in connection with battered spouses who kill their abusers in nonconfrontational circumstances (e.g., while the latter are asleep) and, when prosecuted, attempt to invoke self-defense. Those incidents do not happen often. A comprehensive study of appellate cases revealed only forty-five convictions in the period from 1902 to 1991. In each of these cases, female defendants alleged that although they suffered no attack immediately prior to the homicide, they killed their abusive spouses or domestic partners in self-defense.[24] The actual number of such killings may be higher, as the study did not include cases that were not prosecuted, were dismissed before trial, were resolved by a plea bargain, or resulted in acquittal.[25] But regardless of their frequency, these cases demand principled resolution.[26]

Traditional law of self-defense does not authorize the use of deadly force unless the actor reasonably believed that he was in imminent danger of death or serious bodily harm; thus, in cases of nonconfrontational killings, battered spouses are usually denied self-defense.[27] The MPC has replaced the requirement of imminence of harm with that of immediate necessity to defend oneself.[28] Most states, however, have rejected the MPC formulation.[29]

Advocating the MPC standard, Paul Robinson argued that we should focus not on the immediacy of threat but on the immediacy of the need for response: "If a threatened harm is such that it cannot be avoided if the intended victim waits until the last moment, the principle of self-defense must permit him to act earlier—as early as is required to defend himself effectively."[30] Richard Rosen took this logic one step further to conclude that neither the imminence of the attack nor the immediacy of the need to prevent it should be required for successful invocation of self-defense if the defendant can present substantial evidence that the killing was necessary even though the danger was not urgent.[31] And Stephen Morse, while rejecting across-the-board abolition of the imminence requirement in nonconfrontational cases,[32] advocated the following standard: "If death or serious bodily harm in the relatively near future is a virtual certainty *and* the future attack cannot be adequately defended against when it is imminent *and* if there really are *no* reasonable alternatives, traditional self-defense doctrine ought to justify the pre-emptive strike."[33]

It is hard not to be sympathetic to these and other efforts to provide a defense to a person who, in fact, could neither escape nor fend off repetitive attacks and thus had only a moment *between* the attacks to strike back. Consider, for instance, the widely cited, tragic case of Judy Norman who shot her husband, J.T. Norman, to death while he was asleep. Judy married J.T. when she was fourteen and lived with him for twenty-five years. The following are some facts provided by the North Carolina Court of Appeals:

> Norman was an alcoholic. He had begun to drink and to beat defendant five years after they were married. The couple had five children, four of whom are still living. When defendant was pregnant with her youngest child, Norman beat her and kicked her down a flight of steps, causing the baby to be born prematurely the next day.
>
> Norman, himself, had worked one day a few months prior to his death; but aside from that one day, witnesses could not remember his ever working. Over the years and up to the time of his death, Norman forced defendant to prostitute herself every day in order to support him. If she begged him not to make her go, he slapped her. Norman required defendant to make a minimum of one hundred dollars per day; if she failed to make this minimum, he would beat her.
>
> Norman commonly called her "Dogs," "Bitches," and "Whores," and referred to her as a dog. Norman beat defendant "most every day," especially when he was drunk and when other people were around, to "show off." He would beat defendant with whatever was handy—his fist, a fly swatter, a baseball bat, his shoe, or a bottle; he put out cigarettes on defendant's skin; he threw food and drink in her face and refused to let her eat for days at a time; and he threw glasses, ashtrays, and beer bottles at her and once smashed a glass in her face. Defendant exhibited to the jury scars on her face from these incidents. Norman would often make defendant bark like a dog, and if she refused, he would beat her. He often forced defendant to sleep on the concrete floor of their home and on several occasions forced her to eat dog or cat food out of the dog or cat bowl.
>
> Norman often stated both to defendant and to others that he would kill defendant. He also threatened to cut her heart out.[34]

The day before the killing, J.T. beat Judy so badly, she called the police. The police arrived but could not arrest J.T. because Judy refused to file a formal complaint, saying that if she did, J.T. would kill her. An hour later, the police had to come back because Judy took an overdose of sleeping pills. When paramedics arrived, J.T. tried to interfere with their efforts, screaming: "Let the bitch die. . . . She ain't nothing but a dog. She don't deserve to live."[35] The next day, violence escalated. J.T. beat Judy all day long, poured beer onto her head, smashed a doughnut on her face, and put out a cigarette on her chest. He also threatened to cut off Judy's breasts, to slit her throat, and to kill her.

> In the late afternoon, Norman wanted to take a nap. He lay down on the larger of the two beds in the bedroom. Defendant started to lie down on the smaller

> bed, but Norman said, "No bitch . . . Dogs don't sleep on beds, they sleep in [*sic*] the floor." Soon after, one of the Normans' daughters, Phyllis, came into the room and asked if defendant could look after her baby. Norman assented. When the baby began to cry, defendant took the child to her mother's house, fearful that the baby would disturb Norman. At her mother's house, defendant found a gun. She took it back to her home and shot Norman.[36]

Judy was convicted of voluntary manslaughter and sentenced to six years of imprisonment. The Supreme Court of North Carolina affirmed her conviction, rejecting Judy's claim that the jury should have been instructed on self-defense.[37] The court explained that the defense was not available to Judy because she was not in "imminent" danger of death or great bodily harm. Quoting *Black's Law Dictionary*, the court said that "imminent" in this context means "immediate danger, such as must be instantly met, such as cannot be guarded against by calling for the assistance of others or the protection of the law."[38]

The court opined that Judy was not faced with an instantaneous choice between killing her husband and being killed or seriously injured by him.

> Instead, *all* of the evidence tended to show that the defendant had ample time and opportunity to resort to other means of preventing further abuse by her husband. There was no action underway by the decedent from which the jury could have found that the defendant had reasonable grounds to believe either that a felonious assault was imminent or that it might result in her death or great bodily injury. Additionally, no such action by the decedent had been underway immediately prior to his falling asleep.[39]

Judy's subjective belief in "what might be 'inevitable' at some indefinite point in the future"[40] was held to be insufficient to satisfy the requirement of imminence. Under the approaches suggested by Rozen (killing of an offender may be necessary even when the threat of harm is not urgent), Robinson (killing of an offender may be justified as the last opportunity to defend the victim against future threat), and Morse (killing of an offender may be justified if there was "no reasonable alternative"), Judy might be able to successfully invoke self-defense. Morse argued, for instance, that she should have been acquitted "because her killing was no more preemptive than the present theory of self-defense, properly understood, already permits."[41]

> Judged by the rationale of a rational imminence standard, the harm was imminent. Judy had nowhere to hide and no other reasonable, lawful alternative,

> including waiting for the next deadly attack. It was simply too risky. . . . Judy Norman had no reasonable alternative and justifiably killed J.T.[42]

For Morse, Rozen, Robinson, and some other scholars, the requirement of imminence is not self-standing but rather a proxy,[43] a translator,[44] a modification,[45] a "component and corollary of the requirement of necessity."[46] Many advocates for battered women have promoted such interpretation and corresponding changes to the self-defense doctrine. Despite the compelling need to aid and empower victims like Judy Norman, the wisdom of this revision in the law of self-defense appears questionable. As Kim Kessler Ferzan insightfully pointed out, necessity is only a limitation on one's right to defend oneself—if killing the aggressor is not necessary in order to save the life of the victim, such killing would not be justified—but necessity alone does not provide an independent ground for a preventive strike.[47]

Take, for example, Morse's proposal. Morse would dispose of the requirement of imminence if death or serious bodily harm in the "relatively near future" is a "virtual certainty," the future attack cannot be effectively resisted when it becomes imminent, and there are "really no reasonable alternatives."[48] Numerous qualifiers—*relatively* near future, *virtual* certainty, *really* no alternatives—strive to soften the harshness of the proposed revision and make the new standard fit under the umbrella of traditional self-defense doctrine. But how is it self-defense if there was no attack or attempted attack, if an attack is about to happen only in a relatively near future? Besides, if the future is only *relatively* near, how can the death or serious bodily harm be a certainty, even if a *virtual* certainty?

From early on, intentional killing of an unoffending victim has been a moral and legal taboo in our culture—an act that is "at once dangerous, immoral, and opposed to all legal principle and analogy."[49] Even when killing of one unoffending person could save the lives of many, such killing has been ruled unacceptable,[50] at least in the circumstances when, but for the killing, the victim would have been alive.[51] Invoking necessity as justification for nonconfrontational killing presents a serious moral problem: how can a court conclude that, in the absence of a present threat of death or serious bodily harm, one life may be sacrificed for the sake of another? And even if the court could make this determination, should it?

A few years ago, the English Court of Appeal had to decide a case of newborn Siamese twins, Jodie and Mary. The twins were joined at the abdomen, and each had a separate set of all vital organs except for the shared bladder.

However, Mary's heart barely functioned, and her lungs did not function at all. She was surviving only as a result of Jodie's heart pumping blood around her body. If the girls had not been separated, Jodie's heart would have eventually failed and they would have both died within a few months. The only way to save Jodie was by separating, and thus instantly killing, Mary. The girls' parents, devout Catholics, rejected the operation on religious grounds, and the hospital sought permission from a court. The permission was granted and sustained on appeal. The girls were separated, Jodie survived, and Mary died.

The case inspired a lot of soul-searching and debate regarding the role of courts in resolving complicated moral dilemmas. Lord Justice Ward, writing the appellate opinion, was the first to acknowledge: "There has been some public concern as to why the court is involved at all. We do not ask for work but we have a duty to decide what parties with a proper interest ask us to decide."[52] He recognized that the hospital authorities were entitled to seek the court's ruling, but he explicitly pointed out that they were under no duty to do so: "Other medical teams may well have accepted the parents' decision. Had St Mary's done so, there could not have been the slightest criticism of them for letting nature take its course in accordance with the parent's wishes."[53] What Lord Justice Ward seemed to be saying, and what resonated with many public voices, is that perhaps in the absence of an unlawful act courts should not be asked to choose who is to live and who is to die.[54]

By the same token, should courts be asked to legitimize killing a person who presents no immediate threat? And yet, if the defendant is charged with a serious crime, the judge has no choice but to conduct a trial and, in the end, issue jury instructions. What should those instructions read in a case like Judy Norman's? Should J.T.'s perennial mistreatment of Judy be taken into account in determining the scope of her culpability? Wasn't J.T. at least in part responsible for what she did? Justice Martin raised these issues in his dissenting opinion, arguing that deliberation of self-defense had been improperly taken away from the jury:

> By his barbaric conduct over the course of twenty years, J.T. Norman reduced the quality of the defendant's life to such an abysmal state that, given the opportunity to do so, the jury might well have found that she was justified in acting in self-defense for the preservation of her tragic life.[55]

Justice Martin was probably right: some jurors might have felt that way. Whether criminal doctrine should provide room for these feelings is a separate question. If nonconfrontational killing were justifiable, then a battered woman who hired a contract killer to take her husband's life should also be justified.[56] Moreover, the contract killer should be justified too because justification, unlike excuse, is a universal defense, namely, those who assist in justified conduct are shielded from punishment by the same privilege as those who are entitled to it in the first place. This would be an absurd outcome.

I agree with Joshua Dressler that a battered woman should not have a right "to kill today because sooner or later that batterer will inevitably kill her."[57] However, I agree with this view for a reason that differs from Dressler's. Dressler rejects self-defense in cases like Judy Norman's because of his general opposition to the theory of forfeiture. For him, to say that J.T. has lost his right to life is to pronounce that "a human life is expendable," and we can swat J.T. "like a fly and toss him in the garbage without guilt feelings."[58] For me, as discussed earlier, forfeiture, or rather involuntary loss, of rights in cases of self-defense means only that for a period while the aggressor poses threat to a nonaggressor, the former loses moral parity with the latter, which justifies saving the nonaggressor's life over the aggressor's if only one life may be spared. The reason I cannot justify the killing of J.T. stems from the time break between J.T.'s aggression and Judy's response.

Unlike the state, which may enforce a wrongdoer's loss of rights at a much later time (e.g., revoke a reckless driver's license in a proceeding that takes place weeks after his misconduct), an individual may not benefit from a wrongdoer's loss of rights after the wrongful act is over. The law does not, and should not, authorize private retaliation. The victim's conduct may work as a liability mitigator only when it is an integral part of the criminal episode. Wrongdoers do not lose their rights for good. For instance, the MPC limits one's privilege to use defensive force if he provoked his adversary with the purpose of killing or seriously injuring him. This limitation applies, however, only to *the same encounter*.[59] A commentary explains that "the assailant will regain his privilege of self-defense by so far breaking off the struggle that any renewal by the other party can be viewed as a distinct engagement."[60] The crucial question for the involuntary reduction of rights is, therefore, whether the wrongful act of the victim was a part of the same episode as the perpetrator's violent response. If it was not, the victim's conduct is largely irrelevant for the mitigation of the perpetrator's liability.

Does that mean that Judy Norman was correctly convicted of manslaughter? Not at all. She was not entitled to a defense of justification, but considering all circumstances, she could have a reasonable claim for excuse. Dressler suggests that all excuse defenses are based on the defendant's lack of either (i) "substantial capacity" or (ii) "fair opportunity," in each case, to understand the facts relating to his conduct, appreciate that his conduct violates society's mores, or conform his conduct to the dictates of the law.[61] The first group of excuses takes into account the defendant's internal incapacity (e.g., insanity or infancy); the second recognizes an external limitation (e.g., duress). Dressler makes a plausible case for excusing Judy Norman based on the lack of fair opportunity. Under his theory, jurors should decide: "Could Judy have avoided the situation by walking out the door?"

> To answer *that* question, the jury would likely ask itself other questions: Did Judy Norman have children, thus making it more difficult for her to leave? Yes. She had four living at the time of J.T.'s death. What then were her options? Leave them with J.T.? That would be unthinkable for any loving parent. Leave *with* them? Where would she have gone? How would she have supported the children? What safety nets had been set up in her community to make such an option realistic? Moreover, what would have prevented J.T. from finding her and "punishing" her for her departure? Rather than leave, could she have called the police for help? *She did,* and they did nothing to protect her. And, so on.[62]

Assuming this defense worked similarly to the paradigmatic "lack of fair opportunity" defense, namely, duress, the jurors could acquit Judy if they found that she acted under the pressure that a person of reasonable firmness would have been unable to withstand. However, if this defense were applied similarly to duress, Judy most likely would not be able to raise it: in the absolute majority of American jurisdictions, duress does not excuse murder.[63] The MPC takes the opposite view, and a commentary explains: "It is obvious that even homicide may sometimes be the product of coercion that is truly irresistible."[64]

Interestingly, common law and civil law countries are sharply divided on how they treat duress. Unlike the common law, the civil law jurisdictions tend to allow duress as a full (e.g., France and Germany) or partial (e.g., Norway and Poland) defense, regardless of the severity of the committed offense. As for a broader community, a few years ago, the United Nations War Crimes Tribunal for the Former Yugoslavia concluded that there is no rule of customary international law governing the availability of duress as a defense to killing of innocent civilians and refused to grant a complete excuse for war-crime killings committed under compulsion.[65] In addition, two judges of the tribunal writing separately opined that an offender who acted under an imminent threat to his life is less blameworthy than an offender who committed a crime under a more remote threat of reprisal.[66] Similarly, imminence of harm is an element of duress in the majority of American penal codes, while the MPC rule once again differs.[67] A commentary to the MPC provision recognizes that "long and wasting pressure may break down resistance more effectively than a threat of immediate destruction."[68]

For a defendant like Judy Norman, this means that only in a jurisdiction that neither disqualifies homicide from the defense of duress nor limits the defense to situations of imminent threat would she stand a chance of acquittal under Dressler's proposal. Even there, her acquittal would require the legislature or the court to equate the severity of pressure and coercion in a situation of "no fair opportunity" with that of duress in the traditional sense.

Perhaps, if Judy's incapacity were viewed as an internal, rather than external, limitation, the success of her defense would be more certain. In fact, this is exactly what women in Judy's situation historically used to do: they presented evidence of the "battered wives'" syndrome and pleaded temporary insanity or diminished capacity. This defense strategy, albeit relatively successful, has been criticized by many feminists. Anne Coughlin, for example, found it objectionable because it "relieves the accused woman of the stigma and pain of criminal punishment only if she embraces another kind of stigma and pain: she must advance an interpretation of her own activity that labels it the irrational product of a mental health disorder."[69]

The internal limitation, however, does not have to be framed as a mental abnormality. It could be, as Jeremy Horder points out, the way "*ordinary* people, be they long-term hostages or battered women, tend to think and act in a certain kind of exceptional situation."[70] Unlike Horder, I do not believe that this reasonably (meaning, understandably) distorted perception provides grounds for justification. Instead, I would use Horder's test for an *excusatory* defense based on an internal limitation. Such a defense, full or partial, would fairly incorporate specific circumstances of the battered women's situation without imposing on them the stigma of abnormality.

The proposed defense would certainly not preclude an alternative excusatory mitigation based on a clinical psychological condition. Such mitigation, advocated, for example, by Stephen Morse, would be appropriate when the defendant's capacity for rationality was substantially diminished at the time of the crime and the diminished rationality substantially affected his criminal conduct.[71]

The issue of defenses for battered women who kill their abusers continues to be heatedly debated. Fairness requires that at least in some circumstances these women be acquitted. However, in order to achieve the desired outcome, we should be careful not to compromise the moral meaning of justification and specifically self-defense. The requirement of imminence serves to ensure that only responsive violence be justified. Consistently with the principle of conditionality of rights, the victim may lose his right not to be assaulted, injured, or killed *only* for the period of his own aggression.

• • •

In a nutshell, the victim's conduct prior to, at the time of, or subsequent[72] to the injury may be relevant to the level of the perpetrator's liability. Consent to a particular act should remain valid for the time reasonably necessary to complete that act, unless the consent-giver has communicated his wish to modify or revoke his consent. The victim's involuntary limitation of rights with respect to the perpetrator should continue for as long as the victim encroaches on the rights of the perpetrator or imminently threatens to do so. However, the defense of comparative liability should not be available to a perpetrator who used force in response to the victim's wrongdoing if that wrongdoing is not a part of the same encounter.

6 THE DEFENSE OF COMPARATIVE CRIMINAL LIABILITY

FACTORS RELEVANT TO THE MITIGATION OF THE PERPETRATORS' LIABILITY

In the earlier chapters of this book, my goal was to explore and formulate a general principle – that the victim's conduct can change the balance of rights and responsibilities between the victim and the perpetrator, and as a result, mitigate or eliminate the perpetrator's liability. Yet this general principle may not be translated into a criminal defense unless a more particular question is addressed: assuming the victim was instrumental in producing his own injury, how shall we compare his involvement with that of the perpetrator's, and *to what extent* shall we reduce the perpetrator's liability? To answer this question, one needs to weigh numerous factors, such as the magnitude of the affected rights of the perpetrator and the victim; the respective causative roles played by the perpetrator and the victim; and their relative culpability (including the nature of their conduct, the knowledge possessed by the participants, their individual capacities to avoid harm, the significance and value of purposes sought by their activities, the foreseeability and magnitude of the risk, and other factors).[1] Depending on the specifics of each case, different considerations may be more or less important.

The Magnitude of the Affected Rights

The "rights" question involves two inquiries: does the law recognize the affected rights of the perpetrator and the victim, and what is the comparative value assigned by the law to those rights? For example, I have a legally protected right not to be slapped on the face. This right, like any right to bodily integrity, is situated quite high in the hierarchy of rights, and its violation may subject the offender to a criminal punishment.[2] Thus, if I overreact as a result of being slapped, I would be partially justified. I would be more justified if I only slap the offender back, and less justified if I kill him.

In contrast, adultery is not criminally punishable in most states. Whatever claim I may have that my husband not cheat on me, this claim has very little legal ground.[3] Therefore, if I throw a heavy object at my husband upon witnessing his infidelity, my justification argument would be significantly less persuasive than in the previous example. That is not to say I will not have any defense. My defense, however, will be based predominantly on the excusatory "heat of passion" rationale. If explicitly incorporated into law, this approach would resolve a number of problems associated with provocation cases. For example, triggers of provocation would no longer represent an outdated list of equally valued historical incidents.[4] Instead, jurors would view any provoking event from the perspective of the perpetrator's rights. Only those acts that violate the perpetrator's legal rights would qualify for mitigation of his liability. Moreover, the extent of mitigation would depend, in part, on the place of the offended right on the continuum of currently recognized rights.

The relative significance of rights can be demonstrated by the defense of protection of property, which is authorized by all states and the MPC. Under a typical statute, an actor is justified in using force against another person if he reasonably believes that the force is immediately necessary to prevent or terminate the other person's trespass on or criminal interference with property lawfully in the actor's possession.[5] No state allows the use of deadly force solely for the protection of property.[6] In a mid-nineteenth-century North Carolina case, the defendant threatened a constable with an axe when the constable came to the defendant's home to seize a gun. The trial court held that, if the constable's actions were unlawful, the defendant was justified in protecting his property and thus not guilty of assault.[7] The appellate court, however, reversed the trial court's decision, opining:

> [W]hen it is said that a man may rightfully use as much force, as is necessary for the protection of his person or property, it should be recollected that this rule is subject to this most important modification, that he shall not, except in extreme cases, endanger human life or great bodily harm. It is not every right of person, and still less of property, that can lawfully be asserted, or every wrong, that may rightfully be redressed by extreme remedies. There is a recklessness—a

> wanton disregard of humanity and social duty—in taking or endeavoring to take the life of a fellow being, in order to save one's self from a comparatively slight wrong—which is essentially wicked, and which the law abhors. You may not kill, because you cannot otherwise effect your object, although the object sought to be effected is right. You can only kill to save life or limb, or prevent a great crime, or to accomplish a necessary public duty.[8]

The fact that various human interests enjoy unequal legal protection does not mean that the law always favors the more important interest. For example, an interest in living is considered to be more important than an interest in sexual inviolability, yet the law authorizes the victim of a sexual assault to use all necessary force, including deadly force, against the attacker. Nonetheless, a person may not be justified in the use of force if the magnitude of his interest is *grossly disproportionate* to that of his adversary. The MPC, for instance, provides that the "use of force to prevent or terminate trespass is not justifiable . . . if the actor knows that the exclusion of the trespasser will expose him to substantial danger of serious bodily harm."[9] Thus, although the mountaineers who found refuge in a deserted cabin during a dangerous snowstorm violated the cabin owner's property rights, he may not use force to evict them. His interest in the inviolability of his property is grossly disproportionate to the mountaineers' interest in staying alive.

For similar reasons, the New Jersey Supreme Court reversed the trespass conviction of two government employees who entered private property to aid migrant farm workers and refused to leave when confronted by the owner. The court said: "Property rights serve human values. They are recognized to that end, and are limited by it. Title to real property cannot include dominion over the destiny of persons the owner permits to come upon the premises. Their well being must remain the paramount concern of a system of law."[10]

Analogous arguments have been used in connection with the defense of provocation. In *People v. Epps*,[11] the defendant contended that his murder conviction should be reduced to manslaughter. The victim, a young boy, broke some branches from a tree in the defendant's yard. That apparently provoked a confrontation and severe beating of the defendant by the boy's father. When the defendant threatened the father with a knife, the father jumped into his truck and drove off. The defendant then went inside his house, returned with a gun, and shot the boy to death. The court rejected the defendant's claim of provocation. The father's conduct was held to be irrelevant because he was not the victim. As for the boy's conduct, the court quite sensibly opined that breaking tree branches was not sufficient provocation to mitigate responsibility for taking a human life.[12]

It is important to highlight that the hierarchy of rights and their violations must be determined from the objective point of view, not from the individual preferences of the victim. Some may say that harm is in the eye of the victim, and accordingly, the injuries or losses that the victim likes least are most harmful, while the harms the victim can tolerate most are least harmful. Yet the preference-based scale of rights and harms inevitably produces absurd results, as Leo Katz's elegant hypotheticals show.

In one of them, a man is about to rape a woman. At the last moment, the woman pleads: "I would rather die than be violated," so he obligingly kills her. At his trial, the defense argues that, although the defendant is certainly guilty of a heinous crime, his punishment should be no more severe than punishment for rape. After all, the victim herself preferred murder to rape, that is, regarded it as a lesser harm. In the opposite hypothetical, the perpetrator rapes the woman despite her desperate plea to take her life instead. At the trial, the prosecutor demands the death penalty for the defendant. He argues that, although ordinarily the death penalty may not be imposed for rape of an adult woman, this case of rape is worse than murder: didn't the victim herself feel so?[13]

Obviously, neither argument should succeed. Partly because the "victim cares only about one dimension of the perpetrator's activities—the expected harm,"[14] whereas criminal law cares about harm as one of several criteria of a wrongdoing.[15] And partly because the meaning of harm in criminal law is not limited to each victim's idiosyncratic perception of harm. Criminal law embodies a uniform hierarchical set of moral and legal principles based in part on the values assigned by society to specific rights.

Comparative Causation

Tests for Comparing Causation The scope of one's responsibility for particular harm is largely an issue of causation. Yet criminal law has chosen to ignore the causative role of the victim and instead has attributed the entire fault to the defendant who was *a* "but for" cause and *a* proximate cause of the victim's injury or loss.

Recently, Aya Gruber has proposed a defense that would change this rule and mitigate the defendant's culpability when the victim's wrongful conduct "caused the defendant to commit the charged offense," which he was otherwise "not predisposed" to commit.[16] Despite my strong support for a criminal defense based on the victim's conduct, I find these specific requirements conceptually flawed.

The requirement that the defendant not be *predisposed* to commit the offense is objectionable like any requirement that conditions the defendant's penalty not on his criminal act but rather on his propensity for crime or violent thoughts. If a court took this requirement seriously, it would have to deny the defense to a woman who escaped rape by shooting her attacker simply because she was *predisposed* to shoot any SOB who tried to rape her.

Still more problematic is the way Gruber treats causation. Only if the victim had *caused* the defendant to commit the offense would the defense apply. Even putting aside the doubtful proposition that one may *cause* another free and independent agent to do anything,[17] there remains a bigger issue: why should not the defense apply, at least partially, when *both* the defendant and the victim contributed to the harmful outcome? Is it fair or realistic to impose full causative responsibility on one party?

All our experience tells us that causation is almost never an all-or-nothing issue. Many factors work together to bring about a result. Thus, in the words of Judith Jarvis Thomson, it is "no wonder it has seemed such a hard problem to work out the truth-conditions for 'X is the cause of Y'—for it is doubtful that 'X is the sole cause of Y' can ever be true."[18] To bring criminal law in accord with reality, we need to adopt a comparative approach to causation. Simply shifting the entire burden from the perpetrator to the victim, as Gruber implicitly proposes, would not overcome the crudeness of the current black-and-white dichotomy.

But can the causative importance of various events ever be compared? There is a view that denies this possibility. Under that view, causation is not a relative concept; either it exists or it does not, and if it does exist, one may not speak of degrees of causation.[19] If certain events were necessary to produce a result, it is impossible to tell which event was more necessary.[20] Thus, if "it took malaria-bearing mosquitoes and the spread of Christianity to undo the Roman Empire, the mosquitoes were as necessary as the Christians and neither is paramount to the other."[21]

To be sure, it is not always easy to name the determinative cause among other causes, yet in many contexts we manage to compare events as being more or less important for certain consequences:

> We might wish to say, for instance, that Lenin's participation in the Bolshevik Revolution was a more important cause of its success than was Stalin's, or that the absence of a skilled labor force is a more important cause of economic backwardness than is limited natural resources. Or, we might have reason to say that James is happier today than he was last week partly because he earned an A on his torts exam, but more because his love life has improved.[22]

Scholars have suggested various ways to compare the importance of contributing causes in torts.[23] Some of these methods, although not completely importable to penal theory, may serve as models for developing a comparative theory of causation in criminal law. Among those are: counterfactual similarity, the "necessary element of a sufficient set," and relative responsibility.

The method of counterfactual similarity "involves using imaginative alternatives to the actual course of events to determine whether something similar to the event would have occurred in the absence of a particular cause."[24] For example:

> [T]he change in James' love life was a more important cause of his current happiness than was his torts grade, since had James not earned an A on his torts exam, his mood would more closely approximate his current level of happiness than it would had his love life not improved.[25]

Under the "necessary element of a sufficient set" test, "a particular condition was a cause of (condition contributing to) a specific consequence if, and only if, it was a necessary element of a set of antecedent actual conditions that was sufficient for the occurrence of the consequence."[26] This method does not offer a mechanism for comparing multiple causes; it is valuable, however, in eliminating noncauses and limiting the circle of responsible parties.

Finally, under the relative responsibility method, the more important of two causes is the one that is more responsible for their effect. The term *responsible* in this context means something other than making the biggest factual difference toward the occurrence of an event.[27] It is instead "the statement of a moral and legal conclusion that a particular cause ought to be held more accountable than other causes for the effect. It is an unabashedly normative interpretation of more important cause, and it bears a close kinship to traditional notions of proximate cause."[28]

The outlined approaches capture important aspects of how we attribute causal weight to various events. We measure the importance of a cause by

(1) the factual difference it makes ("necessary element of a sufficient set" and counterfactual similarity) and (2) the legal and moral weight we assign to different types of behavior (relative responsibility). Both considerations come into play as we look at the victim's acts or omissions and their impact on the outcome of the criminal interaction.

Victim's and Perpetrator's Contemporaneous Actions The current legal rule states that the victim's conduct is irrelevant, unless it is the sole proximate cause of the suffered harm. If what the victim did was merely a substantial contribution, the court would not take the victim's actions into account. Consider, for example, *Everett v. State*,[29] in which the defendant challenged his vehicular homicide conviction. The defendant admitted that he did not wear glasses at the time of the accident and that he had drunk some beer and smoked marijuana shortly before the accident, but he claimed that his driving was not impaired. The victim was a pedestrian, apparently intoxicated, who stepped out of a bar and was trying to cross the street. According to witnesses, had the victim not abruptly stopped in the middle of the road, he probably would not have been struck. On appeal, the court acknowledged that the victim's "jay-walking was a significant factor in the accident"[30] and that "the conduct of decedent contributed to his own demise."[31] However, since the evidence did not support a conclusion that the victim was the *sole* cause of his death, the court approved the trial judge's decision not to instruct the jury on the victim's jaywalking and blood alcohol level.[32]

In contrast with the victim's conduct, the perpetrator's conduct constitutes the proximate cause of the victim's injury if it is merely a *substantial factor* in bringing about that injury. As one court said, "[s]o long as the defendant's acts are found by the jury to rise to the high level of 'culpable negligence' and so long as the defendant's acts actually constitute a substantial factor in causing the death, absent any factors to justify or excuse, there is liability for the negligence."[33]

Considering that criminal law ignores the victim's own negligence, this disparity in the treatment of the victim's and the perpetrator's causative impacts is disturbing. Just as in cases of drag racing, it would be more fair and consistent with the general principles of responsibility to take into account *all* contributing causes, whether culpable or nonculpable. To illustrate the last point, consider a driver who runs a stop sign while driving a seriously injured passenger to the hospital. The driver's conduct is justified under the principle of the balance of evils. However, if, as a result of ignoring the stop sign, he collides with another car and suffers an injury, it would be unfair to disregard his causative role in the accident, whether or not the second driver was at fault. This does not certainly mean that a defendant like Everett should escape responsibility for his victim's death; this only means that his responsibility should be proportionate to his causal role in that death.

Victim's Intervening Acts and Omissions When the harmful result is produced not by contemporaneous but by consecutive actions (or omissions) of the perpetrator and the victim, the court must decide: has the chain of causation been broken? Is the perpetrator responsible for all the eventual harm even though, when he stopped acting, the victim was in a much better position than he ended up being in and, but for his own actions (or omissions), would not have suffered the higher amount of harm?

Victims' omissions are usually not assigned much causative weight. In part, this is so because omissions do not, literally speaking, "cause" anything. Quoting Francis Bohlen, "by failing to interfere in the plaintiff's affairs, the defendant has left him as he was before; no better off, it is true, but still in no worse position; he has failed to benefit him, but he has not caused him any new injury nor created any new injurious situation."[34] Under this view, by failing to save a drowning child, I do not "cause" his death. If I were nowhere around, the child would have drowned all the same.

And yet, numerous examples support our intuition that sometimes (1) an omission can make a difference in the course of events, and (2) it may be fair to hold a person responsible for the harm that would not have happened but for the omission. Say Jones, the signalman, gets drunk and does not pull a lever, as he is supposed to do in order to make a train turn right. As a result, the train crashes. Can we say that Jones's failure to pull the lever caused the crash?[35] Perhaps not: after all, as Thomson phrases it, everyone else also failed to pull the lever, "a certain paraplegic, Bloggs, also did not pull the lever. My typewriter also did not pull the lever."[36] So if our collective failure to pull the lever did not cause the crash, why did Jones's?

The key to this question may lie in the difference between Jones and others: Jones, unlike the rest of the world, had a duty to pull the lever. Moreover, unlike Bloggs and the typewriter, he was capable of pulling it. In other words, there seems to be an important connection between causation, duty, and capacity, and even if we cannot say that *Jones's omission* caused the crash, we can still say that *Jones* caused the crash because he was behind the chain of events that he was both capable of preventing and under a duty to prevent.[37]

These examples help us to understand why the victim's omission plays such a minor causative role in the formula of comparative liability: even if the victim can prevent harm to himself, he is under no duty to do so. Unlike a tort victim or a victim of a contractual breach, a victim of a criminal offense has no duty to mitigate harm. Thus, the victim's failure to seek medical treatment does not reduce the perpetrator's liability.[38] In *Regina v. Blaue*, the victim, a Jehovah's Witness, died from a stab wound after having refused blood transfusion, and the defendant was convicted of manslaughter.[39] The court stated:

> It does not lie in the mouth of the assailant to say that his victim's religious beliefs which inhibited him from accepting certain kinds of treatment were unreasonable. The question for decision is what caused her death. The answer is the stab wound. The fact that the victim refused to stop this end coming about did not break the causal connection between the act and death.[40]

This conclusion is in accord with the general principle of criminal law that ordinarily an omission does not break the chain of causation. Moreover, in the absence of a duty to act, omission does not satisfy the requirements of a voluntary act and thus is irrelevant for purposes of criminal responsibility.[41] The *Blaue* victim certainly owed no duty to her assailant. Consequently, her refusal of treatment did not affect the perpetrator's liability for the resulting harm.

However, when victims not merely fail to mitigate harm but instead affirmatively do something that exacerbates it, the analysis changes. Consider the following two cases. In *State v. Perez-Cervantes*, the victim's stab wounds were treated at a hospital; the victim was released and, despite doctors' warnings, returned to his habitual cocaine use. The drug raised his blood pressure and caused internal injuries, of which he shortly died.[42] In *Regina v. Dear*, the defendant slashed the victim with a knife several times after learning that the victim had sexually molested his twelve-year-old daughter. When the victim's wounds started to heal, he reopened them and soon died of blood loss.[43] In each case, the defendant was convicted of murder.

These decisions appear to be erroneous. In both *Perez-Cervantes* and *Dear*, the victim's initial injuries were not life-threatening. What made them fatal were the intervening self-destructive acts of the victims. By the time they were committed, each victim was already in the position of "apparent safety."

Under the doctrine of apparent safety, the defendant is not liable for the ultimate harm to the victim if some of the harmful events occurred after "the defendant's active force has come to rest in a position of apparent safety."[44] In the paradigmatic case of *State v. Preslar*, a woman escaped home after her husband violently assaulted her. She intended to stay with her father; however, when she almost reached his house, she changed her mind and decided not to enter it until the next morning. She spent the night outside, in bitter cold, and later died. The court held that the defendant was not responsible for his wife's death because "there was nothing to prevent her from going in, but she chose, of her own accord, to remain out all night, exposed on the damp ground."[45]

Based on this doctrine, in both *Perez-Cervantes* and *Dear*, the victims' conduct should break the chain of causation, provided, of course, their conduct can be qualified as "free, deliberate, and informed."[46] Conduct is usually qualified this way if the accompanying culpability of the intervening actor reaches beyond ordinary negligence.[47] This is certainly the case in both *Perez-Cervantes* and *Dear*: by taking cocaine, the victim of *Perez-Cervantes* exhibited conscious disregard of substantial and unjustifiable risk to his health, namely, recklessness (assuming he was not addicted to the drug to such an extent that his drug use was no longer voluntary), and the victim in *Dear* intentionally opened his wounds in order to stop the process of healing. Accordingly, the defendants in these two cases (to a much higher degree than the defendant in *Preslar* who could be merely negligent) should have been held responsible for the aggravated assault on their victims but not for the victims' deaths.

Yet, if we change, even slightly, the balance of causative contributions by the perpetrator and the victim (the factual impact of their actions, as well as their relative responsibility), the outcome may be totally different. The famous case of *Stephenson v. State*[48] provides good material for showing how these comparative considerations may work. In that case, the victim, Madge Oberholtzer, took poison after being kidnapped, beaten, humiliated, and nearly raped.[49] She was denied medical help by her kidnapper and eventually died.[50] Factors that contributed to Madge Oberholtzer's death were summarized as "shock, loss of food, loss of rest, action of the poison on her system and her lack of early treatment."[51] According to medical testimony, it was unlikely that any one factor would have resulted in death on its own.[52]

The jury found the defendant guilty of second-degree murder, and the Supreme Court of Indiana affirmed the verdict.[53] Some commentators have harshly criticized that decision, which, in their view, undermined the requirement of proximate causation by holding Stephenson responsible for an intervening act of the victim.[54] From the perspective of *comparative causation*, however, Stephenson's verdict was correct.

A jury instructed to view causation comparatively would have to consider (1) the comparative impact of Stephenson's and Madge's actions and (2) Stephenson's and Madge's comparative accountability for her death. It is likely that such a jury would find Stephenson's actions at least as substantial a cause of Madge Oberholtzer's death as her own—but for him, she would not have taken the poison. More importantly, even after she took the poison, she still could be saved had he not denied her medical treatment.

It is even more likely that Stephenson would be found primarily liable for Madge's death as the jury compared the legal and moral significance of cold-blooded, premeditated offenses committed by Stephenson and hysterical, semirational actions undertaken by Madge in response to Stephenson's assault. The jury would also take into account that Stephenson had not only the moral but also the legal duty to rescue his victim. Generally, one has no legal duty to aid others, even when the aid can be rendered without danger or inconvenience to the actor. However, there are circumstances that give rise to such a duty. For example, one acquires a duty to help another person if he puts that person in peril or if he voluntarily takes control over that person and moves him to a place of isolation where other people cannot help him.[55]

In *Jones v. State*,[56] for instance, the defendant raped a girl, who then, in distress, either fell or jumped into a creek. The defendant could have saved her but chose not to. The girl drowned, and the defendant was convicted of murder. The Supreme Court of Indiana (the same court that a few years earlier decided *Stephenson*) affirmed the conviction, saying: "Can it be doubted that one who by his own overpowering criminal act has put another in danger of drowning has the duty to preserve her life?"[57]

The duty to rescue was also found in *People v. Oliver*,[58] a case in which the defendant brought home an intoxicated man, let him inject heroine in her bathroom, and later, when he collapsed, had him dragged outside, where he died of an overdose. The Court of Appeal of California concluded that the defendant owed the victim a duty of care because she took him from a public place, where others could have prevented him from injuring himself, to a private place, her home, where only she could provide medical assistance.[59] *Stephenson* combines elements of both cases: it was Stephenson's continuous assault that put Madge Oberholtzer's health and life in the position of danger, and it was his "absolute and complete"[60] "control and domination"[61] over her that made him about the only person who could summon a doctor and save her life.

Had the *Stephenson* trial court explicitly taken these considerations into account and instructed the jury to compare the causative impact of the defendant's and the victim's actions, as well as their respective responsibility for those actions, the Supreme Court of Indiana would have had a much stronger legal basis to affirm the conviction and conclude that "[t]o say that there is no causal connection between the acts of appellant and the death of Madge Oberholtzer, and that the treatment accorded her by appellant had no causal connection with the death of Madge Oberholtzer would be a travesty of justice."[62]

Multiple Perpetrators Another comparative culpability issue of significant interest involves multiple defendants. Addressing my arguments for comparative criminal liability, Kenneth Simons raised a question: "If a single defendant's liability is properly mitigated because of the victim's fault, should it not also be mitigated if a second defendant's faulty or wrongful conduct contributed to a victim's harm (apart from whether the victim's own conduct is properly considered a mitigation)?"[63]

There may be several possible scenarios involving multiple defendants. One, for example, is when these defendants are accomplices or coconspirators. The theories of accessorial and conspiratorial liability provide an unequivocal answer to why one defendant may not benefit from the actions of another. Pursuant to these theories, one is guilty because, by his own intentional actions—an agreement or some aid—he "adopts" the crime of his cofelons. Naturally, the more criminal acts one "adopts," the higher is his criminal liability. Those criminal acts are imputed to the defendant and become "his own"; therefore, multiple perpetrators may only increase, but not decrease, the defendant's culpability.

The second situation in which apportionment of liability may become relevant is when the harm is divisible, for example, when two unrelated, independently acting defendants are responsible for different harms. Suppose, as a result of attending a restaurant, the victim has suffered a theft of a wallet and severe food poisoning. The thief and the restaurant owner would obviously be responsible for two different wrongs—the thief for the theft, and the restaurant owner for the injury to the victim caused by the unsanitary condition of the establishment. The liability of neither of them would be affected by the actions of the other.

The third scenario is known in legal literature as overdetermination.[64] In a classic case of preemptive overdetermination, two people set a building on fire, but one fire "reaches the victim's house first and destroys it; the other fire then arrives sufficient to have destroyed the house if it were still standing, but there is no house left to destroy."[65] The first fire here has preempted the harm and precluded the liability of the second arsonist, but only the liability for the completed crime. The second arsonist would be still guilty of attempted arson.

The case that Simons had in mind belongs to yet another type called concurrent overdetermination. In a case of this type, two unrelated fires, each sufficient to burn down the building, join and *together* destroy it.[66] Specifically, Simons asks: "If two independent speeding drivers collide and cause the victim's death, in circumstances where the speeding of either alone would have been sufficient to cause the harm, should the punishment for each be mitigated, because of the causal contribution and fault of the other?"[67] Simons apparently thinks that the tenet of comparative liability would mandate such mitigation. This is an odd proposition. In the concurrent overdetermination case envisioned by Simons, each defendant's actions are independent in terms of both causation and culpability and do not increase or reduce the ultimate harmful result. Accordingly, the conduct of any additional actor—a perpetrator or the victim—does not have any effect on the liability of a particular defendant. Each driver's negligence is a "but for" and proximate cause of the fatal accident *attributable to him*.[68] In the words of Jerome Hall,

> The fact is that both actions caused the death. That either would have caused it in the absence of the other does not imply that neither was in fact a cause. It does not imply that this is an exception to the causal principle. It only signifies that the usual simple application of the "but for" formula is not relevant to this situation, that it would be superficial and misleading to apply it here in a sense carried from single-cause situations.[69]

In Simons's hypothetical, each collision is causally sufficient and independent from the other, but it is *not necessary*: if the other driver did not exist, the victim would still be dead. Conversely, outside the overdetermination context, when a collision results from negligent actions of a driver and the victim, the causal contribution of each party is a necessary condition of the resulting harm. If the victim acted differently, he would not be harmed.

More importantly, in Simons's hypothetical, wrongful actions of one defendant toward the victim do not reduce the obligations of the other defendant not to act wrongfully toward the same victim. Accordingly, each of them is guilty of violating the victim's rights. In contrast, the principle of conditionality of rights allows mitigating the perpetrator's liability only when the victim has acted in such a way as to eliminate or reduce some of his rights, thus eliminating or reducing the perpetrator's responsibility for interfering with the interests protected by those rights.

Pursuant to this same logic, each defendant would be responsible for the entire harm in the non-overdetermination context as well—say, when two independent speeding drivers collide and cause the victim's death in circumstances in which the speeding of either alone would *not* have been sufficient to cause the harm. Each driver would be guilty of homicide because each of them was involved in criminal conduct that violated the victim's right to life and resulted in combined indivisible harm, the victim's death. It is not essential that the harm caused by each driver separately was not sufficient to kill the victim. In part, it is not essential simply because no criminal act by itself is ever sufficient for the harmful result. Many other conditions must be present (and absent) for that harmful result to materialize. Quoting Michael Moore, "A spark is not sufficient for an explosion, because oxygen and fuel are necessary as well. These three together are not sufficient for the explosion because the absence of large amounts of inert material is also required. And so on."[70]

Yet a more important reason for holding each speeding driver responsible for the victim's death is the same as the one behind a whole number of criminal law doctrines—such as the "egg shell victim" doctrine or the "legal wrong" doctrine—which extend the perpetrator's liability to cover *all* the harm suffered by the victim. Pursuant to these doctrines, the perpetrator who culpably engages in unlawful conduct is deemed to have assumed the risk that the resulting harm may turn out to be more severe than what he anticipated. Similarly, each independently acting defendant should be responsible for the entire harm, which his illegal actions helped to bring about, regardless of how many other defendants were involved. The principle of conditionality of rights would not provide grounds for any mitigation of the defendant's liability in these circumstances.

Comparative Culpability

In some instances, the comparative culpability of the participants may affect the value of their rights and the seriousness of encroachments on those rights. The clearest example is provocation. In part, the provoker's loss or reduction of rights may be explained by his assault on the rights of others and in part, by assumption of risk. By hitting you, I assume the risk that you may hit me back and that, being angered by the undeserved assault, you may hit me harder than I hit you.

That semivoluntary rationale may mandate a somewhat different treatment of innocent aggressors in situations of provocation compared to self-defense. As we have seen, in the case of self-defense, the culpability of the aggressor is irrelevant to the rights of the target.[71] The very fact that, if not stopped, the aggressor will violate the most essential rights of an innocent party triggers the condition that makes the aggressor lose his rights. That outcome may be different in a provocation scenario.

Since the target of provocation is not presented with a risk to his life, we may choose not to recognize *as a justifying event* (or give reduced weight to) provocation by certain groups of people, just as we often do not recognize consent of some groups of people (e.g., minors or insane). For example, it is offensive when someone intentionally spits on you, and we can easily understand that such provoking conduct, coming from an adult man, may partially justify a violent response. It is, however, significantly less offensive when the offender is a young child. Accordingly, the level of mitigation to which the defendant may be entitled should reflect that.

Negligent, reckless, or even intentional behavior that normally reduces the victim's right not to be hurt may be given little or no weight if the victim was a minor. As the U.S. Supreme Court said, "[a] lack of maturity and an underdeveloped sense of responsibility are found in youth more often than in adults and are more understandable among the young. These qualities often result in impetuous and ill-considered actions and decisions."[72] Because of that, a child's involvement in a dangerous activity should not be characterized as full-fledged assumption of risk, particularly when other participants are much older and play an active role in bringing the child into the activity. In *Commonwealth v. Malone*,[73] for example, the defendant, a seventeen-year-old boy, was convicted of second-degree murder for killing a thirteen-year-old companion in the course of playing Russian Poker (a version of Russian roulette). It was the defendant who proposed the game. The victim merely replied: "I don't care; go ahead."[74] The defendant then placed a revolver against the victim's temple and pulled the trigger three times. The third time turned out to be fatal. I think that, in a case like this, the young age of the victim, the significant age difference between the victim and the perpetrator, and the passive involvement of the victim in the reckless game create a strong presumption that the victim's consent was not quite free, deliberate, and informed; and thus his own culpability should not provide grounds for mitigation of the perpetrator's offense.

Moreover, the level of the provoker's culpability should probably be taken into account in any case of mitigation based on the victim's provocative conduct. There is a difference in how we perceive the fault of a defendant who killed his victim after being physically attacked by an intentional actor as opposed to a merely negligent actor. Just like in cases of the assumption of risk, the less conscious the victim's engagement in a dangerous (provoking) activity, the more appropriate it may be to treat his behavior as an involuntary, rather than a voluntary, reduction of rights. And, as suggested before, perhaps fewer rights should be alienable involuntarily than voluntarily.[75]

These considerations should be taken into account in other circumstances as well. When the perpetrator and the victim are equally culpable (e.g., in cases of drag racing, dueling, or Russian roulette), the conduct of the victim should be a stronger mitigator than when the perpetrator is more culpable than the victim (e.g., in a case of a car crash, in which the perpetrator drove recklessly whereas the victim was merely negligent). Conversely, when the victim is more culpable than the perpetrator, the court should be reluctant to impose full liability.

In *State v. Munnell*,[76] for instance, the defendant struck and killed the victim, who was lying unconscious on the road. The driver's blood alcohol concentration was 0.11 percent (0.01 percent above the state limit), while the victim's was at least 0.24 percent. The defendant was charged with vehicular homicide. The trial court certified to the appellate court several questions, including this: "Is being less at fault than the deceased victim a defense to a prosecution"[77] under the state statute? The Minnesota Appellate Court held that it was not.

This decision strikes me as wrong. Both criminal law and morality assign significant weight to one's culpability. As Justice Holmes once put it, even a dog knows the difference between being stumbled over and being kicked.[78] Defendants who commit identical acts and cause identical harm, yet with different mens rea, are normally convicted of offenses of different gravity. For example, in a case of accidental deadly shooting, the defendant's verdict may vary from murder to manslaughter to negligent homicide to (arguably) not guilty based entirely on his level of culpability. Similarly, in our everyday life, when assigning responsibility, we pay significant attention to who is at fault. So how can a fair verdict disregard the jury's finding that the victim was more at fault than the defendant?[79]

In determining the respective culpability of the perpetrator and the victim, jurors should be instructed to compare the nature of the participants' conduct, their respective capacities to avoid harm, the significance and value of purposes sought by their activities, and the foreseeability and magnitude of the risk they took. For example, if a fatal car crash happened because the perpetrator exceeded the speed limit and hit the victim's car parked in the middle of a highway, the level of mitigation of the perpetrator's liability may depend on a number of facts. It would be higher if the perpetrator was in a rush to deliver a sick child to a hospital whereas the victim took an impromptu nap at the wheel after a few shots of tequila. And it would be lower if the perpetrator was hurrying home for a favorite television show whereas the victim had suffered a heart attack in his car. These are, of course, extreme examples serving only to demonstrate how individual culpability can change the liability equation.

PRACTICAL IMPLEMENTATION OF COMPARATIVE LIABILITY

Finally, in what form should criminal law adopt the theory of comparative liability? I suggest that the victim's rights-reducing conduct should function as an affirmative defense. In some circumstances, it would provide a complete justification, whereas in other circumstances, it would only mitigate the defendant's liability. In either case, the defendant would bear the burden of production. As for the burden of persuasion, it may be more appropriate to follow the MPC practice and allocate it to the prosecution, unless specified otherwise.[80]

Some scholars have expressed concerns about practical implementation of the defense. For example, Douglas Husak tried to envision how the mechanism of mitigation would work in a case of partial reduction of criminal liability. He correctly noted that the structure of homicide offenses provides an ideal solution. "When persons commit homicides, fault mitigators such as provocation function as 'imperfect defenses,' allowing defendants to be convicted of a lesser-included offense like manslaughter."[81] He then went on to caution that "lesser-included offenses are rare outside the context of homicide; there usually is no hierarchy of offenses for which defendants whose fault is mitigated might be convicted."[82]

I agree with Husak that the structure of homicide offenses provides a convenient paradigm for applying any partial defense, not just the one related to the victim's conduct. However, I do not think that to incorporate a partial defense there is no other alternative but "to double the size of the substantive criminal law by enacting lesser-included offenses across the entire spectrum of crimes."[83]

One way to proceed in the case of successful invocation of the defense of comparative liability is to permit downgrading of an offense charged to a lower degree or to another lesser-related offense, regardless of whether or not it is also lesser included (an offense is considered lesser included only if "the elements of the lesser offense are a subset of the elements of the charged offense"[84]). This solution would not require too much legislative effort, since the majority of nonvictimless crimes—and the defense of comparative responsibility, by definition, applies only to those—already have some less serious analogues, particularly in jurisdictions whose penal codes are modeled on the MPC. For example, Article 211 of the MPC includes aggravated assault (a felony of the second or third degree), a simple assault (a misdemeanor or petty misdemeanor), and reckless endangerment (a misdemeanor). When warranted by facts, the charge of aggravated assault could be reduced to a simple assault or even reckless endangerment.

True, recent decisions have purported to limit jury instruction on lesser offenses to those that meet the strict requirements for lesser-included offenses.[85] Yet, as one commentator has pointed out, these decisions typically rely on statutes or rules and have not considered that a lesser offense may constitute a defense or a defense theory.[86] Pursuant to the well-developed body of federal law, the Fifth, Sixth, and Fourteenth Amendments guarantee an individual the right to have the jury instructed on his theory of defense. Therefore, a statute or rule that precludes instruction on a nonincluded offense ought not to be applied when it interferes with the defendant's constitutional right to present a defense.

For example, in *Sanborn v. Commonwealth*,[87] the defendant was charged, among other things, with kidnapping and rape of the victim. The defendant sought a jury instruction on the lesser-related (but nonincluded) offense of abuse of a corpse because, according to his theory of the case, the charged criminal acts were committed after the victim was already dead. The trial judge refused the instruction, the conviction was later reversed, and the Supreme Court of Kentucky opined:

> Sanborn could hardly expect the jury to exonerate him in the face of his criminal misconduct, and this was the reason why his counsel requested instructions on a crime that presented a middle ground between the offense more severely punished and acquittal. It is fundamental that in a criminal case it is the duty of the court "by the instructions to give to the accused the opportunity for the jury to determine the merits of any lawful defense which he has."[88]

In sum, the failure to instruct on a nonincluded offense when such instruction is necessitated by a defense theory (including the defense theory of comparative liability) may violate the defendant's constitutional rights to due process, compulsory process, and fair trial by jury. In addition, the U.S. Supreme Court has consistently held that state rules of evidence should not deprive the defendant of a fair trial.[89] The Court has applied a balancing test to resolve conflicting interests of the defendant and the state. Exclusion of evidence has been held to be arbitrary or disproportionate "where it infringed upon a weighty interest of the defendant."[90] Accordingly, even if the rules or statutes precluding a lesser nonincluded offense are not unconstitutional per se, the high stake of the defendant in adequately presenting his defense theory would most likely outweigh competing interests of the state.

In addition to using lesser offenses to mitigate the defendant's liability in a case in which the victim is partially responsible for the resulting harm, various grades of the same offense can also be used. Current state codes commonly recognize as many as ten or more offense grades, and proper grading of offenses is considered to be a requirement of fair and consistent punishment.[91] Some codes already take the victim's conduct into account when assigning various degrees of an offense, but these instances are rare and random. The MPC, for example, treats the offense of simple assault as a misdemeanor. If, however, it is committed in a fight or scuffle entered into by mutual consent, it is only a petty misdemeanor.[92] Similarly, in Pennsylvania, assault is a misdemeanor in the second degree, but if it is committed in a fight or scuffle entered into by mutual consent, it is a misdemeanor of the third degree.[93]

Another concern that has been expressed in connection with the proposed defense is that, by asking jurors to apply a multifactor test, a comparative fault-like inquiry on a case-by-case basis, we would give them too much discretion over the gravity of criminal punishments.[94] I do not think those worries are warranted. In practically any criminal trial, jurors have to deal with multifactor tests. They have to decide who had rights to what, who was at fault, and who was causally responsible for the harm. They often have to use a "comparative fault-type inquiry" in order to determine whether the defendant acted reasonably.

Moreover, in many instances, that inquiry directly translates into the verdict and the gravity of criminal punishments. For example, in a case of involuntary homicide, the difference between the defendant's non-negligent conduct, negligence, recklessness, and recklessness manifesting extreme indifference to the value of human life determines the choice between no liability, negligent homicide (a felony of the third degree), manslaughter (a felony of the second degree), and murder (a felony of the first degree).[95]

• • •

In this part, I sought to provide a conceptual framework for the defense of comparative criminal liability. This defense should be available to a defendant when the victim was, at least in part, responsible for the suffered harm. The victim may be responsible for the harm if he either waived his right not to be harmed voluntarily or lost or reduced it involuntarily. The waiver of rights is in effect, in the case of consent, for the time reasonably necessary to complete the authorized act, unless the victim has communicated his wish to modify or withdraw consent. The involuntary loss or reduction of rights continues for as long as the victim encroaches on the rights of the perpetrator or imminently threatens to do so.

The defense of comparative liability may serve as full or partial justification. Factors relevant to the determination of the scope of available mitigation include the magnitude of the affected rights of the perpetrator and the victim, the relative causative roles played by the perpetrator and the victim, and their comparative culpability (including the nature of their conduct, the knowledge possessed by the participants, their respective capacities to avoid harm, the significance and value of purposes sought by their activities, and the foreseeability and magnitude of the risk).

CONCLUSION

THE CRIMINAL LAW doctrine maintains that victims' conduct does not mitigate perpetrators' liability. However, upon close examination, this declaration is only partially correct. Furthermore, to the extent it is correct, it produces legal rules that are in direct conflict with fundamental principles of criminal liability, factual findings by social scientists, public perceptions of right and wrong, and developments in other areas of law. Considerations of fairness and effectiveness mandate that criminal law integrate victims into its theory of liability. If victims by their own actions have reduced their rights not to be harmed, defendants should be allowed to raise that as an affirmative defense at their trial.

In this book, I attempted to describe and apply the principle, which I believe to be a general principle of criminal law, the principle of conditionality of rights. This principle is a function of our collective living and our interaction with each other as citizens and individuals. As a principle, it is absolute: in any community, people should be entitled to go about their lives with the expectation that their rights will be respected by other members of the community, provided that they equally respect the rights of others. The implementation of this principle, however, may differ both historically and culturally. Law, and criminal law in particular, reflects moral and social norms of the community. It is, therefore, only to be expected that the scope of individual rights protected by the law and the comparative weight assigned to specific rights may vary from country to country and may undergo transformation as the time goes by.

As it stands, American criminal law does not supply cohesive answers to many situations involving the interplay or conflict of individual rights. Some of these situations were discussed in this book. Among them are assisted suicide and consensual injuries, homicide motivated by adultery, postpenetration rape, and killing of domestic abusers in nonconfrontational circumstances. Of course, the proposed defense of comparative liability will not automatically ensure the fair and consistent treatment of the victims and perpetrators of these and other harmful acts; it will, however, provide the conceptual framework for systematic incorporation of individual rights into the criminal theory.

This revision will bring victims into the focus of criminal law and convey to the community respect for their rights. For example, consent of the victim will be explicitly recognized as a complete or partial justification. A defendant wishing to invoke this defense will have to establish that the victim's consent was voluntary and rational. This condition will both give people an opportunity to control their own lives and protect vulnerable individuals from abuse. Particularly serious and irreversible harm may necessitate formal proof of the rationality and voluntariness of the victim's choice. To accommodate this requirement, the law will need to develop a set of standards and procedures governing consensual harmful actions. For example, consent to a cosmetic surgery may involve meeting with a psychologist and signing a simple medical consent form, whereas consent to active euthanasia may be deemed valid only subject to a psychiatric evaluation of the victim by several independent doctors, a legal consultation, and a document, similar to a living will, properly executed and witnessed.

Another group of cases that will be affected by the revision of the law includes those involving the victim's assumption of risk. In cases of this type, the victim either voluntarily participates in dangerous activities together with the defendant (e.g., Russian roulette) or inadvertently suffers a mishap through his own fault as well as the fault of the defendant (e.g., an accident in which a speeding driver hits a drunken pedestrian). These cases should be distinguished from situations in which the victim merely does not take sufficient precautions against crime and falls prey to intentional wrongdoing (e.g., a person who strolls through a high-crime area late at night and is mugged). In the latter type of cases, the victims' lack of caution does not diminish their rights because the law may not require people to live their lives so as to anticipate and accommodate crime. Accordingly, under the principle of conditionality of rights, the victims' conduct will mitigate the perpetrators' fault in a case of Russian roulette or a car accident but not in a case of mugging.

Beyond the cases of consent and assumption of risk, the defense of comparative liability should be available only when the victim has attacked or was about to attack some legal rights of the perpetrator. Accordingly, cases of homicide motivated by spousal infidelity or continuous but not imminent domestic abuse will not qualify for either full or partial justification. In both instances, the defendants will have to rely only on the theory of excuse. Similarly, the perpetrators who disregard their partners' revocation of sexual consent will not be entitled to justificatory mitigation of rape charges.

Naturally, the degree of mitigation to which the perpetrator may be entitled should depend on a number of factors. At a minimum, the court should conduct comparative evaluation of the victim's and the perpetrator's affected rights, causative roles, and culpability. In some cases, the perpetrator will be completely exculpated; in other ones, his fault will be merely mitigated.

Undoubtedly, there will remain numerous cases that will not yield a straightforward solution; this is inevitable whenever we apply any rules or categories to the complexity of human interaction. It would be unfeasible to suppose that the defense of comparative liability can turn the proverbial "hard cases" that make bad law into easy ones. It is my hope, though, that, if implemented, this defense will bring the criminal theory in accord with the general notions of moral fairness and result if not in "good," then at least in a substantially better—more consistent, just, and effective—body of criminal law.

REFERENCE MATTER

NOTES

Introduction

1. Mendelsohn, "Victimology," 24.

2. Fletcher, *Grammar of Criminal Law*, 121 (for example, *Dchiyah* in Arabic; *Opfer* in German; *offiera* in Polish; *zhertva* in Russian).

3. Ibid. at 129.

4. Johnson, "Criminals Target Each Other."

5. *Beul v. ASSE Intern., Inc.*, 233 F.3d 441, 451 (7th Cir. 2000).

6. See Adams and Osborne, "Victims' Rights and Services," 675–76.

7. For a map of states that have adopted victims' rights amendments see http://www.nvcap.org/stvras.htm.

8. Dubber, "Victim in American Penal Law," 3. Among those who discussed the victim's contribution to the criminal act are Harel, "Efficiency and Fairness"; Gruber, "Victim Wrongs"; Gruber, "Righting Victim Wrongs."

9. Schafer, *Victimology*, 5.

10. Ortiz de Urbina Gimeno, "Old Wine in New Wineskins?" *2.

11. Fletcher, "Place of Victims," 51.

12. See Dubber, *Victims in the War on Crime*, 3 (opining that "any satisfactory solution to this problem will require a new integrated theory of penal law that assigns victim and offender their proper place in each aspect of penal law in light of that aspect's purpose or purposes, as well as the general requirements of constitutionality and legitimacy").

13. See, e.g., Dubber, *Victims in the War on Crime*; Fletcher, "Place of Victims"; Moore, "Victims and Retribution"; Schünemann, "Role of the Victim," 39–40; Westen, *Logic of Consent*.

Chapter 1

1. Haney, "Mitigation and the Study of Lives," 351.

2. Ibid.

3. Schafer, *Victimology*, 25.

4. Cesare Lombroso described a type of criminal who acted under the influence of victim-provoked emotions. Raffaele Garofalo discussed victim behavior that could provoke the offender to commit a criminal act. Gabriel Tarde pointed out the possibility that some victims' conduct could be responsible for the crime. August Goll and Josef Kohler analyzed a number of Shakespearean villains whose crimes were motivated by their own victims. These works certainly broke new ground in criminology, but at the same time most of them "suffered from the lack of organized imagination." The subject was treated with "only vague and oversimplified allusions, which have not shed any clear light upon the nature of the criminal-victim relationship." Ibid., 2–3; 34.

5. Mendelsohn himself might object to this characterization. He argued in favor of separating victim-related factors of a crime from criminal-related factors into a new science parallel to criminology or even "the reverse of criminology." See Schafer, *Victimology*, 35, citing Mendelsohn, "Victimology," 25–26.

6. Karmen, *Crime Victims*, 8.

7. Claster, *Bad Guys and Good Guys*, 160; Schafer, *Victimology*, 34–35.

8. See Schafer, *Victimology*, 36, citing Mendelsohn, "Victimology," 105–7.

9. Von Hentig, *Criminal and His Victim*, 418. Apparently, von Hentig's fascination with the complexities of the victim-perpetrator relationship was triggered by Franz Werfel's famous novella "Not the Murderer," a story of a father-son conflict that led to patricide. See Schafer, *Victimology*, 34. The title of the novella came from an old Albanian proverb: "Not the murderer but the murdered is the guilty one." See Wagener, *Understanding Franz Werfel*, 74.

10. See von Hentig, *Criminal and His Victim*, 383–450.

> The law assumes that the perpetrator is always the directing agent at the back of any move. It takes for granted that the "doer" is always, and during the whole process which ends in the criminal outcome, active, the "sufferer" always inactive. It is characteristic of our legalistic thinking that the notion of provocation has been allowed to enter into our criminal codes, only in a very limited way. (419)

11. Ibid., 384.

12. See Schafer, *Victimology*, 41–47 (analyzing various victim typologies, including those authored by Ezzat Abdel Fattah, Thorsten Sellin, and Marvin E. Wolfgang, Robert A. Silverman, Gilbert Geis, and Hans Joachim Schneider and setting forth his own typology). See also Karmen, *Crime Victims*, 106–10.

13. Karmen, *Crime Victims*, 100.

14. Ibid., 110–34.

15. See generally Wolfgang, *Patterns in Criminal Homicide*.

16. Karmen, *Crime Victims*, 104. Here are some typical examples from Philadelphia police reports:

> A husband threatened to kill his wife, then attacked her with a knife. In the ensuing struggle he fell on his own weapon and bled to death.
>
> The person who ended up the victim was the one who had started a barroom shoving match. His friends tried to break up the fight, but he persisted. Finally the tide turned, and the aggressor was knocked down; he hit his head on the floor and died from his injuries.
>
> A man demanded money that he believed was owed to him. The other man maintained that he had repaid the debt and, incensed over the accusation, drew a knife. The creditor pulled out a gun and shot him as he lunged.

Ibid.

17. See ibid., 106.

18. Victim precipitation was defined as a situation in which, in the case of a homicide, the killed person was the first to resort to force; in the case of an aggravated assault, the seriously injured person was the first to use physical force or offensive language and gestures; in the case of an armed robbery, the victim "clearly had not acted with reasonable self-protective behavior in handling money, jewelry, or other valuables"; and, in the case of a rape, the victim "at first agreed to sexual relations, or clearly invited them verbally and through gestures, but then retracted before the act." Karmen, *Crime Victims*, 106–7, citing Mulvihill et al., *Offender and His Victim*, and Mulvihill et al., *Crimes of Violence*. The research indicated that victim precipitation accounted for 22 percent of all murders, 14 percent of all aggravated assaults, 11 percent of all robberies, and 4 percent of all forcible rapes. Karmen, *Crime Victims*, 106–7.

19. See generally Anttila, "Victimology," 5–14; Toch, *Violent Men*; Wexler, "Patients, Therapists, and Third Parties,"1–28; Baumer et al., "Role of Victim Characteristics," 297.

20. U.S. Department of Justice, *Murder in Families*, 4.

21. Silverman, "Victim Precipitation," 99–112.

22. Arison, "Victims of Homicide," 55–68.

23. Claster, *Bad Guys and Good Guys*, 163.

24. Curtis, "Victim Precipitation and Violent Crime," 597.

25. Johnson, "Criminals Target Each Other."

26. Ibid.

27. One reason people may "blame the victim" lies in their need to believe that the world is just and innocent people do not become victims of crime. Therefore, if a person is victimized, he must be partially responsible for his own plight. See generally Lerner, "Desire for Justice," 205.

28. Kalven, Jr., and Zeisel, *American Jury*, 193–347. That study was based on questionnaires filled out by 555 judges presiding, in sum, over 3,576 criminal jury trials. The

judges were asked, among other things, how they would decide each case over which they presided had it been tried before them without a jury. Ibid., 45, 50–51.

29. Baumer et al., "Role of Victim Characteristics," 303.

30. The counties were widely scattered, from Los Angeles and San Diego, Denver and Dallas, to Philadelphia and Dade County (Miami). A little over half of all murders in the nation occur in these seventy-five counties. Consequently, survey results summarized in this report have broad relevance because they are from the courts where the majority of the nation's murder trials are held. U.S. Department of Justice, *Spouse Murder Defendants.*

31. Ibid., 5, 9, 10, 13.

32. Ibid., iv, 21–22.

33. The reporters stated their conclusions in cautious terms, explaining that thorough analysis requires more cases and more details than what was available from the study's database. For instance, the survey did not show "which defendant actually claimed self-defense; which of the spouses in each case was the first to strike or threaten the other; which defendants received a charge or sentence reduction because prosecutors, judges, or juries decided victim provocation was present; which claims of self-defense were supported by strong evidence; which defendants claiming self-defense had the option of fleeing rather than using deadly force." Ibid., 26. The survey, however, did document instances when the prosecutor screened out the case expressly because of victim provocation. Ibid., 26 n. 15.

34. Under *Restatement (Third) of Torts: Apportionment of Liability*, § 3, the assumption of risk defense has been abolished as an independent doctrine that bars a faulty plaintiff's recovery and instead is integrated into the doctrine of comparative fault. See *Restatement (Third) of Torts: Apportionment of Liability*, § 3 cmt. c.

35. See, e.g., ibid., cmt. d (proposing plaintiff no-duty rules); *Hennessey v. Pyne*, 694 A.2d 691 (R.I. 1997) (holding that, by living near a golf course, a homeowner does not assume the risk of being injured by a negligent duffer); *Lynch v. Scheininger*, 744 A.2d 113 (N.J. 2000) (concluding that a woman cannot be charged with fault for conceiving a child even if she knows that, because of a physician's negligence, it is risky to do so); *Hutchinson ex. rel. Hutchinson v. Luddy*, 763 A.2d 826, 848–49 (Pa. Super. Ct. 2000) (holding that a victim of sexual assault had no duty to avoid being harmed and that even a negligent codefendant could not raise the plaintiff's comparative negligence as a defense). See also Dobbs, *Law of Torts*, 503 (explaining that plaintiff no-duty cases are "cases in which the plaintiff has a liberty (or right) to be free from constraints imposed by the defendant"); Bublick, "Citizen No-Duty Rules," 1478–83 (advocating complete plaintiffs' no-duty rule in civil rape cases).

36. See, e.g., *Graham v. Stephens*, 779 So. 2d 649, 651 (Fla. Dist. Ct. App. 2001) ("the duty that arises in the unattended motor vehicle cases is one that extends to members of the public using the highways" and not "to the unauthorized user of the

vehicle"); *Rushink v. Gerstheimer*, 82 A.D.2d 944, 944–45 (N.Y. App. Div. 1981) (statute which "prohibits a person in charge of a vehicle from leaving it unattended without removing or hiding the key, was enacted to deter theft and injury from the operation of motor vehicles by unauthorized persons" but not "to protect such unauthorized users from the consequences of their own actions").

37. See, e.g., *State v. Crace*, 289 N.W.2d 54, 59 (Minn. 1979) ("It is well settled that the contributory negligence of the victim is never a defense to criminal prosecution"); *State v. Malone*, 819 P.2d 34 (Alaska Ct. App. 1991) (the victim's contributory negligence is no defense to criminal negligence); *People v. Maire*, 705 P.2d 1023 (Colo. Ct. App. 1985) (the victim's contributory negligence is no defense to vehicular homicide); *State v. Plaspohl*, 157 N.E.2d 579 (Ind. 1959) (the victim's contributory negligence is no defense to reckless homicide prosecution arising out of a drag race).

38. See, e.g., *People v. Tims*, 534 N.W.2d 675, 682 (Mich. 1995) (holding that "defendant's conduct need only be 'a' proximate cause of death" over the dissent's view that, for defendant's conviction, his conduct has to sufficiently dominate the other contributing factors); *State v. Dionne*, 442 A.2d 876, 887 (R.I. 1982) (unless it amounts to an independent intervening cause, the victim's conduct is irrelevant).

39. The term *victim* in the context of valid consent is somewhat of a misnomer; in this book it is used for the consistency of the terminology to mean an individual who has suffered a consensual injury to a legally recognized welfare interest.

40. Perkins, *Criminal Law*, 962.

41. See, e.g., *Model Penal Code*, § 2.1 (providing that consent is a defense "if such consent negatives an element of the offense or precludes the infliction of the harm or evil sought to be prevented by the law defining the offense").

42. See ibid., § 2.11 cmt. 1 (noting that, for many crimes, including rape, false imprisonment, and criminal trespass, "it is essential to the commission of the crime that there be an unwilling victim of the actor's conduct").

43. *Model Penal Code*, § 2.11 cmt. 1 (pointing out that consent to homicide "does not operate to prevent consummation of the crime"). See also Stephen, *History of the Criminal Law in England*, 16 (observing that consent to one's own death "is wholly immaterial to the guilt of the person who causes it").

44. *Model Penal Code*, § 2.11 cmt. 1.

45. Blackstone, *Commentaries on the Laws of England*, 133.

46. See LaFave, *Substantive Criminal Law*, § 15.6, 543 n. 3 ("No state has a statute making successful suicide a crime"). Suicide is apparently still a common-law crime in Virginia, Rhode Island, and possibly Illinois. See *Wackwitz v. Roy*, 418 S.E.2d 861, 864 (Va. 1992); *Clift v. Narragansett Television L.P.*, 688 A.2d 805, 808 (R.I. 1996); *Burnett v. People*, 68 N.E. 505, 509–11 (Ill. 1903).

47. Callahan and White, "Legalization of Physician-Assisted Suicide," 28–29.

48. *Washington v. Glucksberg*, 521 U.S. 702, 731–32 (1997).

49. See, e.g., Miller et al., "Regulating Physician-Assisted Death," 120 (arguing in favor of legitimizing voluntary euthanasia upon adoption of "clear criteria, rigorous procedures, and adequate safeguards" protecting individuals' right to decide for themselves).

50. See, e.g., *Washington v. Glucksberg*, 521 U.S. 702, 730–34 (1997) ("The State has an interest in preventing suicide, and in studying, identifying, and treating its causes").

51. Ibid., 736 (O'Connor, J., concurring) (interpreting the Court's decision to recognize that "our Nation's history, legal traditions, and practices" do not support one's right to commit a suicide).

52. See *Cruzan v. Dir., Mo. Dep't. of Health*, 497 U.S. 261, 279 (1990) (confirming one's constitutionally protected right to refuse lifesaving hydration and nutrition).

53. Feinberg, "Voluntary Euthanasia," 112.

54. *Model Penal Code*, § 211.1(1).

55. *Haw. Rev. Stat. Ann.* § 707–712 (Michie 2003) (charging third-degree assault as a misdemeanor, unless resulting from a fight or scuffle, in which case it is a petty misdemeanor); *Neb. Rev. Stat.* § 28-310 (1989) (following the MPC); *N.H. Rev. Stat. Ann.* 631:2-a (1996) (following the MPC); *N.J. Stat. Ann.* § 2C:12-1 (West 2003) (following the MPC); 18 *Pa. Cons. Stat.* § 2701 (1998) (following the MPC); *Vt. Stat. Ann.* tit. 13, § 1023 (following the MPC).

56. See *Miss. Code Ann.* § 97-3-7 (1999) (closely following MPC § 211.1 but containing no provision for mutual combat); *Mont. Code Ann.* § 45-5-201 (2003) (same); *S.D. Codified Laws* § 22-18-1 (2001) (same).

57. See, e.g., *N.C. Gen. Stat.* § 14-33(a) (1983) (specifically provides that punishment for assault does not depend on whether the assault is a result of mutual combat); *Utah Code Ann.* § 76-5-104 (2003) (specifically states that mutual combat is not a defense to assault).

58. *Model Penal Code*, § 2.11(2)(a).

59. *Model Penal Code*, § 2.11(2)(b).

60. *Model Penal Code*, §§ 2.11(2)(c), 3.08(4).

61. Thirteen states explicitly recognize a general defense of consent in their statutes. See *Ala. Code* § 13A-2-7 (2005); *Colo. Rev. Stat.* § 18-1-505 (2004); *Del. Code Ann.* tit. 11 §§ 451–53 (2001); *Haw. Rev. Stat.* §§ 702-233-235 (1993) (omits equivalent of subsection (2)(a)); *Me. Rev. Stat. Ann.* tit. 17-A, § 109 (2006) (omits equivalent of Subsection (3) (c)); *Vernon's Ann. Miss. Stat.* § 565.080; *Mont. Code Ann.* § 45-2-211 (2005); *N.H. Rev. Stat. Ann.* § 626:6 (1996) (omits equivalent of subsections [3][c] and [3][d]); *N.J. Stat. Ann.* § 2C:2-10 (West 2005) (omits equivalent of subsection [3][c]); *N.D. Cent. Code* § 12.1-17-08 (1997) (omits equivalent of subsection 3[c]); *Pa. Cons. Stat. Ann.* § 311 (1998) (omits equivalent of subsection [2][a]); *Tenn. Code Ann.* § 39-13-104 (2003) (omits equivalent of subsection 2[c] and 3); *Texas Penal Code Ann.* § 22.06 (Vernon 2003) (omits equivalent of subsection 2[c] and 3). Other states have incorporated the concept of

consent in the special part of their penal codes, making nonconsent an element of an offense or providing for the defense of consent with respect to specific crimes. See, e.g., 720 *Ill. Comp. Stat.* 5/12-17 (2002) ("It shall be a defense to any offense under Section 12-13 through 12-16 of this Code [sexual crimes] where force or threat of force is an element of the offense that the victim consented"). Where the statute does not explicitly mention consent, case law usually defines in what circumstances consent may function as a defense. Compare *Cal. Penal Code* § 240 ("An assault is an unlawful attempt, coupled with a present ability, to commit a violent injury on the person of another") with *People v. Gordon*, 11 P. 762, 762 (Cal. 1886) (stating that an attempt made with the victim's consent "will not constitute an assault").

62. *Model Penal Code*, § 210.0(3). Following the MPC, many states have adopted an identical or similar definition. See, e.g., *N.J. Stat. Ann.* § 2C:11-1(b) (West 2005); *Tex. Penal Code* § 1.07(46) (Vernon 2005).

63. *In re J.A.P.*, No. 03-02-00112-CV, 2002 Tex. App. LEXIS 7374, at *3 (Tex. Crim. App. Oct. 17, 2002).

64. Ibid., *12–13.

65. Ibid., *10 (citing *Brown v. State*, 605 S.W.2d 572, 575 [Tex. Crim. App. 1980]).

66. Ibid., *10 (quoting Tex. Penal Code § 1.07[a]46) (Vernon 2005) (which defines serious bodily injury as an "injury that creates a substantial risk of death or that causes death, serious permanent disfigurement, or protracted loss or impairment of the function of any bodily member or organ").

67. *Model Penal Code*, § 2.11 cmt. 2 n. 8. The commentary points out that the MPC provision does not explicitly foreclose resort to such judgments, though the envisioned emphasis is on the amount of injury itself. Ibid.

68. *State v. Collier*, 372 N.W.2d 303, 304 (Iowa Ct. App. 1985). See also *R. v. Donovan* (1934) 2 Eng. Rep. 498, 503 (K.B.) ("seven or eight red marks" on the body of a participant of a sadomasochistic encounter found to be sufficient for an assault conviction); *R. v. Emmett*, [1999] EWCA (Crim.) 1710 (Eng.) (bloodshot eyes and a burn, which had completely healed by the time of the trial, sufficed for an assault conviction of a participant of consensual sadomasochistic sex); *R. v. Boyea* (1992), 156 J.P. 505 (bruising to the interior and exterior of the vagina was found to be sufficient to preclude consent as a defense to indecent assault).

69. *State v. Collier*, 372 N.W.2d 303, 309 (Iowa Ct. App. 1985) (Schlegel, J., dissenting).

70. See, e.g., *Model Penal Code*, § 210.0(2); *Wash. Rev. Code* § 9A.04.110(4)(a) (2004) ("'Bodily injury,' 'physical injury,' or 'bodily harm' means physical pain or injury, illness, or an impairment of physical condition").

71. *State v. Guinn*, No. 23886-1-II, 2001 Wash. App. LEXIS 502 (Wash. Ct. App., March 30, 2001).

72. Ibid., *34.

73. Ibid.

74. *People v. Jovanovic*, 263 A.D.2d 182, 197 n. 5, (N.Y. App. Div. 1999).

75. Ibid., 197, 204. See also ibid., 207 (Mazzarelli, J., concurring in part and dissenting in part) (pointing out that the court's decision goes against the rule adopted in many jurisdictions).

76. *Model Penal Code*, § 2.11(2)(b).

77. Ibid.

78. Ibid., cmt. 2 n. 10. See also American Law Institute, "39th Annual Meeting," 97–104 (explaining the need to broaden the language to permit activities like stunt flying or professional wrestling); *State v. Malone*, No. M2000-02265-CCA-R3-CD, 2001 Tenn. Crim. App. LEXIS 901, *9–10 (Tenn. Crim. App. November 16, 2001) (holding that Tennessee Code Annotated allows consent to serve as a defense only "within the context of sporting activities, and the like, in which two parties agree to engage in conduct where some contact is expected or anticipated").

79. American Law Institute, "39th Annual Meeting," 99–101.

80. Wozniak, "Annotation, Validity, Construction, and Application," 689.

81. United Kingdom Law Commission, "Consent in the Criminal Law," 10.1.

82. Ibid. (quoting *William Fraser* [1847] Ark. 280, 302).

83. See Hilton, "RELIGION: Good Friday"; Dizon, "Tourists Here to See Filipinos Crucify Selves."

84. See Ruppe, "Opus Dei on the Rise."

85. Ibid.

86. See United Kingdom Law Commission, "Consent in the Criminal Law," 10.4.

87. *United States v. Meyers*, 906 F. Supp. 1494, 1496 (D. Wyo. 1995); see also *Ogletree v. State*, 440 S.E.2d 732, 733 (Ga. Ct. App. 1994) (opining that, even had the victim consented, the severe beating ordered by a pastor would still constitute battery).

88. 720 *Ill. Comp. Stat. Ann.* 5/12-32(a) (West 2005) (emphasis added).

89. United Kingdom Law Commission, "Consent in the Criminal Law," 131.

90. Ibid.

91. See, e.g., *People v. Samuels*, 58 Cal. Rptr. 439, 447 (Ct. App. 1967) (ruling that "consent of the victim is not generally a defense to assault or battery, except in a situation involving ordinary physical contact or blows incident to sports such as football, boxing or wrestling").

92. See *State v. Collier*, 372 N.W.2d 303, 307 (Iowa Ct. App. 1985).

93. *Foronda v. Haw. Int'l Boxing Club*, 2001 Haw. App. LEXIS 117, *48 (Int. Ct. App. Hi 2001).

94. Ibid.

95. *R. v. Brown*, [1994] 1 A.C. 212, 278 (H.L.) (opinion of Lord Slynn, L.J.).

96. Freeman, "Bug Chasers."

97. Weiss, "Criminalizing Consensual Transmission of HIV," 389–90.

98. Those states are Florida, Idaho, Illinois, Iowa, Nevada, North Dakota, South Dakota, and Tennessee. See Wolf and Vezina, "Crime and Punishment," 854.

99. Those states are Arkansas, California, Georgia, Louisiana, Michigan, Missouri, New Jersey, Ohio, Oklahoma, and South Carolina. Ibid.

100. Ironically, the quintessential "recognized" form of treatment offered during the discussion of the relevant MPC provision at the ALI meeting in 1962 is highly controversial today: electric shock therapy in cases of "mental trouble." American Law Institute, "39th Annual Meeting," 92.

101. Noah, "Informed Consent," 377.

102. See *Jane L. v. Bangerter*, 61 F.3d 1493, 1500–2 (10th Cir. 1995), *rev'd on other grounds sub nom. Leavitt v. Jane L.*, 518 U.S. 137 (1996); *Margaret S. v. Edwards*, 794 F.2d 994, 999 (5th Cir. 1986) ("The whole distinction between experimentation and testing, or between research and practice, is . . . almost meaningless in the medical context"); *Lifchez v. Hartigan*, 735 F.Supp. 1361, 1364–66 (N.D. Ill. 1990), *aff'd mem.*, 914 F.2d 260 (7th Cir. 1990).

103. See, e.g., Brody, "Why Cancer-Free Women Have Breasts Removed."

104. Ziegler and Kroll, "Primary Breast Cancer," 453 (discussing controversial nature of prophylactic mastectomy and comparing it with less radical alternatives).

105. Ibid., 452.

106. See Hatcher et al., "Psychosocial Impact," 76.

107. "When It Feels Right," 15.

108. Ibid.

109. But see Bayne and Levy, "Amputees by Choice," 84–85 (arguing that, as long as people are legally sane, they should be allowed to have their limbs amputated by a surgeon).

110. Elliot, "New Way to Be Mad," 73–74.

111. See *G.B. v. Lackner*, 145 Cal. Rptr. 555, 557 (Ct. App. 1978). ("The severity of the problem of transsexualism becomes obvious when one contemplates the reality of the male transsexual's desperate desire to have normally functioning male genitals removed because the male sex organs are a source of immense psychological distress.")

112. See Bridy, "Confounding Extremities," 155. ("To the extent that society and its institutions remain committed to a norm of bodily integrity that excludes the disabled body, it will remain very difficult to collectively imagine that elective amputation could be good medicine for apotemnophiles.")

113. Elliott, "A New Way to Be Mad," 73.

114. See, e.g., Mill, *On Liberty*, ch. IV, ¶¶ 10–11.

> [W]ith regard to the merely contingent, or, as it may be called, constructive injury which a person causes to society, by conduct which neither violates any specific

duty to the public, nor occasions perceptible hurt to any assignable individual except himself; the inconvenience is one which society can afford to bear, for the sake of the greater good of human freedom.

Ibid.

115. Finn, "Cannibal Case Grips Germany," A26.

116. Ibid.

117. Cook, "Moral Mayhem," 17.

118. Ibid.

119. Landler, "Cannibal Convicted of Manslaughter," 3. Explaining the verdict, the judge said: "This was an act between two extremely disturbed people who both wanted something from each other." Ibid. For the legal opinion, see *Bundesgerichtshof* [BGH] [Federal Court of Justice], April 22, 2005, 50 Entscheidungen des Bundesgerichtshofes in Strafsachen [BGHST] 80, available at http://www.bundesgerichtshof.de using Aktenzeichen: 2 StR 310/04.

120. See CNN, "Perverse Cannibal Killer Gets Life." For an official press release, see "Kannibale von Rotenburg' jetzt rechtskräftig wegen Mordes verurteilt," Bundesgerichtshof Pressemitteilung Nr. 26/2007 (February16, 2007), available at http://www.bundesgerichtshof.de/.

121. This decision is available at http://www.bundesgerichtshof.de using Aktenzeichen: 2 StR 518/06.

122. See *R. v. Brown*, [1994] 1 A.C. 212 (H.L.) (citing Attorney-General's Reference (No. 6 of 1980) [1981] Q.B. 715, 719).

123. See *R. v. Brown*, [1994] 1 A.C. 212 (H.L.).

124. Roberts, "Philosophy, Feinberg, Codification, and Consent," 210–11. Paul Roberts served as a consultant to the Law Commission for England and Wales.

125. United Kingdom Law Commission, "Criminal Law Consent and Offences against the Person," Part X.

126. United Kingdom Law Commission, "Consent in the Criminal Law," 1.

127. Roberts, "Philosophy, Feinberg, Codification, and Consent," 248.

128. Ibid., 233.

129. United Kingdom Law Commission, *Eighth Programme of Law Reform*, 44.

130. See discussion in Chapter 2 under "Consistency of Criminal Sanctions."

131. See *Model Penal Code*, § 3.04(2)(b).

132. See LaFave and Scott, Jr., *Criminal Law*, § 5.7(e).

133. See, e.g., Fletcher, *Rethinking Criminal Law*, § 10.5, 869–70; Fletcher, "Proportionality and the Psychotic Aggressor," 375 (arguing that self-defense killing of innocent aggressors is justified); McMahan, "Self-Defense," 256–85 (discussing various justificatory theories of killing an innocent aggressor in self-defense).

134. See discussion in Chapter 3 under "The Case of Innocent Aggressors: Justification or Excuse?"

135. See Alexander, "Propter Honoris Respectum," 1482.

136. Ibid., 1483.

137. See LaFave, *Criminal Law*, § 10.4(i) at 550.

138. *Model Penal Code*, § 3.09(2).

139. See, e.g., Fletcher, *Rethinking Criminal Law*, 696–97, 762–69 (arguing that even a reasonable mistake regarding the presence of justifying conditions negates justification); Robinson, "Criminal Law Defenses," 239–40 (arguing that mistaken self-defense should be treated as an excuse rather than a justification); Alexander, "Propter Honoris Respectum,"1483–84 (supporting Robinson's argument). Alexander has persuasively argued that mistaken self-defense should not be viewed as a justification:

> If this were not the case—if, instead, the law took seriously its characterization of the mistaken self-defender as "justified" and his use of force as legally "privileged"—a third party, seeing A about to employ force against an innocent B because of a mistaken belief that B was attacking him, would be justified in coming to the mistaken A's rather than the innocent B's aid. Indeed, on one reading of the Model Penal Code, B himself could not use self-defensive force against A because A's use of force against B would be "privileged." (1484, footnote omitted)

For an opposite view, see, e.g., Greenawalt, "Distinguishing Justifications from Excuses," 102 (arguing that "the actor's blameless perception of the facts ought to be sufficient to support a justification"); Greenawalt, "Perplexing Borders," 1907–9 (arguing that a reasonable mistake should be justified because the actor's harmful conduct was warranted); Dressler, "New Thoughts," 92–95 (critiquing Fletcher's theory of justification and excuse for, among other things, denying justification to a reasonably mistaken actor). See also Morawetz, "Reconstructing the Criminal Defenses," 289–90 (proposing an alternative way of treating reasonable mistakes as "justified wrongs"); Sendor, "Mistakes of Fact," 766–71 (attempting to reconcile Greenawalt's and Dressler's views with those of Fletcher and Robinson and proposing a theory of responsibility that treats reasonable mistakes as an excuse but denies wrongfulness of the actor's conduct).

140. See *Model Penal Code*, § 210.3(1)(b) ("Criminal homicide constitutes manslaughter when . . . a homicide which would otherwise be murder is committed under the influence of extreme mental or emotional disturbance for which there is reasonable explanation or excuse"). See also ibid., § 210.3 cmt. 3 (noting that the MPC has significantly enlarged "the class of cases which would otherwise be murder but which could be reduced to manslaughter under then existing law because the homicidal act occurred in the 'heat of passion' upon 'adequate provocation' ").

141. Ibid., § 210.3(1)(b).

142. See Austin, "Plea for Excuses," 2–3. ("Is [the provoker] partly responsible, because he roused a violent impulse or passion in me, so that it wasn't truly or merely

me acting 'of my own accord' [excuse]? Or is it rather that, he having done me such injury, I was entitled to retaliate [justification]?")

143. See ibid. ("In the one defence, . . . we accept responsibility but deny that it was bad: in the other, we admit that it was bad but don't accept full, or even any, responsibility.")

144. Hart, *Punishment and Responsibility*, 13.

145. Austin, "Plea for Excuses," 6.

146. For contrasting views as to whether justification applies only to the "right" or also to the "tolerable" conduct, see, e.g., Fletcher, "Should Intolerable Prison Conditions," 1358–59 (arguing that conduct that is merely permissible or tolerable is not justified); and Dressler, "New Thoughts," 81–87 (arguing that justification should apply to the "tolerable" as well as the "right" conduct).

147. Uniacke, *Permissible Killing*, 13.

148. Ibid., 14 (opining that the fact that a successful plea of provocation results in conviction of an offense is sufficient to identify provocation as an excuse).

149. Husak, "Partial Defenses," 169.

150. Even in cases of complete justification, wrongfulness of an act may be above zero. See, e.g., ibid., 172. ("No one who believes that killings in self-defense are completely justified need suppose that the quantum of wrongfulness in all such killings is equivalent to that in, say, scratching one's head.")

151. Ibid., 70.

152. Ibid.

153. Ibid.

154. See, e.g., Uniacke, *Permissible Killing*, 13 (noting that the usual interpretation of provocation is excusatory); Nourse, "Reconceptualizing Criminal Law Defenses," 1717; Huigens, "Homicide in Aretaic Terms," 132 (noting the shift toward treating provocation as a partial excuse); Dubber, "Victim in American Penal Law," 12 (noting that American law treats provocation as a partial excuse).

155. Dressler, "Rethinking Heat of Passion," 458; Dressler, "Battered Women and Sleeping Abusers," 465–68. See also Uniacke, *Permissible Killing*, 13 (completely rejecting justificatory rationale of provocation and criticizing Dressler for "conced[ing] too much to the claim that provocation functions as a partial justification").

156. See *Model Penal Code*, §§ 210.2, 210.5 (murder is a felony of the first degree, whereas causing or aiding suicide is a felony of the second degree). See also *Pain Relief Promotion Act of 1999*, pt. 1, at 4 n. 11. Numerous states treat assisting a suicide as manslaughter rather than murder. See, e.g., *Alaska Stat.* § 11.41.120(a)(2) (Michie 2002) (defining intentionally aiding another to commit suicide as manslaughter); *Ariz. Rev. Stat.* § 13-1103(A)(3) (2001) ("A person commits manslaughter by . . . [i] ntentionally aiding another to commit suicide"); *Ark. Code Ann.* § 5-10-104(a)(2) (Michie 1997) (treating purposefully causing or aiding another to commit suicide as

manslaughter); *Cal. Penal Code* § 401 (West 1999) (distinguishing assisted suicide from murder); *Colo. Rev. Stat.* § 18-3-104 (West 1999) (treating intentionally causing or aiding another to commit suicide as manslaughter); *Conn. Gen. Stat.* § 53a-56(2) (2001) ("A person is guilty of manslaughter in the second degree when . . . he intentionally causes or aids another person, other than by force, duress or deception, to commit suicide"); *Haw. Rev. Stat. Ann.* § 707-702(1)(b) (Michie 2003). ("A person commits the offense of manslaughter if . . . [h]e intentionally causes another person to commit suicide.")

157. See discussion in Chapter 3.

158. Dressler, "Rethinking Heat of Passion," 458.

159. Ibid.

160. That is equally true for the MPC version of the defense, which focuses on the "extreme mental or emotional disturbance" of the defendant "for which there is reasonable explanation or excuse." *Model Penal Code*, § 210.3(1)(b).

161. Shakespeare, *Romeo and Juliet*, Act 2, Scene II.

162. See Dietz et al., "Homicide," § 49 (listing among emotions that mitigate a murder to voluntary manslaughter "anger, rage, resentment, or terror sufficient to obscure the reason of ordinary man").

163. Perkins, *Criminal Law*, 54.

164. *Model Penal Code*, §§ 3.04, 3.06(3)(d).

165. Ibid., § 2.09 cmt. 4 at 381.

166. A commentary to the MPC explicitly narrows down the question of the defense of duress to "whether there are cases where the actor cannot justify his conduct under [the necessity defense], as when his choice involves an equal or greater evil than that threatened, but where he nonetheless should be excused because he was subject to coercion." *Model Penal Code*, § 2.09 cmt. 2 at 373.

167. *Model Penal Code*, § 210.3(1)(b). See *Ark. Code Ann.* § 5-10-104(a)(1) (Michie 1987); *Conn. Gen. Stat. Ann.* § 53a-54a(a) (West 2001); *Del. Code Ann.* § 641 (2003); *Haw. Rev. Stat. Ann.* § 707-702(2) (Michie 2003); *Ky. Rev. Stat. Ann.* § 507.020(1)(a) (Michie 1999); *Mont. Code Ann.* § 45-5-103(1) (2003); *N.Y. Penal Law* § 125.25(1)(a) (McKinney 2003); *N.D. Cent. Code* § 12.1-16-01(2) (2003); *Or. Rev. Stat.* §163.135(1) (2003); *Utah Code Ann.* § 76-5-203(4)(a)(i) (2003).

168. See, e.g., Dressler, *Understanding Criminal Law*, 231.

169. See Dietz et al., "Homicide," § 111. ("Extreme emotional distress without legally recognized provocation will not reduce murder to manslaughter.") See also *MacEwan v. State*, 701 So. 2d 66, 69–70 (Ala. Crim. App. 1997).

170. *People v. Spurlin*, 156 Cal. App. 3d 119 (Cal. Ct. App. 1984).

171. *Regina v. Dudley and Stephens*, 14 Q.B.D. 273 (1884), reprinted in [1881-5] All. E.R. Rep. 61.

172. Ibid., 67.

173. Ibid., 64.

174. See Kadish, Schulhofer, and Steiker *Criminal Law and Its Process*, 825.

175. See Dietz et al., "Homicide," § 115. ("It is generally held that neither duress, coercion, nor compulsion are defenses to murder.") (Footnotes omitted.) See also *Schertz v. State*, 380 N.W.2d 404 (Iowa 1985); *State v. Chism*, 436 So. 2d 464 (La. 1983); *State v. McCartney*, 684 So. 2d 416, 425 (La. Ct. App. 3d Cir. 1996) (noting that the defense of compulsion is unavailable in murder prosecutions); *State v. Weston*, 219 P. 180, 185 (Or. 1923) (stating that "[f]ear, duress or compulsion due to the act of another, seems to be considered no excuse for taking the life of a third person"); *State v. Nargashian*, 58 A. 953, 955 (R.I. 1904) (stating that no justification for murder is present when a defendant undertakes a voluntary course of action).

176. Dietz et al., "Homicide," § 115 (stating that duress does not mitigate murder to manslaughter). See *United States v. LaFleur*, 971 F.2d 200, 206 (9th Cir. 1991) (holding that duress cannot mitigate first-degree murder to manslaughter); *State v. Rocheville*, 425 S.E.2d 32, 35 (S.C. 1993) (finding that duress cannot serve to reduce murder to manslaughter).

177. See *United States v. LaFleur*, 971 F.2d 200, 206 (9th Cir. 1991) (concluding that "consistent with the common law rule, a defendant should not be excused from taking the life of an innocent third person because of the threat of harm to himself").

178. At least ten states by statute (Alaska, Arizona, Colorado, Delaware, Illinois, Missouri, Ohio, Pennsylvania, Texas, Wisconsin) and another fifteen by case law (California, Georgia, Kansas, Louisiana, Maryland, Minnesota, New Mexico, Nebraska, Oklahoma, Rhode Island, South Carolina, Tennessee, Vermont, Virginia, Wyoming) authorize mitigation from murder to a lesser offense only if the provocative act is attributable to the victim, the victim's accomplice, or the intended victim. See *Ariz. Rev. Stat.* § 13-1103(A)(2) (victim only); *Ohio Rev. Code Ann.* § 2903.03(A) (victim only); *S.C. Code Ann.* § 16-3-20(C)(b)(8) (victim only); *Mo. Rev. Stat.* § 565.002(7) (victim or accomplice); *Tex. Penal Code Ann.* § 19.02(a)(2) (victim or accomplice); *Ill. Comp. Stat.* § 9-2(1) (victim or intended victim); 18 *Pa. Cons. Stat.* § 2503 (a)(1), (2) (same); Alaska Stat. § 11.41.115(a) (same); *Colo. Rev. Stat.* § 18-3-103(3)(b) (same); *Wis. Stat. Ann.* § 939.44(1)(b) (same). See also *Foster v. State*, 444 S.E.2d 296, 297 n. 2 (Ga. 1994) ("[I]t appears that the voluntary manslaughter statute *OCGA* § 16-5-2[a] should be construed so as to authorize a conviction for that form of homicide only where the defendant can show provocation by the homicide victim"); *State v. Follin*, 947 P.2d 8, 16-17 (Kan. 1997) (determining that trial court appropriately declined to extend instruction on manslaughter when defendant killed a nonprovoking victim); *State v. Charles*, 787 So. 2d 516, 519 (La. App. 3 Cir. 2001) ("Case law requires that there be some act or series of acts by the victim sufficient to deprive a reasonable person of cool reflection"); *Tripp v. State*, 374 A.2d 384, 389 (Md. Ct. App. 1977) ("Except for rare instances of 'transferred intent,' where one aims at A, misses and hits B by mistake, a defendant seeking

to extenuate an intentional killing upon the theory that he killed in hot-blooded rage brought on by the provocative acts of his victim is limited to those killings where the victim is the provocateur"); *State v. Auchampach*, 540 N.W.2d 808, 1815 (Minn. 1995) ("[A] defendant's emotional state alone is not sufficient to mitigate murder to manslaughter; rather, the words and acts of a victim must have been enough to provoke a person of ordinary self-control"); *State v. Bautista*, 227 N.W.2d 835, 839 (Neb. 1975) (indicating that a jury instruction on provocation is only appropriate when the victim caused the provocation); *Krucheck v. State*, 702 P.2d 1267, 1269 (Wy. 1985) ("[T]he heat of passion, anger, rage, or hot blood 'must have been entertained toward the person slain, and not toward another'"); *People v. Steele*, 47 P.3d 225, 240 (Cal. 2002) ("But it does not satisfy the objective, reasonable person requirement, which requires provocation by the victim"); *State v. Gutierrez*, 541 P.2d 628, 631 (N.M. Ct. App. 1975) (accepting rule against allowing provocation defense for killing persons other than the provoker); *Hawkins v. State*, 46 P.3d 139, 146 (Okla. Crim. App. 2002) ("[M]anslaughter . . . requires adequate provocation *on the part of the deceased* toward the defendant, not some implied provocation on the part of a third person sitting in a car a considerable distance away"); *State v. Winston*, 252 A.2d 354, 358 (R.I. 1969) ("[A]n essential element of [voluntary manslaughter] is the presence of provocation offered by the person slain"); *Arnold v. Commonwealth*, 560 S.E.2d 915, 919 (Va. Ct. App. 2002). ("While it is true that 'malice and heat of passion are mutually exclusive,' we have held that where it is not the victim of the crime who invoked the defendant's heat of passion, there was no evidence to support a finding of heat of passion.")

179. See, e.g., Torcia, *Wharton's Criminal Law*, § 156; LaFave and Scott, Jr., *Criminal Law*, § 7.10(g).

180. Perkins, *Criminal Law*, 69.

181. Hart and Honore, *Causation in the Law*, 58. ("It is . . . an integral part of the idea of provocation that one person arouses another's passions and *makes* him to lose his normal self-control.")

182. Perkins, *Criminal Law*, 69

183. See discussion in this chapter under "Self Defense."

184. *Model Penal Code*, § 210.3(1)(b) (defining manslaughter as a homicide which would otherwise be murder when it is "committed under the influence of extreme mental or emotional disturbance for which there is reasonable explanation or excuse").

185. Ibid., § 210.3 cmt. 5(a). "By eliminating any reference to provocation in the ordinary sense of improper conduct by the deceased, the MPC avoids arbitrary exclusion of some circumstances that may justify reducing murder to manslaughter." Ibid.

186. See, e.g., *Ark. Code Ann.* § 5-10-104(a)(1) (Michie 1987); *Conn. Gen. Stat. Ann.* § 53a-54a(a) (West 2001); *Del. Code Ann.* § 641 (2003); *Haw. Rev. Stat. Ann.* § 707-702(2) (Michie 2003); *Ky. Rev. Stat. Ann.* § 507.020(1)(a) (Michie 1999); *Mont. Code Ann.* § 45-5-103(1) (2003); *N.Y. Penal Law* § 125.25(1)(a) (McKinney 2003); *N.D. Cent. Code* §

12.1-16-01(2) (2003); *Or. Rev. Stat.* § 163.135(1) (2003); *Utah Code Ann.* § 76-5-203(4)(a)(i) (2003).

187. See, e.g., *Del. Code Ann.* tit. 11, § 641 (2003) (providing that "emotional distress is not reasonably explained . . . when there is no causal relationship between the provocation, event or situation which caused the extreme emotional distress and the victim of the murder"). See also *State v. Stewart*, 624 N.W.2d 585, 590–91 (Minn. 2001) (the state statute was based on the MPC; however, the court noted that "a heat of passion that provokes an assailant to kill the provocateur will not necessarily satisfy the subjective or objective elements of heat-of-passion manslaughter as to other victims" and concluded that the situation at bar was such a case).

188. *People v. Spurlin*, 156 Cal. App. 3d 119, 126 (Cal. Ct. App. 1984).

189. *Maher v. People*, 10 Mich. 212 (Mich. 1862) (Manning, J., dissenting) (emphasis added).

Chapter 2

1. Moore, "Victims and Retribution," 65–66 ("the role of the victim of crime . . . is to be ascertained by thinking through the theory of punishment").

2. See, e.g., Greenawalt, "Punishment," 1336 ("a retributivist claims that punishment is justified because people deserve it; a utilitarian believes that justification lies in the useful purposes that the punishment serves").

3. Kant, *Philosophy of Law*, 195–96.

4. See, e.g., Moore, *Law and Psychiatry*, 239 (explaining that a consistent utilitarian would have to punish an innocent look-alike in place of a skyjacker who cannot be caught if that would deter skyjacking).

5. See, e.g., Darley et al., "Incapacitation and Just Deserts."

6. See Warr and Stafford, "Public Goals of Punishment," 99–101.

7. *Tison v. Arizona*, 481 U.S. 137, 149 (1987). ("The heart of the retribution rationale is that a criminal sentence must be directly related to the personal culpability of the criminal offender.")

8. Moore, "Victims and Retribution," 87.

9. Ibid. The opposing school of thought maintains that the amount of harm is irrelevant to the perpetrator's desert: why should one be punished less severely only because, quite fortuitously, his attempted offense failed or caused less harm than it could? See, e.g., Hart, *Punishment and Responsibility*, 131 ("Why should the accidental fact that an intended harmful outcome has not occurred be a ground for punishing less a criminal who may be equally dangerous and equally wicked?"); Kadish, "Criminal Law," 697 (arguing that allowing wrongdoing an independent moral significance is irrational). The debate over the moral and legal significance of the resulting harm has a long history and still continues. See, e.g., Burkhardt, "Is There a Rational Justification,"

556 (remarking that "little progress has been made toward a solution of this issue in the last two hundred years"); Kadish, "Criminal Law," 679 n. 2 (noting that, in fact, the issue is more than a thousand years old—"Plato tried to explain the lesser punishment for a failed attempt to kill as an expression of gratitude to the gods"). For the insightful analysis of advocated positions on both sides of the debate, see, e.g., Moore, *Placing Blame*, 191–247.

10. Kadish, "Criminal Law," 701. Sanford H. Kadish has conceded that

> [w]hile in principle it's difficult to find good reasons for making desert turn on chance, here's the rub: most of us do in fact make judgments precisely of this kind. Doesn't it seem natural for a parent to want to punish his child more for spilling his milk than for almost spilling it, more for running the family car into a wall than for almost doing so? (688)

11. See, e.g., *Model Penal Code*, § 3.02.

12. *Mills v. Maryland*, 486 U.S. 367, 397 (1988). ("If a jury is to assess meaningfully the defendant's moral culpability and blameworthiness, one essential consideration should be the extent of the harm caused by the defendant.")

13. Kalven, Jr., and Zeisel, *American Jury*, 243–44.

14. *Commonwealth v. Atencio*, 189 N.E.2d 223 (Mass. 1963).

15. Ibid., 224.

16. Ibid.

17. Ibid.

18. See Harel, "Efficiency and Fairness," 1193.

> Efficiency requires the distribution of the costs of precautions between the state and potential victims in a way that minimizes the total costs of crime. Without appropriate incentives, potential victims will invest less in precautionary measures than is socially optimal. That is, potential victims will expose themselves to risks which are unjustified from the perspective of efficiency.

19. Ibid., 1196.

20. Ibid., 1197.

21. See, e.g., Robinson and Darley, "Utility of Desert," 477 ("The criminal law must earn a reputation for [1] punishing those who deserve it under rules perceived as just, [2] protecting from punishment those who do not deserve it, and [3] where punishment is deserved, imposing the amount of punishment deserved, no more, no less"); Robinson and Darley, *Justice, Liability, and Blame*, 5–7 (arguing that community views are important, from both the retributivist and the utilitarian perspectives, to what criminal law rules ought to be).

22. Robinson and Darley, "Utility of Desert," 457.

23. Schünemann, "Future of the Victimological Approach," 150.

24. Ibid., 150–51.
25. Ibid., 152.
26. See Schünemann, "Role of the Victim," 39–40.
27. See Schünemann, "Future of the Victimological Approach," 150–51, 158.
28. Robinson and Darley, "Utility of Desert," 456.
29. Ibid., 457.

The criminal law can have a second effect in gaining compliance with its commands. If it earns a reputation as a reliable statement of what the community, given sufficient information and time to reflect, would perceive as condemnable, people are more likely to defer to its commands as morally authoritative and as appropriate to follow in those borderline cases in which the propriety of certain conduct is unsettled or ambiguous in the mind of the actor.

30. Kalven, Jr., and Zeisel, *American Jury*, 242–57.
31. Ibid.
32. Sundby, "Capital Jury and Empathy," 357–58.
33. Ibid.
34. See Simons, "Relevance of Community Values," 653–59 (discussing the complexity of the connection between community views and punishment rationales).
35. Schanberg, "Let's Be Outraged," 94.
36. Kalven, Jr., and Zeisel, *American Jury*, 254.
37. Ibid., 249. In Kalven, Jr., and Zeisel's study, only three out of forty-two defendants charged with simple rape were convicted of it. Ibid., 253. The judge's disagreement with the jury verdict on the major charge approached 100 percent. Ibid., 253–54.
38. See Kalven, Jr., and Zeisel, *American Jury*, 249–51. See also Whatley, "Victim Characteristics," 91.
39. See ibid., 249–51.
40. See Field and Bienen, *Jurors and Rape*, 54. See also Williams and Holmes, *Second Assault*, 118 (conducting a cross-cultural survey of attitudes toward rape, in which most respondents, including victims, named women's behavior and/or appearance as the second [after the perpetrator's mental illness] most frequent cause of rape).
41. See Schafran, "Writing and Reading About Rape," 995 n. 58 (citing Telephone Survey of 500 Adult Americans by Yankelovich Partners, Inc., for Time/CNN [May 8, 1991]).
42. Nemeth et al., "Chilling the Sexes," 42, 44.
43. Robinson and Darley, "Utility of Desert," 456.
44. See discussion in this chapter under "Utilitarian Considerations."
45. Robinson and Darley, "Utility of Desert," 473. In a diverse society that role may be particularly important. See ibid., 457 (noting that "in a society as diverse as ours,

the criminal law may be the only society-wide mechanism that transcends cultural and ethnic differences").

46. Ibid., 473–74.

47. See *Ohio Rev. Code Ann.* § 2903.12 (Anderson 2001) (reducing a charge from felonious assault to aggravated assault in case of serious provocation by the victim); *Ky. Rev. Stat.* § 508.040 (Michie 1999) (allowing a reduction in charge when an assault is committed under extreme emotional disturbance); *Mo. Rev. Stat.* § 565.060 (1999) (allowing a charge of second-degree assault instead of first-degree assault if the defendant acted under "sudden passion arising out of adequate cause"); *Colo. Rev. Stat.* § 18-3-202(2)(a) (West 1999) (reducing first-degree assault from a class three to a class five felony if committed in the heat of passion); *Colo. Rev. Stat.* § 18-3-203(2)(a) (West 1999) (reducing second-degree assault from a class four to a class six felony if committed in the heat of passion).

48. See *Alaska Stat.* § 12.55.155(d)(6) (Michie 2002); *La. Code Crim. Proc. Ann.* art. 894.1(24), (26) (West 1997); *N.C. Gen. Stat.* § 15A-1340.16(e)(8) (2002); *Tenn. Code Ann.* § 40-35-113(2) (2003); *Wash. Rev. Code Ann.* § 9.94A.535(1)(a) (West 2001).

49. *Model Penal Code*, § 211.1(1).

50. See, e.g., *State v. Friedman*, 996 P.2d 268, 272 (Haw. 2000) (confirming that a quarrel during which participants were pushing each other and slapping each other constituted "mutual affray").

51. *Haw. Rev. Stat. Ann.* § 707-712 (Michie 2003) (charging third-degree assault as a misdemeanor, unless resulting from a fight or scuffle in which case it is a petty misdemeanor); *Neb. Rev. Stat.* § 28-310 (1989) (following the MPC), *N.H. Rev. Stat. Ann.* 631:2-a (1996) (following the MPC); *N.J. Stat. Ann.* § 2C:12-1 (West 2003) (following the MPC); 18 *Pa. Cons. Stat.* § 2701 (1998) (following the MPC); *Vt. Stat. Ann.* tit. 13, § 1023 (following the MPC).

52. See *Miss. Code Ann.* § 97-3-7 (1999) (closely following MPC § 211.1 but containing no provision for mutual combat); *Mont. Code Ann.* § 45-5-201 (2003) (same); *S.D. Codified Laws* § 22-18-1 (2001) (same).

53. See *N.C. Gen. Stat.* § 14-33(a) (1983) (specifically punishes assault the same way regardless of whether the assault arose as a result of mutual combat or not); *Utah Code Ann.* § 76-5-104 (2003) (specifically states that mutual combat is not a defense to assault).

54. See, e.g., *Ga. Code Ann.* § 16-7-21 (2003) (criminal trespass) and § 16-7-23(a)(1) (criminal damage to property in the second degree); *Kan. Crim. Code Ann.* § 21-3720 (West 1999) (criminal damage to property); *La. Rev. Stat. Ann.* § 14:56 (1997) (simple criminal damage to property); *N.C. Gen. Stat.* § 14-127 (willful and wanton injury to real property) and § 14-160 (willful and wanton injury to personal property); *W. Va. Code Ann.* § 61-3-30 (Michie 2000) (injury to or destruction of property). See also *Model Penal Code*, § 220.3(1)(b) (providing that a person is guilty of criminal mischief

if he purposely or recklessly tampers with tangible property of another so as to endanger person or property).

55. *Model Penal Code*, § 3.10. See also ibid. cmt. (explaining that in this area the penal law must on the whole accept and build upon the privileges recognized in torts and property, except in rare situations where a penal law departure from the civil law position is made clear).

56. See, e.g., *Thomas v. State*, 30 Ark. 433, 435 (1875) (malicious mischief not committed when the act was done under provocation); *Mosley v. State*, 28 Ga. 190, 192 (1859) (injuries inflicted upon personal property in a passion, or under reasonable provocation, stand on different footing); *State v. Martin*, 53 S.E. 874, 876 (N.C. 1906) (malicious mischief is not committed when such act is prompted or done under the influence of sudden aroused passion). In each of these cases, provocation completely exonerated the defendant, a result quite different from its usual effect.

57. See cases cited in note 56.

58. *Richmond v. State*, 623 A.2d 630, 633 (Md. App. 1993).

59. Ibid., 634 (holding that "mitigation that will reduce one offense to another is a concept peculiar to criminal homicide cases").

60. See *Brown v. United States*, 584 A.2d 537 (D.C. App. 1990). For contrary treatment of the same issue, see, for example, *Denny v. State*, 486 S.E.2d 417, 420 (Ga. App. 1997) (holding that "standard charges on provocation do not pertain to property offenses"); *State v. Bourg*, 615 So. 2d 957, 961 (La. Ct. App. 1st Cir. 1993) (holding that harassment of the defendant by the victim was not a defense to a charge of aggravated criminal damage to property). The District of Columbia also authorizes the defense of provocation, in the unemployment compensation context, to employees' misconduct resulting in their termination. See *Georgia-Pacific Corp. v. Employment Div.*, 533 P.2d 829 (D.C. App. 1975); *Williams v. District Unemployment Compensation Bd.*, 383 A.2d 345, 350 (D.C. 1978).

61. *Brown v. United States*, 584 A.2d 537, 544 (D.C. App. 1990).

62. Ibid., 543–44.

63. Ibid., 539.

64. Ibid., 539 n. 2. But see *Richmond v. Maryland*, 623 A.2d 630, 633–34 (Md. App. 1991) (rejecting provocation in a mayhem case).

65. *Federal Sentencing Guidelines 1999*, 18 *U.S.C.* § 5K2.10.

66. *Model Sent. and Corr. Act* § 3-108, 10 *U.L.A.* 396 (2001).

67. *Model Penal Code*, § 7.01 (2)(e).

68. See *Ala. Code* § 13A-5-51(3) (1994); *Cal. Penal Code* § 190.3(e) (West 1988); *Fla. Stat. Ann.* § 921.141(6)(c) (West 1985); 720 *Ill. Comp. Stat. Ann.* § 5/9-1(c)(3) (Smith-Hurd Supp. 1993); *Ind. Code Ann.* § 35-50-2-9(c)(3) (Michie 1993); *Ky. Rev. Stat. Ann.* § 532.025(b)(3) (Michie 1990); *Md. Code Ann.* § 413(g)(2) (Supp. 1993); *Miss. Code Ann.* § 99-19-101(6)(c) (Supp. 1993); *Mo. Ann. Stat.* § 565.032(3)(3) (West Supp. 1993); *Mont. Code Ann.*

§ 46-18-304(5) (1987); *Neb. Rev. Stat.* § 29-2523(2)(f) (1989); *Nev. Rev. Stat. Ann.* § 200.035(3) (Michie 1992); *N.H. Rev. Stat. Ann.* § 630:5 (1996); *N.J. Stat. Ann.* § 2C:11-3 (West 2003); *N.M. Stat. Ann.* § 31-20A-6 (Michie 1978); *N.C. Gen. Stat.* § 15A-2000(f)(3) (1983); *Ohio Rev. Code Ann.* § 2929.04 (Anderson 2001); 42 *Pa. Stat. Ann.* § 9711(e)(6) (West Supp. 1993); *S.C. Code Ann.* § 16-3-20(C)(b)(3) (Law. Co-op. Supp. 1993); *Tenn. Code Ann.* § 39-13-204(j)(3) (1991); *Va. Code Ann.* § 19.2-264.4(B)(iii) (Michie 1990); *Wash. Rev. Code* § 10.95.070 (2001); *Wyo. Stat. Ann.* § 6-2-102(j)(iii) (Michie Supp. 1993); 18 *U.S.C.* § 3592(a)(7) (1999).

69. See, e.g., *Model Penal Code*, § 210.6(4)(c) (it is a mitigating factor when "[t]he victim was a participant in the defendant's homicidal conduct or consented to the homicidal act").

70. Ibid., commentaries, 140–41. Mitigating factors for capital sentencing purposes recognized under the MPC are the following:

a. The defendant has no significant history of prior criminal activity.
b. The murder was committed while the defendant was under the influence of extreme mental or emotional disturbance.
c. The victim was a participant in the defendant's homicidal conduct or consented to the homicidal act.
d. The murder was committed under circumstances which the defendant believed to provide a moral justification or extenuation for his conduct.
e. The defendant was an accomplice in a murder committed by another person and his participation in the homicidal act was relatively minor.
f. The defendant acted under duress or under the domination of another person.
g. At the time of the murder, the capacity of the defendant to appreciate the criminality [wrongfulness] of his conduct or to conform his conduct to the requirements of law was impaired as a result of mental disease or defect or intoxication.
h. The youth of the defendant at the time of the offense.

Ibid., § 210.6(4). The same factors or their variations permeate most state death penalty statutes. See Acker and Lanier, "In Fairness and Mercy," 313–33. Other factors present in some state statutes are: (1) absence of intent to commit a murder, (2) the offender's lack of future dangerousness or likelihood of rehabilitation, (3) cooperation with authorities, (4) the fact that another defendant equally culpable in the crime will not be punished by death, and (5) the fact that the act of the defendant was not the sole proximate cause of the victim's death. Ibid., 333–37.

71. Acker and Lanier, "In Fairness and Mercy," 320. By now, there are thirty-one such jurisdictions, including federal legislation. See 18 *U.S.C.S.* § 3592(a)(7) (1999); *Ala. Code* § 13A-5-51(3) (1994); *Ariz. Rev. Stat.* § 13-703(G) (2001); *Ark. Code Ann.* § 5-4-605 (Michie 1997); *Cal. Penal Code* § 190.3(e) (West 1999); *Colo. Rev. Stat. Ann.* § 18-1.3-1201(4)

(West 1999); *Conn. Gen. Stat.* § 53a-46a(d) (2001); *Fla. Stat. Ann.* § 921.141(6)(c) (West 2001); 720 *Ill. Comp. Stat.* 5/9-1(c)(3) (1993); *Ind. Code Ann.* § 35-50-2-9(c)(3) (West 1998); *Ky. Rev. Stat. Ann.* § 532.025(2)(b)(3) (Michie 1999); *La. Code Crim. Proc. Ann.* art. 905.5 (West 1997); *Md. Code Ann.* § 2-303(h)(2)(ii) (2002); *Miss. Code Ann.* § 99-19-101(6)(c) (West 1999); *Mo. Rev. Stat.* § 565.032(3)(3) (1999); *Mont. Code Ann.* § 46-18-304(1)(e) (2003); *Neb. Rev. Stat.* § 29-2523(2)(f) (2003); *Nev. Rev. Stat. Ann.* § 200.035(3) (Michie 2001); *N.H. Rev. Stat. Ann.* § 630:5(VI)(h) (1996); *N.M. Stat. Ann.* § 31-20A-6(E) (Michie 1978); *N.Y. Crim. Proc. Law* § 400.27(9) (McKinney 1994); *N.C. Gen. Stat.* § 15A-2000(f)(3) (1983); *Ohio Rev. Code Ann.* § 2929.04(B)(1) (Anderson 2001); *Or. Rev. Stat.* § 163.150(1)(c)(A) (1997); 42 *Pa. Cons. Stat.* § 9711(e)(6) (1998); *S.C. Code Ann.* § 16-3-20(C)(b)(3) (Law. Co-op. 2003); *Tenn. Code Ann.* § 39-13-204(j)(3) (2003); *Utah Code Ann.* § 76-3-207(4) (2003); *Va. Code Ann.* § 19.2-264.4(B)(iii) (Michie 2003); *Wash. Rev. Code* § 10.95.070(3) (2001); *Wyo. Stat. Ann.* § 6-2-102(j)(iii) (Michie 1993).

72. Acker and Lanier, "In Fairness and Mercy," 320. See also *Ala. Code* § 13A-5-51(3) (1982); *Cal. Penal Code* § 190.3(e) (West 1988); *Fla. Stat. Ann.* § 921.141(6)(9)(c) (West 1985); 720 *Ill. Comp. Stat.* 5/9-1(c)(3) (West Supp. 1993); *Ind. Code Ann.* § 35-50-2-9(c)(3) (Michie 1993); *Ky. Rev. Stat. Ann.* § 532.025(b)(3) (Michie 1990); *Md. Code Ann.* art. 27, § 413(g)(2) (Supp. 1993); *Miss. Code Ann.* § 99-19-101(6)(c) (Supp. 1993); *Mo. Ann. Stat.* § 565.032(3)(3) (West Supp. 1993); *Mont. Code Ann.* § 46-18-304(5) (1987) *Neb. Rev. Stat.* § 29-2523(2)(f) (1989); *Nev. Rev. Stat. Ann.* 200.035(3) (Michie 1992); *N.C. Gen. Stat.* § 15A-2000(f)(3) (1983) (specifically requiring the victim's voluntary participation in the defendant's homicidal conduct); 42 *Pa. Cons. Stat. Ann.* § 9711(e)(6) (West Supp. 1993); *S.C. Code Ann.* § 16-3-20(C)(b)(3) (Law. Co-op. Supp. 1993); *Tenn. Code Ann.* § 39-13-204(j)(3) (1991); *Va. Code Ann.* § 19.2-264.4(B)(iii) (Michie 1990); *Wyo. Stat. Ann.* § 6-2-1304(j)(3) (Michie 1991); *Wyo. Stat. Ann.* § 6-2-102(j)(iii) (Michie Supp. 1993). No reference is made to the victim's conduct as a potential mitigating factor in the death penalty laws of Arizona, Arkansas, Colorado, Connecticut, Louisiana, Oregon, or Utah. See Acker and Lanier, "In Fairness and Mercy," 320–21. However, both Colorado and Louisiana have statutory mitigating factors to the effect that the offender reasonably believed that there was a moral justification or extenuation for his conduct, and the homicide victim's conduct may be relevant to such circumstances.

73. *Model Penal Code*, § 210.6(4)(c).

74. See Acker and Lanier, "In Fairness and Mercy," 320–21. See also *N.H. Rev. Stat. Ann.* § 630:5(VI)(h) (Supp. 1993); *Wash. Rev. Code Ann.* § 10.95.070(3) (West Supp. 1993); 21 *U.S.C.A.* § 848(m)(9) (West Supp. 1993).

75. *N.M. Stat. Ann.* § 31-20A-6(E) (Michie 1990).

76. *Ohio Rev. Code Ann.* § 2929.04(B)(1) (Anderson 1993).

77. See *N.J. Stat. Ann.* § 2C:11-3(c)(5)(b) (West Supp. 1993) ("The victim solicited, participated in or consented to the conduct which resulted in his death"); *S.C. Code Ann.* § 16-3-20(C)(b)(8) (Law. Co-op. Supp. 1993) (including the MPC's victim par-

ticipation or consent provision and also a separate circumstance that considers whether "[t]he defendant was provoked by the victim into committing the murder").

78. Lynch, "Sentencing Guidelines," *1.

79. Ibid.

80. See generally Robinson, "Functional Analysis of Criminal Law."

81. Ibid., 857.

82. Ibid.

83. *Model Penal Code*, §§ 210.2, 210.3.

84. Ibid., §§ 210.3, 210.4.

85. Robinson, "Functional Analysis of Criminal Law," 857.

86. *Model Penal Code*, § 1.02.

87. Ibid., § 1.02 cmt. at 20.

88. See Robinson, "Functional Analysis of Criminal Law," 907.

89. Ibid.

90. Ibid.

91. See *Model Penal Code*, §§ 210.3(b), 2.09, 210.6(4).

92. Huigens, "Rethinking the Penalty Phase," 1195.

93. Ibid.

94. Ibid., 1196.

95. Ibid., 1251.

96. Ibid.

97. See ibid., 1228.

98. Ibid., 1252.

99. See, e.g., *Model Penal Code*, § 1.02 cmt. at 20 (recognizing that, "in its effect on the offender's status in society, the law delineating . . . distinctions [between serious and minor offenses] has an impact second only to that which establishes that proscribed conduct will be criminal").

100. See, e.g., *Mullaney v. Wilbur*, 421 U.S. 684, 697–98 (1975) (acknowledging that criminal law "is concerned not only with guilt or innocence in the abstract but also with the degree of criminal culpability").

101. Husak, "Partial Defenses," at 169.

102. See, e.g., Kalven, Jr., and Zeisel, *American Jury*, 243–45.

103. Kalven, Jr., and Zeisel, *American Jury*, 62 (study shows that, taken together, cases with disagreement on guilt [19.1 percent], hung juries [5.5 percent] and disagreement on charge [5.2 percent] equal 29.8 percent of all included cases). It is worth noting that out of that 29.8 percent, the judge would be more lenient in only 4 percent of cases. Ibid.

104. Ibid.

105. Ibid. (at the penalty stage, the judge is more lenient than the jury in 1.5 percent of cases, whereas jurors are more lenient than the judge in 2.5 percent of cases).

106. The survey does not provide similar data for provoked husband defendants because there were too few cases for a reliable estimate. See U.S. Department of Justice, *Spouse Murder Defendants*, 22 n. 11.

107. Ibid., 22.

108. *Federal Sentencing Guidelines 2006*, 18 *U.S.C.* § 5K2.10. Victim's Conduct (Policy Statement). Courts are to consider the conduct of both the victim and the offender, including the following:

1. The size and strength of the victim, or other relevant physical characteristics, in comparison with those of the defendant;
2. The persistence of the victim's conduct and any efforts by the defendant to prevent confrontation;
3. The danger reasonably perceived by the defendant, including the victim's reputation for violence;
4. The danger actually presented to the defendant by the victim;
5. Any other relevant conduct by the victim that substantially contributed to the danger presented; and
6. The proportionality and reasonableness of the defendant's response to the victim's provocation.

109. U.S. Sentencing Commission, *2001 Sourcebook*, Table 25.

110. See ibid., Table 27. The departures included in this calculation do not include those granted for the substantial assistance to the prosecution.

111. *Blakeley v. Washington*, 542 U.S. 296; *United States v. Booker*, 543 U.S. 220. See also Klein, "Redrawing the Criminal-Civil Boundary," 679–80.

112. See U.S. Sentencing Commission, *1999 Sourcebook*, Table 24–25.

113. Klein, "Redrawing the Criminal-Civil Boundary," 679–80.

114. See generally Malone, "Ruminations on the Role of Fault," 2.

115. See Finkelstein, "New Perspectives and Legal Implications," 965. ("While both tort and criminal law recognize that there are harms that should not generate liability, harm appears to be at least a necessary condition for liability in both areas.")

116. See Grey, "New Federalism Jurisprudence," 519. ("Although tort law thus moved away from the criminal law, it remains rooted in seeking to punish those who violate societal norms.")

117. See Hall, *General Principles of Criminal Law*, 254–57 (discussing similarities and differences in how causation is understood in criminal law and tort law).

118. Stephens, "Conceptualizing Violence," 582. See also *Smith v. Wade*, 461 U.S. 30, 51 (1983) (noting that punitive damages are appropriate where defendant's conduct is willful, wanton, or malicious, or demonstrates a reckless indifference to the rights of others or an evil motive).

119. Nadel, "Annotation, Statutes," 63.

120. Mostaghel, "Wrong Place, Wrong Time," 88.

121. Sisk, "Comparative Fault and Common Sense," 30.

122. Ibid., 31. ("If a plaintiff was at fault in part, he had to be treated as at fault in whole, and this contributory negligence barred recovery.")

123. Prosser, "Joint Torts and Several Liability," 418.

124. Best et al., *Comparative Negligence Law and Practice*, § 1-1[4] (noting that contributory negligence remains to be the rule only in a small geographic cluster of jurisdictions: Alabama, the District of Columbia, Maryland, North Carolina, and Virginia).

125. *Goetzman v. Wichern*, 327 N.W.2d 742, 746 (Iowa 1982); *Scott v. Rizzo*, 634 P.2d 1234, 1241 (N.M. 1981).

126. *Goetzman v. Wichern*, 327 N.W.2d 752; *Bradley v. Appalachian Power Co.*, 256 S.E.2d 879, 882 (W. Va. 1979).

127. *Li v. Yellow Cab Co.*, 532 P.2d 1226 (Cal. 1975); *Hoffman v. Jones*, 280 So. 2d 431, 436 (Fla. 1973).

128. *Bradley v. Appalachian Power Co.*, 256 S.E.2d 879, 884 (W. Va. 1979).

129. *Kaatz v. State*, 540 P.2d 1037, 1047 (1975); *Goetzman v. Wichern*, 327 N.W.2d 742, 747 (Iowa 1982); *Scott v. Rizzo*, 634 P.2d 1234, 1241 (N.M. 1981).

130. See, e.g., *Restatement (Second) of Torts*, §§ 479–84 (excluding from the contributory fault rule [i] intentional or reckless injury; [ii] nuisance; [iii] strict liability offense; [iv] violation of a statute; and [v] situation when defendant had the last clear chance to avoid injury).

131. See Sobelsohn, "Comparing Fault," 413.

132. Best et al., *Comparative Negligence Law and Practice*, § 1-1[5][b].

133. See, e.g., *Alibrandi v. Helmsley*, 314 N.Y.S.2d 95, 97 (N.Y. Sup. Ct. 1970).

134. *Hoffman v. Jones*, 280 So. 2d 431, 437 (Fla. 1973); *Alvis v. Ribar*, 421 N.E.2d 886 (Ill. 1981); *Goetzman v. Wichern*, 327 N.W.2d 742, 749 (Iowa 1982).

135. *Li v. Yellow Cab Co.*, 532 P.2d 1226, 1231 (Cal. 1975).

136. Maloney, "From Contributory to Comparative Negligence," 151.

137. Schafer, *Victimology*, 20.

138. See discussion in this chapter under "Utilitarian Considerations."

139. See Maloney, "From Contributory to Comparative Negligence," 151.

140. Ibid., 152. ("The disrespect for law engendered by putting our citizens in a position in which they feel it is necessary to deliberately violate the law is not something to be lightly brushed aside; and it comes ill from the mouths of lawyers, who as officers of the courts have sworn to uphold the law, to defend the present system by arguing that it works because jurors can be trusted to disregard that very law.")

141. *Restatement (Third) of Torts: Apportionment of Liability*, § 1.

142. Bublick, "End Game of Tort Reform," 367. ("Courts in at least twenty-two states have recently faced questions about comparison of defendants' intentional and negligent fault. State legislatures have faced similar questions. Moreover, a number of state courts have examined comparison of intentional and negligent fault between plaintiffs and defendants.") (Footnotes omitted.)

143. *Restatement (Third) of Torts: Apportionment of Liability*, § 1 cmt. c at 7.

144. Ibid., 8.

145. American Law Institute, "76th Meeting," 34 (remarks of Prof. Powers).

146. *Restatement (Third) of Torts: Apportionment of Liability*, § 1 cmt. c at 7 (1999).

147. Ibid.

148. See, e.g., *Comeau v. Lucas*, 455 N.Y.S.2d 871, 873 (N.Y. App. Div. 1982) (comparing disruptive behavior of plaintiff with intentional assault by defendant); *Bonpua v. Fagan*, 602 A.2d 287, 288–89 (N.J. Super. Ct. App. Div. 1992) (comparing negligence of plaintiff in provoking fight with defendant's intentional battery); *Barth v. Coleman*, 878 P.2d 319, 322–23 (N.M. 1994) (comparing negligence of plaintiff with negligence of defendant and intentional assault by other); *Morris v. Yogi Bear's Jellystone Park Camp Resort*, 539 So. 2d 70, 77–78 (La. Ct. App. 1989) (comparing intentional rapist with negligence of thirteen-year-old victim). But see *McLain v. Training and Dev. Corp.*, 572 A.2d 494, 496–97 (Me. 1990) (refusing to compare defendant's responsibility for assault and battery with contributory negligence of plaintiff); *Kelzer v. Wachholz*, 381 N.W.2d 852, 854 (Minn. Ct. App. 1986) (refusing to compare fault of plaintiff with intentional trespasser); *Cartwright v. Equitable Life Assurance Soc'y*, 914 P.2d 976, 996–98 (Mont. 1996) (refusing to compare plaintiff's negligence with defendant's fraud).

149. See, e.g., Bublick, "End Game of Tort Reform," 257; Hollister, "Using Comparative Fault," 121; Sisk, "Comparative Fault and Common Sense," 236; Sobelsohn, "Comparing Fault," 442.

150. See Hollister, "Using Comparative Fault," 127.

151. Juenger, "Brief for Negligence Law Section," 50.

152. *Restatement (Third) of Torts: Apportionment of Liability*, at § 1 cmt. c, reporter's notes at 13.

153. Ibid., 14.

154. Ibid., 13.

155. Ibid., § 3 cmt. d at 53.

156. Ibid., § 8. Similar criteria are central in the *Uniform Comparative Fault Act*. See *Uniform Comparative Fault Act*, 12 *U.L.A.* 33, § 2(b) (1981 Supp.) ("In determining the percentages of fault, the trier of fact shall consider both the nature of the conduct of each party at fault and the extent of the causal relation between the conduct and the damages claimed.")

157. *Restatement (Third) of Torts: Apportionment of Liability*, § 8 cmt. c at 117.

Chapter 3

1. "An example of a duty-based norm is the duty not to be cruel to animals; an example of a rights-based norm is that protecting the right of a person to her own

bodily integrity on which is based the duty of everybody else not to violate that integrity." Moore, "Victims and Retribution," 71.

2. See Ingman, "Defense of Volenti Non Fit Injuria," 8–9.

3. See Fletcher, *Rethinking Criminal Law*, 705; Bergelson, "Right to Be Hurt," 202–6.

4. See, e.g., *Model Penal Code*, § 3.02 cmt 2 at 9.

5. See ibid.

6. See Westen, *Logic of Consent*, 4–5.

7. Although the actor would not be guilty of rape in either case, in the second, unlike in the first one, he would be guilty of attempted rape.

8. See, e.g., Joel Feinberg, *Harm to Self*, 316. In addition to factual consent, the requirement of legally valid consent may be satisfied by establishing imputed consent. Species of imputed consent include constructive consent (the victim's acquiescence to one act presupposes acquiescence to some other act too); informed consent (the victim voluntarily assumes the risk of a certain harm); and hypothetical consent (the victim is incompetent and determination is made for the victim, based on what the victim would have consented to had he been competent or based on the victim's best interests). See Westen, *Logic of Consent*, 269–72.

9. See, e.g., *Model Penal Code*, § 2.11(3) (1980). See also *Model Penal Code*, § 2.11(3) cmt. 3 (1980), 398–99.

10. See Feinberg, *Harm to Self*, 316. ("If he is so impaired or undeveloped cognitively that he doesn't really know what he is doing, or so impaired or undeveloped volitionally that he cannot help what he is doing, then no matter what expression of assent he may appear to give, it will lack the effect of genuine consent.")

11. See ibid., 117–21.

12. Ibid., 124–27. Feinberg wrote:

> In the cases of "presumably nonvoluntary behavior," what we "presume" is either that the actor is ignorant or mistaken about what he is doing, or acting under some sort of compulsion, or suffering from some sort of incapacity, *and* that if that were not the case, he would choose not to do what he seems bent on doing now. (124)

13. Ibid., 62. Those include "interests in the continuance for a foreseeable interval of one's life, and the interests in one's own physical health and vigor, the integrity and normal functioning of one's body, the absence of absorbing pain and suffering or grotesque disfigurement, minimal intellectual acuity, emotional stability" (37).

14. See, e.g., Dan-Cohen, "Basic Values," 770; Dubber, "Toward a Constitutional Law," 568; Duff, "Harms and Wrongs," 39–44; George Wright, "Consenting Adults," 1399.

15. George Wright, "Consenting Adults," 1399; see also Dan-Cohen, "Basic Values," 777–78; Dubber, "Toward a Constitutional Law," 568.

16. See generally Herzog, *Happy Slaves.*

17. Dan-Cohen, "Basic Values," 770. Dan-Cohen defines dignity as "an expressive value demanding that people's behavior, physical and verbal, convey a certain attitude to other people, namely, an attitude of respect" (Ibid., 771).

18. Duff, "Harms and Wrongs," 39.

19. Joel Feinberg, "Mistreatment of Dead Bodies," 31–32.

20. See ibid., 31.

21. See Dubber, "Toward a Constitutional Law," 535. Dan-Cohen makes a similar point when he observes that the term *dignity* should be understood as "moral worth" and not "social status." See Dan-Cohen, *Harmful Thoughts*, 169 n. 23.

22. Dubber, "Toward a Constitutional Law," 535.

23. Feinberg, *Harm to Self*, 172.

24. See, e.g, Gerald Dworkin, "Paternalism," (1971). Dworkin required the government to satisfy a quite demanding burden of proof before paternalistic legislation may be adopted:

> In all cases of paternalistic legislation there must be a heavy and clear burden of proof placed on the authorities to demonstrate the exact nature of the harmful effects (or beneficial consequences) to be avoided (or achieved) and the probability of their occurrence. . . . To paraphrase a formulation of the burden of proof for criminal proceedings—better ten men ruin themselves than one man be unjustly deprived of liberty.

25. Goodman, "Reality TV Hits a Tailspin."

26. *Wolfenden Report*, ¶ 13.

27. Duff, "Harms and Wrongs," 37.

28. Bergelson, "Right to Be Hurt," 219–21.

29. Interestingly, the Universal Declaration of Human Rights makes this distinction quite clear when it states in Article 1: "All human beings are born free and equal in dignity and rights." Universal Declaration of Human Rights, G.A. Res. 217A, at 71, U.N. GAOR, 3d Sess., 1st plen. mtg., U.N. Doc. A/810, Art. 1, December 12, 1948.

30. See discussion in Chapter 1 under "Consent."

31. *People v. Kevorkian*, 639 N.W.2d 291, 298 (Mich. Ct. App. 2001).

32. Ibid., 296.

33. *United States v. Holmes*, 26 F. Cas. 360 (C.C.E.D. Pa. 1842).

34. Ibid. n. 5.

35. *Gilbert v. State*, 487 So. 2d 1185, 1186–87 (Fla. Dist. Ct. App. 1986).

36. Ibid.

37. Ibid. (defendant explained that he used a gun because it causes instantaneous death).

38. Ibid.

39. This second prong is needed to cover a situation in which, say, a doctor performs a necessary surgery but, through no fault of his, fails to save the patient.

40. See, e.g., Uniacke, *Permissible Killing*, 194 ("Something akin to a theory of forfeiture of rights is necessary to the justification of homicide in self-defense: it is necessary to the justification of self-preferential killing"); Nancy Davis, "Abortion and Self-Defense," 202 (stating that unjust aggressors "have in some sense done something that has weakened, forfeited or undermined their prior claims to moral parity" with persons they attack)

41. Feinberg, "Voluntary Euthanasia," 111.

42. See, e.g., Finkelstein, "On the Obligation of the State," 147:

> The innocent threat is a man who has been pushed off the edge of a cliff and is barreling toward you as you sit on a terrace below. The problem is that he is fat, very fat, and if he lands on you he will kill you. The only thing you have time to do is shift the position of an awning over your head. If you do shift the awning, he will be catapulted into a ravine and die, and you will survive. If you do not shift the awning, you will die and he will survive, because you will break his fall. (Ibid., 1369)

43. See, e.g., Fletcher, "Proportionality," 371.

44. See Bergelson, "Rights, Wrongs, and Comparative Justifications," 101 (discussing conflicting justifications).

45. See, e.g., Alexander, "Propter Honoris Respectum," 1481–82 (defining "innocent aggressors" as those "who appear to be attacking me *without legal justification*, but who are legally and morally nonculpable in doing so") (emphasis added).

46. Fletcher, *Rethinking Criminal Law*, 761.

47. The *Model Penal Code* (MPC) leaves the issue open: "While there may be situations, such as rape, where it is hardly possible to claim that greater evil was avoided than that sought to be prevented by the law defining the offense, this is a matter that is safely left to the determination and elaboration of the courts." *Model Penal Code*, § 3.02 cmt. 3, 14. On the other hand, according to the *Model Penal Code*, "the numerical preponderance in the lives saved compared to those sacrificed surely should establish legal justification for the act." Ibid., 15. The numerical preponderance seems to warrant Jack's justification, even if murder is not worse than rape (one count of rape compared to avoiding several counts of murder).

48. Ibid., § 3.04(2)(b).

49. Morris, "Somnambulistic Homicide," 29–30.

50. Ibid.

51. Ibid.

52. Alexander, "Justification and Innocent Aggressors," 1187.

53. *Abbott v. The Queen*, [1976]) 3 All. E.R. 140 at 146, per Lord Salmon giving the judgment of the Privy Council.

54. Greenawalt, "Perplexing Borders," 1915–18.

55. See Fletcher, *Rethinking Criminal Law,* § 10.5, 868–69.

56. See LaFave and Scott, Jr., *Criminal Law,* § 5.8(b).

57. Alexander, "Justification and Innocent Aggressors," 1187–88.

58. Ibid., 1188 ("at least if, assumedly, a proper balancing of short and long-term interests would declare their two lives more important than the victim's one life sufficiently often to warrant an instrumental rule to that effect").

59. Ibid.

60. See, e.g., Kahneman, Knetsch, and Thaler, "Experimental Tests," 1325–48.

61. See Thomson, "Self-Defense and Rights," 40–41.

62. See *Vincent v. Lake Erie Transportation Co.*, 124 N.W. 221 (Minn. 1910). See also *Restatement (Second) of Torts,* § 263; Keeton et al., *Prosser and Keeton,* § 24, 147–48.

63. See Thomson, "Self-Defense and Rights," 42–48; Thomson, "Some Ruminations on Rights," 49–65; Thomson, "Rights and Compensation," 66–77; Thomson, *Realm of Rights,* 348–73.

64. I follow Thomson's distinction between infringement of a right and violation of a right but only to the extent it applies to justifiability of punishment, not to private rights of individuals. Take her own well-known hypothetical in which a person is kidnapped by the Society of Music Lovers to be used for kidney dialysis in order to save the life of a famous violinist. See Thomson, "Defense of Abortion," 48–49, 59–66. If we conclude that the person's rights here were not violated but merely overridden, he should not be justified in fighting for his freedom. At least legally (and, arguably, morally), that outcome would be wrong. Note, however, that a right violation is a necessary, but not sufficient, condition of one's privilege to enforce that right. See discussion in Chapter 6 under "The Magnitude of the Affected Rights."

65. Thomson makes a similar point when she observes: "[S]aying that Aggressor simply ceased to have the right is not the same as saying that Aggressor has forfeited the right." Thomson, "Self-Defense and Rights," 37.

66. Ibid., 42–47.

67. ESPN, "Queens Man in San Francisco."

68. ABC News, "TB Patient Asks Forgiveness."

69. See "Compensation to Crime Victims," available on http://ec.europa.eu/civiljustice/comp_crime_victim/comp_crime_victim_net_en.htm.

70. Dubber, *Victims in the War on Crime,* 316.

71. *In re Beach,* 698 N.E.2d 97, 99 (Ohio Misc. 1994).

72. *Model Penal Code,* § 3.06(3)(b). See also *Neb. Rev. Stat.* § 28-1411(4) (2006); *N.J. Stat. Ann.* § 2C:3-6(b)(2) (West. 2006); 18 *Pa. Cons. Stat.* § 507(c)(2) (2006) (stating a rule that a trespasser may not be expelled in circumstances in which extreme harm is likely to befall him).

73. Fletcher, "Proportionality," 371.

74. But see Alexander, "Justification," 1187.

75. Morris, "Somnambulistic Homicide," 30.

76. See, e.g., *MedlinePlus Medical Encyclopedia*. Psychosis is defined as a severe mental condition characterized by a loss of contact with reality. Persons experiencing a psychotic episode may have hallucinations, hold delusional beliefs, demonstrate personality changes, and exhibit disorganized thinking. Ibid.

77. *Brown v. United States*, 584 A.2d 537, 540 (D.C. Cir. 1990).

78. *Model Penal Code*, § 210.3 cmt. 5(a), 57–58.

79. Dressler, "Why Keep the Provocation Defense?" 969.

80. Dressler, "Battered Women and Sleeping Abusers," 465.

81. See, e.g., Dressler, "New Thoughts," 84–92.

82. Ashworth, "Doctrine of Provocation," 307 ("[t]he claim implicit in partial justification is that an individual is to some extent morally justified in making a punitive return against someone who intentionally causes him serious offense"). I would not limit provocation to an intentional offense, however. An actor may be provoked by an assault caused recklessly or negligently, e.g., when the victim injured the defendant or killed a close relative of the defendant in an accident caused by the victim's reckless or negligent driving. Moreover, even if the victim were justified in his risky driving (e.g., because he was taking a very sick person to a hospital), the rationale for the provocation defense would still apply. The defendant who, because of the victim's careless driving, suffered an injury or witnessed the death of a close relative and in response hit the victim, causing the victim's death, would still be entitled to the defense of provocation. See, e.g., *State v. Madden*, 294 A.2d 609, 622 (N.J. 1972) (stating in dicta that in the event a close relative of the victim of a battery witnessed the beating, the relative would have a plausible defense of provocation); *Commonwealth v. Jenkins*, 26 Phila. 177, 185 (1993) (stating that viewing harm being inflicted on a crippled parent would be sufficient to provoke a reasonable person).

83. *Public Committee Against Torture in Israel v. State of Israel*, HCJ 5100/94 [1999] IsrSC 53(4)817, available at http://www.derechos.org/human rights/mena/doc/torture .html.

84. Ibid.

85. Dressler, "Why Keep the Provocation Defense?" 969.

86. See Blackstone, *Commentaries*, 139.

87. Ibid., 442.

88. Keeton et al., *Prosser and Keeton*, 916.

89. *R. v. Mawgridge* (1707) Kel. 119, 137.

90. Keeton et al., *Prosser and Keeton*, 915–16.

91. D'Emilio and Freedman, *Intimate Matters*, 28,

92. Ibid.

93. Ibid., 138.

94. Blackstone, *Commentaries*, 191.

95. See *N.M. Comp. Laws* § 1076 (1897); *N.M. Penal Code*, § 1468 (1915); *N.M. Stat. Ann.* § 40A-2-1 (1972); 1636 *N.M. Laws* ch. 303, §§ 2–4 (justifying the use of "deadly force upon another who was at the time of the homicide in the act of having sexual intercourse with the accused's wife"); repealed, 1973 *N.M. Laws* ch. 241, § 6; *Utah Comp. Laws* § 1925 (1876); *Utah Comp. Laws* § 4461(3) (1888); *Utah Rev. Stat.* § 4168 (1898); *Utah Comp. Laws* § 8032(4) (1917); *Utah Code Ann.* § 76-30-10 (1953) (justifying homicide when the deceased has committed or attempted to commit the defilement of the wife, daughter, sister, mother, or other female dependent of the accused); repealed, 1973 *Utah Laws* ch. 196, § 76-10-1401; *Tex. Penal Code Ann.* §§ 561–62 (Vernon 1857), § 567 (Vernon 1879), § 672 (Vernon 1895), § 1102 (Vernon 1911), and § 1220 (Vernon 1925) (justifying homicide "when committed by the husband upon one taken in the act of adultery with the wife, provided the killing take place before the parties to the act have separated"); repealed, 1973 *Tex. Gen. Laws* ch. 399, § 3(a); *Ga. Penal Code* § 75 (1910); *Ga. Code Ann.* § 26-1016 (1933), § 21-901(f) (1972). See also *Biggs v. State*, 29 Ga. 723, 728–29 (1860) (interpreting Georgia justifiable homicide statute to include killing of a paramour).

96. *Campbell v. State*, 204 Ga. 399, 403 (1948).

97. *Briggs v. State*, 29 Ga. 723, 729 (1860).

98. *Drysdale v. State*, 10 S.E. 358, 358 (1889).

99. Most states deny the initial aggressor self-defense privilege even when his minor provocation is met by a grossly excessive force. See, e.g., *Ala. Code* § 13A-3-23(c)(2) (2007); *Ind. Code Ann.* § 35-41-3-2(e)(3) (2007); *Mo. Ann. Stat.* § 563.031(1) (West 2007); *N.Y. Penal Law* § 35.15 (McKinney 2007); *Or. Rev. Stat. Ann.* § 161.215(2) (West 2007).

100. *Burger v. State*, 231 S.E.2d 769, 771 (Ga. 1977) (citations omitted).

101. *January v. State*, 181 P. 514, 517 (Okla. 1919).

102. Kalven, Jr., and Zeisel, *American Jury*, 193–347.

103. Ibid., 236.

104. Ibid.

105. Ibid.

106. Ibid. n. 24.

107. *Hamilton v. State*, 244 P.2d 328, 330 (Okla. 1952).

108. Ibid.

109. Ibid., 335.

110. Ibid.

111. Pew Research Center, "Barometer of Modern Morals," 8.

112. Falco, "Road Not Taken," 746.

113. See *Ala. Code* § 13A-13-2 (2007); *Ariz. Rev. Stat.* § 13-1408 (LexisNexis 2007); *Colo. Rev. Stat.* § 18-6-501 (2006); *Fla. Stat. Ann.* § 798.01 (West 2007); *Ga. Code Ann.*

§ 16-6-19 (2007); *Idaho Code* § 18-6601 (2007); 720 *Ill. Comp. Stat. Ann.* 5/11-7 (West 2007); *Kan. Stat. Ann.* § 21-3507 (2006); *Mass. Ann. Laws* ch. 272, § 14 (LexisNexis 2007); *Md. Code Ann.*, Crim. Law § 10-501 (West 2002); *Mich. Comp. Laws Ann.* § 750.30 (West 2007); *Minn. Stat. Ann.* § 609.36 (West 2006); *Miss. Code Ann.* § 97-29-1 (2007); *N.H. Rev. Stat. Ann.* § 645.3 (2003); *N.Y. Penal Law* § 255.17 (McKinney 2007); *N.C. Gen. Stat.* § 14-184 (2007); *N.D. Cent. Code* § 12.1-20-09 (2007); *Okla. Stat. Ann.* tit. 21, § 871 (West 2007); *R.I. Gen. Laws* § 11-6-2 (2007); *S.C. Code Ann.* § 16-15-60 (2006); *Utah Code Ann.* 76-7-103 (2007); *Va. Code Ann.* § 18.2-365 (2007); *W. Va. Code Ann.* § 61-8-3 (LexisNexis 2007); *Wis. Stat. Ann.* § 944.16 (West Supp. 2007).

114. *Mass. Ann. Laws* ch. 272, § 14 (LexisNexis 2007); *Mich. Comp. Laws Ann.* § 750.30 (West 2007); *Okla. Stat. Ann.* tit. 21, § 872 (West 2007); *Wis. Stat. Ann.* § 944.16 (West Supp. 2007).

115. Siegel, "For Better or for Worse."

116. LaFave, *Criminal Law*, 779–80.

117. See *Md. Code Ann.*, Crim. Law § 2-207(b) (West 2002).

118. Wilmot-Weidman, "After a Three-Year Fight," 1.

119. See Patterson, "Putting a Price on Love." The article reports a recent Illinois alienation-of-affection lawsuit in which the husband won an award of $4,802.87 against his wife's lover. Even the husband's attorney was surprised and conceded that "it's kind of remarkable" that the case was not thrown out earlier, as most are. Ibid.

120. See, e.g., *Model Penal Code*, § 2.09(1).

121. See Kadish, Schulhofer, and Steiker, *Criminal Law and Its Process*, 846 (observing that "the great majority of recent cases and statutory revisions continue to exclude the defense in murder prosecutions").

Chapter 4

1. See, e.g., *Model Penal Code*, § 3.09(2) (providing that a defendant who was negligent or reckless in using force may not use self-defense and similar defenses under Article 3 of the MPC in prosecution for negligent or reckless offenses).

2. Buchwald, "Coddling Victims," A15.

3. Ibid.

4. Ibid.

5. "Editorial: Tyson Takes the Count," 253.

6. Harel, "Efficiency and Fairness," 1228.

7. Ibid., 1229.

8. See, e.g., Dietz, et al., "Homicide," art. 105. ("The right to life and to personal security is not only sacred in the estimation of the common law, but it is inalienable.")

9. Thomson, "Self-Defense and Rights," 45.

10. See, e.g., Feinberg, "Voluntary Euthanasia," 122–23.

11. *People v. Samuels*, 58 Cal. Rptr. 439, 442 (Cal. Ct. App. 1967).

12. Ibid., 443.

13. Ibid., 447.

14. See Harding, "Victim of Cannibal Agreed."

15. See ibid.

16. *R. v. Carriere*, [1987] 35 C.C.C. (3d) 276, 286–87 (Can.).

17. *R. v. Brown*, [1994] 1 A.C. 212 (H.L.).

18. See, e.g., *Washington v. Glucksberg*, 521 U.S. 702, 738 (1997) (O'Connor, J., concurring).

19. Gerald Dworkin provided a straightforward definition of paternalism. X acts paternalistically toward Y by doing (omitting) Z if:

> 1. Z (or its omission) interferes with the liberty or autonomy of Y.
> 2. X does so without the consent of Y.
> 3. X does so just because Z will improve the welfare of Y (where this includes preventing his welfare from diminishing), or in some way promote the interests, values, or good of Y.
>
> Gerald Dworkin, "Paternalism" (2005).

20. Hart, *Law, Liberty, and Morality*, 33.

21. Ibid.

22. See West, "Authority, Autonomy, and Choice," 384. Criticizing Posner's interpretation of human nature and comparing Posner's vision of the world with Kafka's, West wrote:

> Kafka's characters usually do what they do—go to work in the morning, become lovers, commit crimes, obey laws, or whatever—not because they believe that by doing so they will improve their own well-being, but because they have been told to do so and crave being told to do so. Whereas Posner's characters relentlessly pursue autonomy and personal well-being, Kafka's characters just as relentlessly desire, need, and ultimately seek out authority. (387)

23. West, "Difference in Women's Hedonic Lives," 97.

24. Roberts, "Philosophy, Feinberg, Codification, and Consent," 228.

25. *Restatement (Second) of Torts*, § 496a cmt. c (discussing the meaning of assumption of risk). See also Simons, "Relevance of Community Values" (analyzing assumption of risk as a fully preferred option).

26. *Restatement (Second) of Torts*, § 496C cmts. b–g.

27. The less conscious the victim's decision to engage in a dangerous activity, the more appropriate it may be to treat his behavior as a case of involuntary, rather than voluntary, reduction of rights.

28. See ibid. § 892a cmt. c.

29. Ibid.

30. Mansfield, “Informed Choice,” 31–32.

31. Hurd, “Blaming the Victim,” 509.

32. Ibid.

33. Ibid., 512.

34. Pound, *Introduction to the Philosophy of Law*, 169.

35. But see Harel, “Efficiency and Fairness,” 127.

36. *State v. Helmenstein*, 163 N.W.2d 85, 89 (N.D. 1968).

37. Ibid.

38. *Wilcox v. Jeffery*, [1951] 1 All E.R. 464.

39. Ibid.

40. See, e.g., *Model Penal Code*, § 2.06(3)(a).

41. *People v. Prettyman*, 926 P.2d 1013, 1019 (Cal. 1996).

42. *Model Penal Code*, § 2.06 cmt., 311.

43. See, e.g., *Commonwealth v. Atencio*, 189 N.E.2d 323 (Mass. 1963).

44. *Model Penal Code*, § 1.13(9)–(10).

45. A similar scheme is adopted for the justificatory defense of necessity under the MPC. See *Model Penal Code*, § 3.02(2).

46. Lacayo, “Rough-Sex Defense,” 55.

47. *Commonwealth v. Peak*, 12 Pa. D. and C.2d 379 (1957).

48. Ibid., 380.

49. Ibid., 380–81. Naturally, if a drag race participant kills not only himself but also a nonparticipating third party, the defendant may be held liable for that latter death through theories of complicity or joint criminal conduct. See, e.g., *State v. McFadden*, 320 N.W.2d 608, 610 (Iowa 1982) (observing that aiding and abetting and joint criminal conduct are vicarious liability theories and that they are sufficient to convict the defendant for the death of a third party). These theories, while completely appropriate in respect of the death of a bystander, are not applicable to the death of a cocompetitor because a standard involuntary manslaughter statute requires the death of “another person.” See ibid., 610 (observing that “[o]bviously, [the victim-competitor] could not have committed involuntary manslaughter with respect to his own death”). In addition, pursuant to the legislative-exemption rule, victims may not be convicted as accomplices. See, e.g., *Model Penal Code*, § 2.06(6)(a). See also *In re Meagan R.*, 42 Cal. App. 4th 17 (Ct. App. 1996). (Meagan R. could not be legally an accomplice in her own statutory rape and thus could not be an accomplice to burglary based on the intent to commit the statutory rape.)

50. *Commonwealth v. Peak*, 12 Pa. D. and C.2d 379, 381 (1957).

51. Ibid., 382.

52. See, e.g., *Commonwealth v. Root*, 170 A.2d 310, 314 (Pa. 1961).

53. Kalven, Jr., and Zeisel, *American Jury*, 243–44.

54. Ibid., 234.

55. See, e.g., *Model Penal Code*, § 210.4(2).

56. *Model Penal Code*, § 211.2.

57. *French v. Camp*, 18 Me. 433, 435 (Me. 1841).

58. Hohfeld, *Fundamental Legal Conceptions*, 38; Thomson, *Realm of Rights*, 323.

59. Universal Declaration of Human Rights, G.A. Res. 217A, at 71, U.N. GAOR, 3d Sess., 1st plen. mtg., U.N. Doc. A/810, Art. 5, December 12, 1948.

60. Universal Declaration of Human Rights, G.A. Res. 217A, at 71, U.N. GAOR, 3d Sess., 1st plen. mtg., U.N. Doc. A/810Art. 5, December 12, 1948. Compare with, for example, Art. 9 ("No one shall be subjected to arbitrary arrest, detention or exile"); Art. 17 ("No one shall be arbitrarily deprived of his property"); or Art. 12. ("No one shall be subjected to arbitrary interference with his privacy, family, home or correspondence, nor to attacks upon his honour and reputation.") Ibid.

61. *Public Committee Against Torture in Israel v. State of Israel*, HCJ 5100/94 [1999] IsrSC 53(4)817, available at http://www.derechos.org/human-rights/mena/doc/torture.html. ¶23.

62. Ibid.

63. *Sensobaugh v. State*, 244 S.W. 379, 379 (Tex. App. 1922).

64. Ibid.

65. Ibid.

66. Husak, "Comparative Fault in Criminal Law," 533.

67. Ibid.

68. *Government Guarantee Fund v. Hyatt Corp.*, 95 F.3d 291, 303 (3d Cir. 1996).

69. *Model Penal Code*, § 213.1(1).

70. See, e.g., Denno, "Sexual Offense Provisions," 209–10 (criticizing the MPC rape rules). In addition to the cited provision, the gender-specific language (*Model Penal Code*, §§ 213.1–213[4]; the marital rape exception §§ 213.1–213[4]; the offense of seduction by promise to marry § 213.3[1][d]; and available in certain instances defense of the victim's sexual promiscuity § 213.6[3]) are, to put it mildly, outdated and embarrassing to see in an influential document like the MPC.

71. See *U.S. Sentencing Guidelines Manual*, § 5K2.10 (1999).

72. *Alaska Stat.* §§ 12.55.155(d)(7), 11.41.410–70 (2002).

73. See Fletcher, "Domination in Wrongdoing," 356.

74. Hohfeld, *Fundamental Legal Conceptions*, 23, 36.

75. See Thomson, *Realm of Rights*, 61–78.

76. Hohfeld, *Fundamental Legal Conceptions*, 36–38.

77. Ibid., 38–50.

78. Ibid., 60.

79. Harel, "Victims and Perpetrators," 494.

80. Ibid.

81. Ibid., 492.
82. Ibid., 493.
83. Ortiz de Urbina Gimeno, "Old Wine in New Wineskins?" 824.
84. Husak, "Comparative Fault in Criminal Law," 535.
85. Ibid.
86. Ibid., 536.
87. Dietz et al., "Homicide," § 170.
88. See Perkins, *Criminal Law*, 1018–19; Blackstone, *Commentaries*, vol. 3, facsimile ed., 3.
89. LaFave, *Criminal Law*, 550.
90. See, e.g., *Ducket v. State*, 966 P.2d 941, 944–45 (Wyo. 1998).
91. *Leeper v. State*, 589 P.2d. 379, 383 (Wyo. 1979).
92. Husak, "Comparative Fault," 537.
93. Simons, "Relevance of Victim Conduct," 559.
94. See discussion about two variations of the defense of provocation in Chapter 3 under "Provocation and Its Triggers: The Case of Adultery."
95. Husak, "Comparative Fault," 537.
96. *Schmidt v. U.S.*, 177 F. F.2d 450, 451 (2d Cir. 1949).
97. *Johnson v. U.S.*, 186 F.2d 588, 589 (2d Cir. 1951).
98. *Schmidt v. U.S.*, 177 F. F.2d 450, 451 (2d Cir. 1949).
99. *Lawrence v. Texas*, 539 U.S. 558 (2003).
100. See ibid., 571.
101. Ibid.
102. Ibid.
103. *Lawrence v. Texas*, 539 U.S. 558, 578 (2003).
104. *Bowers v. Hardwick*, 478 U.S. 186, 193–94 (1986).
105. See Hart, *Law, Liberty and Morality*, 20.
106. Ronald Dworkin, *Liberty and Moralism*, 248.
107. Husak, "Comparative Fault," 533–34.
108. Bergelson "Conditional Rights and Comparative Wrongs," 579–81.
109. Ronald Dworkin, *Liberty and Moralism*, 250.
110. Ibid., 255.
111. Ibid.
112. Ibid.
113. Ibid.
114. *Johnson v. U.S.*, 186 F.2d 588, 589, 590 (2d Cir. 1951).
115. See, e.g., *People v. Phyfe*, 32 N.E. 978 (1893) (holding that a "citizen is entitled to an unequivocal warning before conduct on his part . . . can be made the occasion of a deprivation of his liberty or property"); *People v. Arroyo*, 777 N.Y.S. 2d 836, 844 (2004) (applying the same rule).

116. Dressler, *Understanding Criminal Law*, 39.

117. Ibid., 157.

118. *Regina v. Prince*, L.R. 2 Cr. Cas. Res. 154 (1875).

119. Ibid.

120. See, e.g., Brett, "Criminal Responsibility," 480–81.

121. Gruber, "Victim Wrongs," 713–14.

122. Ibid., 727 n. 360. Since, for Gruber, an act of battery does not necessarily shock the conscience, neither would probably simple trespass or theft.

123. Simons, "Relevance of Victim Conduct," 564.

124. See *Model Penal Code*, § 211.2.

125. See, e.g., *Cox v. State*, 534 A.2d 1333, 1336 (Md. 1988) (an attempt to kill a provoker is punishable as an attempted voluntary manslaughter); *State v. Robinson*, 643 A.2d 591, 597 (NJ 1994) (same).

126. See *Model Penal Code*, § 3.09(3).

127. See Hurd, "Deontology of Negligence," 249–72; Hurd, "Nonreciprocal Risk Imposition"; Hurd, "What in the World," 193–208. See also Perry, "Risk, Harm, and Responsibility."

128. See, e.g., Finkelstein, "New Perspectives and Legal Implications," 987–90; Oberdiek, "Towards a Right Against Risking," forthcoming, see http://www.springerlink.com/content/e046988818363041/?p=a4358958222046e89adf1efaa59d0e6e&pi=3.

129. Raz, *Morality of Freedom*, 398.

130. Oberdiek, "Towards a Right Against Risking," *7–8.

131. Finkelstein, "New Perspectives and Legal Implications," 973.

132. McCarthy, "Rights, Explanation, and Risks," 211 (footnote omitted). This example is also discussed by Robert Nozick and Judith Jarvis Thomson. See Nozick, *Anarchy, State and Utopia*, 82; Thomson, "Some Questions About Government Regulation," 167.

133. Thomson, "Some Questions About Government Regulation," 167.

Chapter 5

1. See, e.g., http://www.publicagenda.org/issues/factfiles_detail.cfm?issue_type=right2die&list=10.

2. Hegland, "Suggestions, Not Demands,"15.

3. Hilfiker, "Allowing the Debilitated to Die," 718.

4. Posner, "Are We One Self," 32.

5. Ibid.

6. Ronald Dworkin, *Life's Dominion*, 220–21.

7. Ibid.

8. Ibid.

9. Most state statutes limit the authority of a living will to withhold or withdraw lifesaving treatment to situations when the patient is in a persistent vegetative state or is suffering a condition that is both terminal and irreversible. See, e.g., *Wright v. Johns Hopkins Health Sys. Corp.*, 728 A.2d 166, 169–70 (Md. 1999). See also Kusmin, "Swing Low, Sweet Chariot," 96.

10. Ronald Dworkin, *Life's Dominion*, 220–21.

11. Feinberg, *Harm to Self*, 181.

12. Cantor, *Advance Directives*, 27.

13. See, e.g., Feinberg, *Harm to Self*, 81-87.

14. See *Uniform Rights of the Terminally Ill Act* 4, 9B *U.L.A.* 616 (1989); *Oregon Death with Dignity Act*, 1995 *Or. Laws* Ch. 3, § 3.07 (I.M. No. 16) (1995).

15. See, e.g., *State v. Way*, 254 S.E.2d 760, 762 (N.C. 1979) (holding that "[i]f the actual penetration is accomplished with the woman's consent, the accused is not guilty of rape, although he may be guilty of another crime because of his subsequent actions"), *Battle v. State*, 414 A.2d 1266, 1270 (Md. App. 1980) (holding that, if a woman "consents prior to penetration and withdraws consent following penetration, there is no rape").

16. *People v. Vela*, 172 Cal. App. 3d 237, 243 (1985).

17. *In re John Z.*, 29 Cal. 4th 756, 786 (2003). See also *State v. Robinson*, 496 A.2d 1067, 1070–71 (Me. 1985); *McGill v. State*, 18 P.3d 77, 84 (Alas. App. 2001); *State v. Siering*, 644 A.2d 958, 963–64 (Conn. App. 1994); *State v. Bunyard*, 133 P.3d 14, 29 (Kan. 2006) (overruled in part by *State v. Gaither*, 156 P.3d 602, 612 [Kan. 2007]). So far, the issue of postpenetration rape has been expressly addressed by courts in eight states (Alaska, California, Connecticut, Kansas, Maine, Maryland, North Carolina, and South Dakota). All but two of them (in Maryland and North Carolina) held that rape may occur after the initial consensual penetration. Courts in two other states, Minnesota and New Mexico, upheld rape convictions notwithstanding appellants' assertions that a procedural error occurred when the judge refused to instruct the jury on the difference between nonconsensual intercourse and revocation of consent during the intercourse. See Davis, "Clarifying the Issue of Consent," 744 n. 125.

18. 720 *Ill. Comp. Stat. Ann.* 5/12–17 (West 2004).

19. *In Re John Z.*, 29 Cal. 4th 756, 763 (2003).

20. Ibid.

21. *State v. Bunyard*, 75 P.3d 750, 756 (Kan. App. 2003).

22. *State v. Bunyard*, 133 P.3d 14, 49 (Kan. 2006).

23. Ibid.

24. Maguigan, "Battered Women and Self-Defense," 394–97.

25. See Dressler, "Battered Women and Sleeping Abusers," 457 n. 1.

26. Several significant works have been published on this subject in recent years alone. See, e.g., Dressler, "Battered Women and Sleeping Abusers"; Ferzan, "Defending

Imminence"; Kaufman, "Self-Defense"; Kraus, "Distorted Reflections"; Lee, *Murder and the Reasonable Man.*

27. See, e.g., *Kansas v. Smith*, 864 P.2d 709, 716 (Kan. 1993) (requiring "an imminent threat or confrontational circumstance involving an overt act by an aggressor" even when long-term domestic abuse is involved). But see *Colorado v. Yaklich*, 833 P.2d 758, 762 (Colo. App. 1991) (finding that whether a battered spouse may claim self-defense in the absence of an immediate physical threat depends on how the jurisdiction defines "imminent danger").

28. *Model Penal Code*, § 3.04 (1) (requiring that the force used by the defendant be "immediately necessary for the purpose of protecting himself against the use of unlawful force . . . on the present occasion").

29. *Model Penal Code*, cmt. 2(c) at 40.

30. Robinson, "Criminal Law Defenses," vol. 2 § 131(c) at 78.

31. Rosen, "On Self-Defense," 405–6.

32. Morse, "Diminished Rationality, Diminished Responsibility," 298.

33. Morse, " 'New Syndrome Excuse' Syndrome," 12.

34. *State v. Norman*, 366 S.E.2d 586, 587 (N.C. Ct. App. 1988).

35. Ibid., 588.

36. Ibid., 588–89.

37. *State v. Norman*, 324 N.C. 253 (N.C. 1989)

38. Ibid., 261 (quoting *Black's Law Dictionary* 676 [5th ed. 1979]).

39. Ibid.

40. Ibid., 261

41. Morse, "Neither Desert nor Disease," 308.

42. Ibid.

43. See ibid.

44. Rosen, "On Self-Defense," 411.

45. Robinson, "Criminal Law Defenses," § 131(B)(3).

46. Rodin, *War and Self-Defense*, 41.

47. Ferzan, "Defending Imminence," 261–62.

48. Morse, " 'New Syndrome Excuse' Syndrome,"12.

49. *R. v. Dudley and Stephens*, 14 Q.B.D. 273 (1884).

50. Ibid.

51. Here I am distinguishing situations in which, but for the acts of the perpetrator, the victim would have lived from situations like the one discussed immediately below in which the victim would have died no matter what. See *In re A (Children) (Conjoined Twins: Surgical Separation)* [2001] Fam. 147.

52. *In re A (Children) (Conjoined Twins: Surgical Separation)* [2001] Fam. 147 at 173 (opinion of Lord Ward L.J.).

53. Ibid.

54. Fitzpatrick, "Jodie and Mary."

55. *State v. Norman*, 378 S.E.2d 8, 21 (N.C. 1989) (Martin, J., dissenting).

56. Dressler, "Battered Women and Sleeping Abusers," 465–66.

57. Ibid., 467.

58. Ibid., 465.

59. *Model Penal Code*, § 3.04(2)(b)(i) (emphasis added).

60. *Model Penal Code*, § 3.04(2)(b)(i) cmt. 4(b) at 52.

61. Dressler, "Battered Women and Sleeping Abusers," 469.

62. Ibid., 470.

63. A few states authorize mitigation from murder to manslaughter when the killing was committed under duress. See, e.g., *Minn. Stat.* 609.20(3) (1987 and Supp. 1999); *Wentworth v. State*, 349 A.2d 421, 427–28 (Md. Ct. Spec. App. 1975).

64. *Model Penal Code*, § 2.09 cmt. 3, 376.

65. *Prosecutor v. Erdemovic*, No. IT-96-22-A (October 7, 1997), 4.

66. Ibid., Separate Opinion of Judge McDonald and Judge Vohrah, para. 66.

67. *Model Penal Code*, § 2.09 cmt. 3, 369–70.

68. *Model Penal Code*, § 2.09 cmt. 3, 376.

69. Coughlin, "Excusing Women," 7.

70. Horder, "Killing the Passive Abuser," 283, 295 (emphasis added).

71. Morse, "Diminished Rationality, Diminished Responsibility," 300.

72. For discussion of victims'conduct after the offense that may affect the perpetrators' liability, see discussion in Chapter 6 under "Comparative Causation."

Chapter 6

1. See Sisk, "Comparative Fault and Common Sense," 40–41 (discussing similar factors considered by the Supreme Court of Louisiana in *Watson v. State Fire & Casualty Insurance Company*, 469 So. 2d 967 [La. 1985], a tort action for wrongful death arising out of a hunting accident).

2. Under the Model Penal Code, a simple assault is a misdemeanor and an aggravated assault is a felony of the third or second degree. See *Model Penal Code*, § 211.1.

3. See discussion supra, in Chapter 3 under "Provocation and Its Triggers: The Case of Adultery."

4. Quoting Justice Oliver W. Holmes,

> It is revolting to have no better reason for a rule of law than that so it was laid down in the time of Henry IV. It is still more revolting if the grounds upon which it was laid down have vanished long since, and the rule simply persists from blind imitation of the past. ("Path of the Law," 469)

5. *Burns Ind. Code Ann.* § 35-41-3-2 (2005).

6. Recent Florida law allows use of deadly force to prevent, among other felonies, carjacking. It is obvious from the context, however, that the purpose of the law is to provide protection against a felony which "involves the use or threat of physical force or violence against any *individual*." *Florida Statutes Title XLVI*, §§ 776.012, 776.06 (emphasis added).

7. *State v. Morgan*, 25 N.C. 186 (1842).

8. Ibid., 193.

9. *Model Penal Code*, § 3.06(3)(b). See also *Neb. Rev. Stat.* § 28-1411(4) (2006); *N.J. Stat. Ann.* § 2C:3-6(b)(2) (West. 2006); 18 *Pa. Cons. Stat.* § 507(c)(2) (2006) (stating a rule that a trespasser may not be expelled in circumstances in which extreme harm is likely to befall him).

10. *State v. Shack*, 277 A.2d 369, 372 (N.J. 1971).

11. *People v. Epps*, 197 Ill. App. 3d 376 (Ill. App. 1990).

12. *People v. Epps*, 197 Ill. App. 3d 376, 383 (Ill. App. 1990).

13. Katz, *Ill-Gotten Gains*, 147.

14. Ibid., 151.

15. Ibid.

16. Gruber, "Victim Wrongs," 652.

17. Gruber recognizes this problem:

> Admittedly, this is quite conceptually prickly when the intervening event is the operation of the defendant's own free will, because it can slip down a slope into speculative arguments about the operation of the human mind and the human will. One is forced to confront the issue of whether one human being's act can truly ever "cause" another person to do anything. (Ibid., 717–18)

18. Thomson, "Causality and Rights," 477. See also Kelman, "Necessary Myth," 579.

19. See Pearson, "Apportionment of Losses," 346.

20. See, e.g., Mackie, *Cement of the Universe*, 128 ("[i]f two factors are each necessary in the circumstances, they are equally necessary"); Kelman, "Necessary Myth," 579 ("there is no obvious way to distinguish, on purely causal grounds, the relative causal contributions of two wholly necessary parties").

21. See Strassfeld, "Causal Comparisons," 919 (citing E. White, *Why Rome Fell* [1927]).

22. Ibid., 920 (citing examples from works by Martin and Nagel).

23. For an in-depth discussion of causation in torts, see "Symposium on Causation in the Law of Torts," 397–680.

24. Sisk, "Comparative Fault and Common Sense," 43. This method has its limitations. See, e.g., Thomson, "Causality and Rights," 482.

25. Strassfeld, "Causal Comparisons," 937.

26. Richard Wright, "Causation in Tort Law," 1790 (emphasis deleted).

27. See Hart and Honore, "Causation in the Law," 66. The authors point out that both in legal usage and in ordinary speech causation means more than just "but for" factual connection: "it is a disguised way of asserting the 'normative' judgment that he is responsible in the first sense, i.e., that it is proper or just to blame or punish him or make him pay."

28. Strassfeld, "Causal Comparisons," 937.

29. *Everett v. State*, 435 So. 2d 955 (Fla. App. 1983).

30. Ibid., 957.

31. Ibid., 958.

32. Ibid.

33. *Wren v. State*, 577 P.2d 235, 240–41 (Alas. 1978).

34. Bohlen, "Moral Duty to Aid Others," 220–21.

35. Thomson, "Causality and Rights," 493–95.

36. Ibid., 495.

37. Ibid.

38. Smith and Hogan, *Criminal Law*, 342. ("The common law rule is that neglect or maltreatment by the injured person of himself does not exempt the defendant from liability for his ultimate death.")

39. *Regina v. Blaue*, 3 All E.R. 446 (C.A. 1975).

40. Ibid., 450.

41. See, e.g., *Model Penal Code*, § 2.01(3).

42. *State v. Perez-Cervantes*, 141 Wn.2d 468, 479–80 (2000).

43. *Regina v. Dear*, [1996] Crim. L.R. 595 (C.A. 1996).

44. Beale, "Proximate Consequences of an Act," 651.

45. *State v. Preslar*, 48 N.C. 421, 428 (N.C. 1856).

46. Hart and Honore, *Causation in the Law*, 326.

47. See LaFave, *Substantive Criminal Law*, 346–47.

48. *Stephenson v. State*, 179 N.E. 633 (Ind. 1932).

49. Ibid., 636.

50. Ibid.

51. Ibid., 645.

52. See ibid., 646–47.

53. Ibid., 637.

54. See, e.g., "Criminal Law and Procedure," 668–74.

55. See ibid.

56. *Jones v. State*, 3 N.E.2d 1017, 1018 (Ind. 1942).

57. Ibid., 1018.

58. *People v. Oliver*, 210 Cal. App. 3d 138 (Cal. App. 1989).

59. Ibid., 149.

60. *Stephenson v. State*, 179 N.E. 633, 649 (Ind. 1932).

61. Ibid.

62. Ibid.

63. Simons, "Relevance of Victim Conduct," 564.

64. See, e.g., Moore, "Causation and Responsibility," 9–13; Richard Wright, "Causation in Tort Law."

65. Moore, "Metaphysics of Causal Intervention," 847.

66. See Moore, "Causation and Responsibility,"10.

67. Simons, "Relevance of Victim Conduct," 564.

68. See, e.g., Moore, "Causation and Responsibility," 29–30. See also *Corey v. Havener*, 65 N.E. 69 (1902) (holding both defendants liable in a case where each rode his motorcycle by the victim's horse and a frightened horse injured the victim, although the noise of even one motorcycle would have been sufficient to produce the same result).

69. Hall, *General Principles of Criminal Law*, 247, 268.

70. Moore, "Metaphysics of Causal Intervention," 859.

71. See discussion in Chapter 3 under "Aggressors and Defenders in Cases of Self-Defense."

72. *Johnson v. Texas*, 509 U.S. 350, 367 (1993).

73. *Commonwealth v. Malone*, 47 A.2d 445 (Pa. 1946).

74. Ibid., 466.

75. See discussion in Chapter 4 under "Involuntary Reduction of Rights."

76. *State v. Munnell*, 344 N.W.2d 883 (Minn. App. 1984).

77. Ibid., 885.

78. Holmes, *The Common Law* 7.

79. Perhaps, recognizing that a jury would be unlikely to deliver a guilty verdict in a case in which the victim was found to be more at fault than the defendant, the prosecutor entered into a plea bargain with the defendant upon remand of the case to the trial level. As a result, homicide charges were dropped; the defendant pleaded guilty to the misdemeanor of driving under the influence and was sentenced to forty-five days in jail and one year of probation. See Commitment upon Sentence, *State v. Munnell* (Minn. Dist. Ct., Itasca County, 9th Judicial Dist., August 16, 1984).

80. See *Model Penal Code*, § 1.12(2)(a). Consent to killing may serve as an example of a situation in which the burden of persuasion should be imposed on the defendant.

81. Husak, "Comparative Fault in Criminal Law," 525.

82. Ibid., 525–26.

83. Ibid., 526.

84. *Schmuck v. U.S.*, 489 U.S. 705, 716 (1989).

85. Lundy, "Jury Instruction Corner," 48. See also *Carter v. U.S.*, 530 U.S. 255 (2000); *Hopkins v. Reeves*, 524 U.S. 88 (1998).

86. See Lundy, "Jury Instruction Corner," 48; *Brown v. Commonwealth*, 555 S.W. 2d 252, 257 (Ky. 1977). ("Evidence suggesting that the defendant was guilty of a lesser offense is, in fact and in principle, a defense against the higher charge.")

87. *Sanborn v. Commonwealth*, 754 S. W.2d 534 (Ky. 1988).

88. Ibid., 549.

89. See Lundy, "Jury Instruction Corner," 48.

90. *United States v. Scheffer*, 523 U.S. 303, 308 (U.S. 1998).

91. See, e.g., *Ariz. Rev. Stat.* § 13-601 (1989) (10 grades of offense); *Del. Code Ann.* tit. 11, §§ 4201, 4202, 4203 (1994) (10 grades); 730 *Ill. Comp. Stat. Ann.* 5/5-5-1 (West 1993) (11 grades); *Neb. Rev. Stat.* §§ 28-105, 28-106 (1995) (15 grades); *N.Y. Penal Law* §§ 55.05, 55.10(3) (McKinney 1998) (10 grades); *Ohio Rev. Code Ann.* § 2901.02 (West 1998) (12 grades). See also Cahill, "Offense Grading and Multiple Liability," 602; Robinson et al., "Five Worst (and Five Best)," 19.

92. *Model Penal Code*, § 211.1(1). Many states follow the same punishment structure. See, e.g., *HRS* § 707-712 (2007), *RSA* 631:2-a (2007), *RSA* 642:9 (2007), *N.J. Stat.* § 2C:12-1 (2007).

93. 18 *Pa.C.S.* § 2701.

94. See Simons, "Relevance of Victim Conduct," 565.

95. *Model Penal Code*, §§ 210.2, 210.3.

BIBLIOGRAPHY

ABC News. "TB Patient Asks Forgiveness but Defends Travel." ABCNews.com. June 1, 2007. http://abcnews.go.com/GMA/OnCall/story?id=3231184&page=1.

Acker, James R., and Charles Lanier. "In Fairness and Mercy: Statutory Mitigation Factors in Capital Punishment Laws." *Criminal Law Bulletin* 30 (1994): 299–345.

Adams, Aileen, and David Osborne. "Victims' Rights and Services: A Historical Perspective and Goals for the Twenty-First Century." *McGeorge Law Review* 33 (2002): 673–88.

Alexander, Lawrence A. "Justification and Innocent Aggressors." *Wayne Law Review* 33 (1987): 1177–89.

———. "Propter Honoris Respectum: A Unified Excuse or Preemptive Self-Protection." *Notre Dame Law Review* 74 (1999): 1475–1505.

American Law Institute. "39th Annual Meeting." *American Law Institute Proceedings.* Philadelphia: American Law Institute, 1962.

———. "79th Annual Meeting." *American Law Institute Proceedings.* Philadelphia: American Law Institute, 1999.

———. *Restatement (Second) of Torts.* St. Paul, Minn.: American Law Institute, 1965.

———. *Restatement (Third) of Torts: Apportionment of Liability, Proposed Final Draft.* Philadelphia: American Law Institute, 1998.

Anttila, Inkeri. "Victimology: A New Territory in Criminology." In *Victimology: A New Focus*, edited by Israel Drapkin and Emilio Viano, 1:5–8. Lexington, Mass.: Lexington Books, 1974.

Arison, Neville H. "Victims of Homicide." In *Victimology: A New Focus*, edited by Israel Drapkin and Emilio Viano, 4:55–68. Lexington, Mass.: Lexington Books, 1974.

Ashworth, Andrew J. "The Doctrine of Provocation." *Cambridge Law Journal* 35 (1976): 292–320.

Austin, John Langshaw. "A Plea for Excuses." *Proceedings of the Aristotelian Society,* n.s., 57 (1956–57): 1–30.

———. "A Plea for Excuses." In *Freedom and Responsibility: Readings in Philosophy and Law,* edited by Herbert Morris, 6–19. Stanford, Calif.: Stanford University Press, 1961.

Baumer, Eric P., et al. "The Role of Victim Characteristics in the Disposition of Murder Cases." *Justice Quarterly* 17 (2000): 281–308.

Bayne, Tim, and Neil Levy. "Amputees by Choice: Body Integrity Identity Disorder and the Ethics of Amputation." *Journal of Applied Philosophy* 22 (2005): 75–85.

Beale, Joseph H. "The Proximate Consequences of an Act." *Harvard Law Review* 33 (1920): 633–58.

Bergelson, Vera. "Conditional Rights and Comparative Wrongs: More on the Theory and Application of Comparative Criminal Liability." *Buffalo Criminal Law Review* 8 (2005): 567–97.

———. "The Right to Be Hurt: Testing the Boundaries of Consent." *George Washington Law Review* 75 (2007): 165–236.

———. "Rights, Wrongs, and Comparative Justifications." *Cardozo Law Review* 28 (2007): 2481–2503.

Best, Arthur, et al. *Comparative Negligence Law and Practice.* Newark, N.J.: Matthew Bender and Company, 2003.

Blackstone, William. *Commentaries on the Laws of England.* Philadelphia: J.B. Lippincott, 1904.

———. *Commentaries on the Laws of England.* Facsimile ed. Chicago: University of Chicago Press, 1979.

Bohlen, Francis. "The Moral Duty to Aid Others as the Basis of Tort Liability." *University of Pennsylvania Law Review* 56 (1908): 217–44.

Brett, Peter. "Criminal Responsibility." *Stanford Law Review* 16 (1964): 470–85.

Bridy, Annemarie. "Confounding Extremities: Surgery at the Medico-ethical Limits of Self-Modification. *Journal of Law, Medicine and Ethics* 32 (2004): 148–55.

Brody, Jane E. "Personal Health: Why Cancer-Free Women Have Breasts Removed." *New York Times,* May 5, 1993, Health section. http://www.proquest.com (accessed November 26, 2007).

Bublick, Ellen M. "Citizen No-Duty Rules: Rape Victims and Comparative Fault." *Columbia Law Review* 99 (1999): 1413–90.

———. "The End Game of Tort Reform: Comparative Apportionment and Intentional Torts." *Notre Dame Law Review* 78 (2003): 355–439.

Buchwald, Art. "Coddling Victims of Crime Underlies Grim Statistics." *Washington Post,* February 4, 1969, section A15.

Burkhardt, Bjorn. "Is There a Rational Justification for Punishing an Accomplished Crime More Severely Than an Attempted Crime?" *Brigham Young University Law Review* 1986 (1986): 553–71.

Cahill, Michael T. "Offense Grading and Multiple Liability: New Challenges for a Model Penal Code Second." *Ohio State Journal of Criminal Law* 1 (2004): 599–610.

Callahan, Daniel, and Margot White. "The Legalization of Physician-Assisted Suicide: Creating a Regulatory Potemkin Village." *University of Richmond Law Review* 30 (1996): 1–83.

Cantor, Norman L. *Advance Directives and the Pursuit of Death with Dignity.* Bloomington: Indiana University Press, 1993.

———. "A Patient's Decision to Decline Life-Saving Medical Treatment: Bodily Integrity Versus the Preservation of Life." *Rutgers Law Review* 26 (1973): 228–64.

Claster, Daniel C. *Bad Guys and Good Guys: Moral Polarization and Crime.* Westport, Conn.: Greenwood Press, 1992.

CNN. "Perverse Cannibal Killer Gets Life." CNN.com. May 9, 2006. http://www.cnn.com/2006/WORLD/europe/05/09/cannibal.trial/index.html.

Committee on Homosexual Offenses and Prostitution. *The Wolfenden Report: Report of the Committee on Homosexual Offenses and Prostitution.* London: HM Stationery Office, 1957.

Cook, Michael. "Moral Mayhem of Murder on the Menu." *Herald Sun,* January 15, 2004, Melbourne, Australia edition, Opinion, 17.

Coughlin, Anne M. "Excusing Women." *California Law Review* 88 (1994): 759–78.

"Criminal Law and Procedure—Homicide—Causal Relation between Defendant's Unlawful Act and the Death." *Michigan Law Review* 31 (1933): 659–82.

Curtis, Lynn A. "Victim Precipitation and Violent Crime." *Social Problems* 21 (1974): 594–605.

Dan-Cohen, Meir. "Basic Values and the Victim's State of Mind." *California Law Review* 88 (2000): 759–78.

———. *Harmful Thoughts: Essays on Law, Self, and Morality.* Princeton, N.J.: Princeton University Press, 2002.

Darley, John M., et al. "Incapacitation and Just Deserts as Motives for Punishment." *Law and Human Behavior* 24 (2000): 659–83.

Davis, Amanda O. "Clarifying the Issue of Consent: The Evolution of Post-Penetration Rape Law." *Stetson Law Review* 34 (2005): 729–66.

Davis, Nancy. "Abortion and Self-Defense." *Philosophy and Public Affairs* 13 (1984): 175–207.

D'Emilio, John, and Estelle B. Freedman. *Intimate Matters: A History of Sexuality in America.* 2d ed. Chicago: University of Chicago Press, 1997.

Denno, Deborah W. "Why the Model Penal Code's Sexual Offense Provisions Should Be Pulled and Replaced." *Ohio State Journal of Criminal Law* 1 (2003): 207–18.

Dietz, Laura, et al. "Homicide." Section 170. *American Jurisprudence.* 2d ed. Eagan, Minn: Thomson West 2007.

Dizon, Nikko. "Tourists Here to See Filipinos Crucify Selves." *Philippine Daily Inquirer*, March 22, 2005, Philippines, front page.

Dobbs, Dan B. *The Law of Torts*. 2 vols. St. Paul, Minn.: West Group, 2001.

Dressler, Joshua. "Battered Women and Sleeping Abusers: Some Reflections." *Ohio State Journal of Criminal Law* 3 (2006): 457–71.

———. "New Thoughts about the Concept of Justification in the Criminal Law: A Critique of Fletcher's Thinking and Rethinking." *UCLA Law Review* 32 (1984): 61–99.

———. "Provocation: Partial Justification or Partial Excuse." *Modern Law Review* 51 (1988): 467–80.

———. "Rethinking Heat of Passion." *Journal of Criminal Law and Criminology* 73 (1982): 421–70.

———. *Understanding Criminal Law*. New York: Lexis Pub., 2001.

———. "When 'Heterosexual' Men Kill 'Homosexual' Men: Reflections on Provocation Law, Sexual Advances, and the 'Reasonable Man' Standard." *Journal of Criminal Law and Criminology* 85 (1995): 726–63.

———. "Why Keep the Provocation Defense? Some Reflections on a Difficult Subject." *Minnesota Law Review* 86 (2002): 959–1002.

Dubber, Markus Dirk. "Toward a Constitutional Law of Crime and Punishment." *Hastings Law Journal* 55 (2004): 509–72.

———. "The Victim in American Penal Law: A Systematic Overview." *Buffalo Criminal Law Review* 3 (1999): 3–31.

———. *Victims in the War on Crime: The Use and Abuse of Victims' Rights*. New York: New York University Press, 2002.

Duff, R. A. "Harms and Wrongs." *Buffalo Criminal Law Review* 5 (2001): 13–44.

Dworkin, Gerald. "Paternalism." In *Morality and the Law*. Belmont, Calif.: Wadsworth, 1971.

———. "Paternalism." *Stanford Encyclopedia of Philosophy* (2005), available at http://plato.stanford.edu/entries/paternalism.

Dworkin, Ronald. *Liberty and Moralism in Taking Rights Seriously*. Cambridge, Mass.: Harvard University Press, 1977.

———. *Life's Dominion: An Argument About Abortion, Euthanasia, and Individual Freedom*. New York: Knopf, 1993.

"Editorial: Tyson Takes the Count." *The Nation*, March 2, 1992, 254.

Elliot, Carl. "A New Way to Be Mad." *Atlantic Monthly*, December 2000, 73–84. http://www.theatlantic.com/doc/prem/200012/madness.

ESPN. "Queens Man in San Francisco for One Day Catches Famous Ball." ESPN.com. Updated August 9, 2007. http://sports.espn.go.com/mlb/news/story?id=2965703.

Falco, Melanie C. "The Road Not Taken: Using the Eighth Amendment to Strike Down Criminal Punishment for Engaging in Consensual Sexual Acts." *North Carolina Law Review* 82 (2004): 723–58.

Feinberg, Joel. "The Mistreatment of Dead Bodies." *Hastings Center Report* 15 (1) (February 1985): 31–37.

———. *The Moral Limits of Criminal Law: Harm to Others*. Vol. 1. New York: Oxford University Press, 1984.

———. *The Moral Limits of Criminal Law: Harm to Self*. Vol. 2. New York: Oxford University Press, 1988.

———. "Voluntary Euthanasia and the Inalienable Right to Life." *Philosophy and Public Affairs* 7 (1978): 93–123.

Ferzan, Kimberly Kessler. "Defending Imminence: From Battered Women to Iraq." *Arizona Law Review* 46 (2004): 213–62.

Field, Hubert S., and Leigh B. Bienen. *Jurors and Rape: A Study in Psychology and Law*. Lexington, Mass.: Lexington Books, 1980.

Finkelstein, Claire. "New Perspectives and Legal Implications: Is Risk a Harm?" *University of Pennsylvania Law Review* 151 (2003): 963–1001.

———. "On the Obligation of the State to Extend a Right of Self-Defense to Its Citizens." *University of Pennsylvania Law Review* 147 (1999): 1361–1402.

Finn, Peter. "Cannibal Case Grips Germany; Suspect Says Internet Correspondent Volunteered to Die." *Washington Post*, December 4, 2003, section A26, Foreign Service edition.

Fitzpatrick, John. "Jodie and Mary: Whose Choice Was It Anyway?" *Spiked Liberties*, June 19, 2001. http://www.spiked-online.com/Articles/00000000540E.htm.

Fletcher, George P. "Corrective Justice for Moderns." *Harvard Law Review* 106 (1993): 1658–78.

———. "Domination in Wrongdoing." *Boston University Law Review* 76 (1996): 347–60.

———. *The Grammar of Criminal Law: American, Comparative, and International*. New York: Oxford University Press, 2007.

———. "The Place of Victims in the Theory of Retribution." *Buffalo Criminal Law Review* 3 (1999): 51–63.

———. "Proportionality and the Psychotic Aggressor: A Vignette in Comparative Criminal Theory." *Israel Law Review* 8 (1973): 367–90.

———. *Rethinking Criminal Law*. Boston: Little, Brown, 1978.

———. "The Right Deed for the Wrong Reason." *UCLA Law Review* 23 (1975): 293–321.

———. "Should Intolerable Prison Conditions Generate a Justification or an Excuse for Escape?" *UCLA Law Review* 26 (1979): 1355–69.

Freeman, Gregory A. "Bug Chasers: The Men Who Long to Be HIV+." *Rolling Stone*, February 6, 2003. http://www.rollingstone.com/news/story/5933610/bug_chasers.

Gibson, Mary. "Rationality." *Philosophy and Public Affairs* 6 (1977): 193–225.

Goodman, Tim. "Reality TV Hits a Tailspin with NBC's 'Fear Factor.'" *San Francisco Chronicle*, June 11, 2001, section E-1, Final edition.

Greenawalt, Kent. "Distinguishing Justifications from Excuses." *Law and Contemporary Problems* 49 (1986): 89–111.

———. "The Perplexing Borders of Justification and Excuse." *Columbia Law Review* 84 (1984): 1897–1927.

———. "Punishment." In *Encyclopedia of Crime and Justice*, edited by Sanford H. Kadish, 4: 1336–45. New York: Free Press, 1983.

Grey, Betsy J. "The New Federalism Jurisprudence and National Tort Reform." *Washington and Lee Law Review* 59 (2002): 475–538.

Gruber, Aya. "Righting Victim Wrongs: Responding to Philosophical Criticisms of the Nonspecific Victim Liability Defense." *Buffalo Law Review* 52 (2004): 433–510.

———. "Victim Wrongs: The Case for a General Criminal Defense Based on Wrongful Victim Behavior in an Era of Victims' Rights." *Temple Law Review* 76 (2003): 645–738.

Hall, Jerome. *General Principles of Criminal Law.* 2d ed. Indianapolis: Bobbs-Merrill, 1960.

Haney, Craig. "Mitigation and the Study of Lives: On the Roots of Violent Criminality and the Nature of Capital Justice." In *America's Experiment with Capital Punishment*, edited by James R. Acker et al., 351–84. Durham, N.C.: Carolina Academic Press, 1998.

Harding, Luke. "Victim of Cannibal Agreed to Be Eaten." *Guardian Unlimited*, December 4, 2003. http://www.guardian.co.uk/germany/article/0,2763,1099477,00.html.

Harel, Alon. "Efficiency and Fairness in Criminal Law: The Case for a Criminal Law Principle of Comparative Fault." *California Law Review* 82 (1994): 1181–1229.

———. "Victims and Perpetrators: The Case Against a Unified Theory of Comparative Liability in Criminal Law." *Buffalo Criminal Law Review* 8 (2005): 489–502.

Hart, H.L.A. *Law, Liberty, and Morality.* Stanford, Calif.: Stanford University Press, 1963.

———. *Punishment and Responsibility: Essays in the Philosophy of Law.* Oxford: Clarendon Press, 1968.

Hart, H.L.A., and Tony Honore. *Causation in the Law.* 2d ed. Oxford: Clarendon Press, 1985.

Hatcher, Mal Bebbington, et al. "The Psychosocial Impact of Bilateral Prophylactic Mastectomy: Prospective Study Using Questionnaires and Semistructured Interviews." *British Medical Journal* 322 (2001): 76–81.

Hegland, Kenney. "Suggestions, Not Demands: Rethinking Living Wills." *Arizona Attorney* 41 (2004): 14–17.

Herzog, Don. *Happy Slaves: A Critique of Consent Theory.* Chicago: University of Chicago Press, 1989.

Hilfiker, David. "Allowing the Debilitated to Die." *New England Journal of Medicine* 308 (1983): 716–19.

Hilton, Ronald. "RELIGION: Good Friday—Viernes Santo. The Philippines." Discussions on Religion, World Association of International Studies, Stanford University, April 14, 2001. http://wais.stanford.edu/Religion/religion_viernessantophilippines41401.html.

Hohfeld, Wesley Newcomb. *Fundamental Legal Conceptions, as Applied in Judicial Reasoning and Other Legal Essays*. New Haven, Conn.: Yale University Press, 1923.

Hollister, Gail D. "Using Comparative Fault to Replace the All-or-Nothing Lottery Imposed in Intentional Torts Suits in Which Both Plaintiff and Defendant Are at Fault." *Vanderbilt Law Review* 46 (1993): 121–74.

Holmes, Oliver W. *The Common Law*. Vol. 7. Mark DeWolfe Howe ed. (Little, Brown & Co., 1963 [1881]).

———. "The Path of the Law." *Harvard Law Review* 10 (1897): 457–78.

Horder, Jeremy. "Killing the Passive Abuser: A Theoretical Defense." In *Criminal Law Theory: Doctrines of the General Part*, edited by Stephen Shute and Andrew Simester, 283–97. Oxford: Oxford University Press, 2002.

Huigens, Kyron. "Homicide in Aretaic Terms." *Buffalo Criminal Law Review* 6 (2002): 97–146.

———. "Rethinking the Penalty Phase." *Arizona State Law Journal* 32 (2000): 1195–1282.

Hurd, Heidi M. "Blaming the Victim: A Response to the Proposal That Criminal Law Recognize a General Defense of Contributory Responsibility." *Buffalo Criminal Law Review* 8 (2005): 503–22.

———. "The Deontology of Negligence." *Boston University Law Review* 76 (1995): 249–72.

———. "Nonreciprocal Risk Imposition, Unjust Enrichment, and the Foundations of Tort Law: A Critical Celebration of George Fletcher's Theory of Tort Law." *Notre Dame Law Review* 78 (2003): 711–29.

———. "What in the World Is Wrong?" *Journal of Contemporary Legal Issues* 5 (1994): 157–216.

Husak, Douglas N. "Comparative Fault in Criminal Law: Conceptual and Normative Perplexities." *Buffalo Criminal Law Review* 8 (2005): 523–40.

———. "Partial Defenses." *Canadian Journal of Law and Jurisprudence* 11 (1998): 167–92.

Ingman, Terence. "A History of the Defense of Volenti Non Fit Injuria." *Juridical Review*, n.s., 26 (1981): 1–28.

Johnson, Kevin. "Criminals Target Each Other, Trend Shows." *USA Today*, August 31, 2007. http://www.usatoday.com/news/nation/2007-08-31-criminal-target_N.htm?csp=34.

Juenger, Friedrich K. "Brief for Negligence Law Section of the State Bar of Michigan in Support of Comparative Negligence as Amicus Curiae, Parsons v. Construction Equipment Company." *Wayne Law Review* 18 (1972): 3–53.

Kadish, Sanford H. "The Criminal Law and the Luck of the Draw." *Journal of Criminal Law and Criminology* 84 (1994): 679–702.

Kadish, Sanford H., Stephen J. Schulhofer, and Carol Steiker. *Criminal Law and Its Processes: Cases and Materials.* New York: Aspen Publishers, 2007.

Kahneman, Daniel, Jack Knetsch, and Richard H. Thaler. "Experimental Tests of the Endowment Effect and the Coase Theorem." *Journal of Political Economy* 98 (1990): 1325–48.

Kalven, Harry, Jr., and Hans Zeisel. *The American Jury.* Boston: Little, Brown, 1966.

Kamisar, Yale. "Euthanasia Legislation: Some Non-Religious Objections." *Minnesota Law Review* 42 (1958): 969–1042.

Kant, Immanuel. *The Philosophy of Law.* Translated by W. Hastie. Edinburgh: T. and T. Clark, 1887.

Karmen, Andrew. *Crime Victims: An Introduction to Victimology.* Belmont, Calif.: Wadsworth/Thomson Learning. 4th ed. 2001.

Katz, Leo. *Ill-Gotten Gains: Evasion, Blackmail, Fraud, and Kindred Puzzles of the Law.* Chicago: University of Chicago Press, 1996.

Kaufman, Whitley R. P. "Self-Defense, Imminence, and the Battered Woman." *New Criminal Law Review* 10(3) (2007): 342–69.

Keeton, W. Page, ed., et al. *Prosser and Keeton on the Law of Torts.* 5th ed. St. Paul, Minn.: West Pub. Co., 1984.

Kelman, Mark. "The Necessary Myth of Objective Causation Judgments in Liberal Political Theory." *Chicago-Kent Law Review* 63 (1987): 579–637.

Klein, Susan R. "Redrawing the Criminal-Civil Boundary." *Buffalo Criminal Law Review* 2 (1990): 679–721.

Kraus, Joan H. "Distorted Reflections of Battered Women Who Kill: A Response to Professor Dressler." *Ohio State Journal of Criminal Law* 4 (2007): 555–72.

Kusmin, Ben. "Swing Low, Sweet Chariot: Abandoning the Disinterested Witness Requirement for Advance Directives." *American Journal of Law and Medicine* 32 (2006): 93–116.

Lacayo, Richard. "The Rough-Sex Defense." *Time*, May 23, 1988. http://www.time.com/time/magazine/article/0,9171,967466,00.html.

LaFave, Wayne R. *Criminal Law.* 4th ed. St. Paul, Minn.: Thompson/West Group, 2003.

———. *Substantive Criminal Law.* 2d ed. Egan, Minn.: Thompson/West Group, 2003.

LaFave, Wayne R., and Austin W. Scott, Jr. *Criminal Law.* 2d ed. St. Paul, Minn.: West Pub. Co., 1986.

Landler, Mark. "Cannibal Convicted of Manslaughter; German Court Orders an 8½-year Sentence." *International Herald Tribune*, January 31, 2004. http://www.lexisnexis.com.

Lawrence, Robert R. "Checking the Allure of Increased Conviction Rates: The Admissibility of Expert Testimony on Rape Trauma Syndrome in Criminal Proceedings." *Virginia Law Review* 70 (1984): 1657–1705.

Lee, Cynthia. *Murder and the Reasonable Man: Passion and Fear in the Criminal Courtroom*. New York: New York University Press, 2003

Lerner, Melvin J. "The Desire for Justice and Reactions to Victims." In *Altruism and Helping Behavior*, edited by Jacqueline Macaulay and Leonard Berkowitz, 205–29. New York: Academic Press, 1970.

Lundy, Thomas. "Jury Instruction Corner: Obtaining Instruction on Non-Included Lesser Offenses." *Champion* 24-DEC (2000): 48–50.

Lynch, Gerald E. "The Sentencing Guidelines as a Not-So-Model Penal Code." *Federal Sentencing Report* 10 (1997): 25–28.

Mackie, J. L. *The Cement of the Universe: A Study of Causation*. Oxford: Clarendon Press, 1980.

Maguigan, Holly. "Battered Women and Self-Defense: Myths and Misconceptions in Current Reform Proposals." *University of Pennsylvania Law Review* 140 (1991): 379–463.

Malone, Wex S. "Ruminations on the Role of Fault in the History of the Common Law of Torts." *Louisiana Law Review* 31 (1970): 1–44.

Maloney, Frank E. "From Contributory to Comparative Negligence: A Needed Law Reform." *Florida Law Review* 11 (1958): 135–74.

Mansfield, John. "Informed Choice in the Law of Torts." *Louisiana Law Review* 22 (1961): 17–76.

McCarthy, David. "Rights, Explanation, and Risks." *Ethics* 107 (1997): 205–25.

McMahan, Jeff. "Self-Defense and the Problem of the Innocent Attacker." *Ethics* 104 (1994): 252–90.

MedlinePlus Medical Encyclopedia. "Psychosis." National Library of Medicine and the National Institutes of Health. http://www.nlm.nih.gov/medlineplus/ency/article/001553.htm. (Last visited February 20, 2009).

Mendelsohn, Benjamin. *A System of Logic*. 8th ed. New York: Harper and Bros., 1874.

———. "The Victimology." *Etudes Internationales de Psycho-Sociologie Criminelle* 1 (1956): 23–26.

Mill, John Stuart. *On Liberty*. London: Longman, Roberts and Green, 1869.

Miller, Franklin G., et al. "Regulating Physician-Assisted Death." *New England Journal of Medicine* 331 (1994): 119–23.

Model Penal Code and Commentaries (Official Draft and Revised Comments). Philadelphia: American Law Institute, 1980–85.

Moore, Michael S. *Act and Crime: The Philosophy of Action and Its Implications for Criminal Law*. Oxford: Clarendon Press, 1993.

———. "Causation and Responsibility." *Social Philosophy and Policy* 16 (1999): 1–51.

———. *Law and Psychiatry: Rethinking the Relationship*. Cambridge: Cambridge University Press, 1984.

———. "The Metaphysics of Causal Intervention." *California Law Review* 88 (2000): 827–77.

———. *Placing Blame: A General Theory of Criminal Law*. Oxford: Clarendon Press, 1997.

———. "Victims and Retribution: A Reply to Professor Fletcher." *Buffalo Criminal Law Review* 3 (1999): 65–89.

Morawetz, Thomas. "Reconstructing the Criminal Defenses: The Significance of Justification." *Journal of Criminal Law and Criminology* 77 (1986): 277–307.

Morris, Norval. "Somnambulistic Homicide: Ghosts, Spiders, and North Koreans." *Res Judicatae* 5 (1951): 29–33.

Morse, Stephen J. "Diminished Rationality, Diminished Responsibility." *Ohio State Journal of Criminal Law* 1 (2003): 289–308.

———. "Neither Desert nor Disease." *Legal Theory* 5 (1999): 265–309.

———. "The 'New Syndrome Excuse' Syndrome." *Criminal Justice Ethics* 14 (1995): 3–15.

———. "Undiminished Confusion in Diminished Capacity." *Journal of Criminal Law and Criminology* 75 (1984): 1–55.

Mostaghel, Deborah M. "Wrong Place, Wrong Time, Unfair Treatment? Aid to Victims of Terrorist Attacks." *Brandeis Law Journal* 40 (2001): 83–140.

Mulvihill, D., et al. *Crimes of Violence*. Staff Report to the National Commission on the Causes and Prevention of Violence. Washington, D.C.: U.S. Government Printing Office 1969.

———. *The Offender and His Victim*. Staff Report to the National Commission on the Causes and Prevention of Violence. Washington, D.C.: U.S. Government Printing Office 1969.

Nadel, Andrea G. "Annotation, Statutes Providing for Governmental Compensation for Victims of Crime." *American Law Reports: ALR 4th*, 20: 63–105. Rochester, N.Y.: Lawyers Co-operative, 1983.

Nemeth, Mary, et al. "Chilling the Sexes: Women's Growing Militancy About Harassment and Date Rape Alarms Many Men." *MacLean's*, February 17, 1992, 42.

New York State Task Force on Life and the Law. *When Death Is Sought: Assisted Suicide and Euthanasia in the Medical Context*. New York: The New York State Task Force on Life and the Law, May 1994.

Noah, Lars. "Informed Consent and the Elusive Dichotomy Between Standard and Experimental Therapy." *American Journal of Law and Medicine* 28 (2002): 361–408.

Nourse, V. F. "Reconceptualizing Criminal Law Defenses." *University of Pennsylvania Law Review* 151 (2003): 1691–1746.

Nozick, Robert. *Anarchy, State and Utopia*. New York: Basic Books, 1974.

Oberdiek, John. "Towards a Right Against Risking." *Law and Philosophy* 28 (2009) *1–26. http://www.springerlink.com/content/e046988818363041/fulltext.pdf.

Ortiz de Urbina Gimeno, Íñigo. "Old Wine in New Wineskins? Appraising Professor Bergelson's Plea for Comparative Criminal Liability." *Pace Law Review* 28 (2008) 815–45.

Patterson, Steve. "Putting a Price on Love." *Chicago Sun-Times*, July 1, 2007. http://www.suntimes.com/news/metro/450874,CST-NWS-sexlaw01.article.

Pearson, Richard N. "Apportionment of Losses Under Comparative Fault Laws—An Analysis of the Alternatives." *Louisiana Law Review* 40 (1980): 343–72.

Perkins, Rollin M. *Perkins on Criminal Law.* 2d ed. Mineola, N.Y.: Foundation Press, 1969.

Perkins, Rollin M., and Ronald N. Boyce. *Criminal Law.* 3d ed. Mineola, N.Y.: Foundation Press, 1982.

Perry, Stephen. "Risk, Harm, and Responsibility." In *Philosophical Foundations of Tort Law*, edited by David G. Owen. Oxford: Clarendon Press, 1995.

Pew Research Center. "A Barometer of Modern Morals: Sex, Drugs, and the 1040." *Pew Research Center Publications.* March 28, 2006. http://pewresearch.org/pubs/307/a<->barometer-of-modern-morals.

Poor Mojo Newswire. "Seagull Body and Fetus Head." August 30, 2005. http://www.poormojo.org/pmjadaily/archives/004388.php.

Posner, Richard A. "Are We One Self or Multiple Selves? Implications for Law and Public Policy." *Legal Theory* 3 (1997): 23–35.

Pound, Roscoe. *An Introduction to the Philosophy of Law.* New Haven, CT: Yale University Press, 1954.

Prosser, William L. "Joint Torts and Several Liability." *California Law Review* 25 (1936–37): 413–43.

Raz, Joseph. *The Morality of Freedom.* New York: Oxford University Press, 1986.

Rizzo, Mario J. "Symposium on Causation in the Law of Torts." *Chicago-Kent Law Review* 63 (1987): 397–406.

Roach, Mary. *Stiff. The Curious Lives of Human Cadavers.* New York: W.W Norton, 2003.

Roberts, Paul. "Philosophy, Feinberg, Codification, and Consent: A Progress Report on English Experiences of Criminal Law Reform." *Buffalo Criminal Law Review* 5 (2001): 173–253.

Robinson, Paul H. "Criminal Law Defenses: A Systematic Analysis." *Columbia Law Review* 82 (1982): 199–291.

———. "A Functional Analysis of Criminal Law." *Northwest University Law Review* 88 (1994): 857–913.

———. "A Theory of Justification: Societal Harm as a Prerequisite for Criminal Liability." *UCLA Law Review* 23 (1975): 266–92.

Robinson, Paul H., Michael T. Cahill, and Usman Mohammad. "The Five Worst (and Five Best) American Criminal Codes." *Northwest University Law Review* 95 (2000): 1–84.

Robinson, Paul H., and John M. Darley. *Justice, Liability, and Blame: Community Views and the Criminal Law.* Boulder, Colo.: Westview Press, 1995.

———. "The Utility of Desert." *Northwest University Law Review* 91 (1997): 453–99.

Rodin, David. *War and Self-Defense.* New York: Oxford University Press, 2002.

Rosen, Richard A. "On Self-Defense, Imminence, and Women Who Kill Their Batterers." *North Carolina Law Review* 71 (1993): 371–411.

Ruppe, David. "Opus Dei on the Rise: Conservative Catholic Group Grows Quietly." *Great Dreams.* June 18, 2001. http://www.greatdreams.com/sacred/Opus_Dei.htm.

Schafer, Stephen. *Victimology: The Victim and His Criminal.* Reston, Va.: Reston Pub. Co., 1977.

Schafran, Lynn Hecht. "Writing and Reading About Rape: A Primer." *St. John's Law Review* 66 (1993): 979–1045.

Schanberg, Sydney H. "Let's Be Outraged At Everyday Rape, Too." *Newsday*, April 28, 1989. Viewpoints section, City edition. http://infoweb.newsbank.com.

Schünemann, Bernd. "The Future of the Victimological Approach to the Interpretation of Criminal Law: The Use of Victimological Considerations as a Comprehensive, Regulative Principle for Limiting the Scope of Certain Crimes." In *Victimology in Comparative Perspective*, 4th ed., edited by K. Miazawa and M. Ohya. Tokyo: Seibundo, 1986.

———. "The Role of the Victim Within the Criminal Justice System: A Three-Tiered Concept." *Buffalo Criminal Law Review* 3 (1999): 33–49.

Sendor, Benjamin B. "Mistakes of Fact: A Study in the Structure of Criminal Conduct." *Wake Forest Law Review* 25 (1990): 707–82.

Shakespeare, William. *Romeo and Juliet*, edited by Brian Gibbons. Walton-on-Thames, Surrey: Thomas Nelson and Sons, 1997.

Siegel, Martin J. "For Better or for Worse: Adultery, Crime and the Constitution." *Journal of Family Law* 30 (1991–92): 45–95.

Silverman, Robert A. "Victim Precipitation: An Examination of the Concept." In *Victimology: A New Focus*, edited by Israel Drapkin and Emilio Viano, vol. 1, 99–109. Lexington, Mass.: Lexington Books, 1974.

Simons, Kenneth W. "The Relevance of Community Values to Just Deserts: Criminal Law, Punishment Rationales, and Democracy." *Hofstra Law Review* 28 (2000): 635–67. "The Relevance of Victim Conduct in Tort and Criminal Law." *Buffalo Criminal Law Review* 8 (2005): 541–65.

Sisk, Gregory C. "Comparative Fault and Common Sense." *Gonzaga Law Review* 30 (1994): 29–51.

Smith, J. C., and Brian Hogan. *Criminal Law.* 7th ed. London: Butterworths, 1992.

Sobelsohn, David. "Comparing Fault." *Indiana Law Review* 60 (1985): 413–62.

Stephen, James. *A History of the Criminal Law in England*. London: Macmillan, 1883.

Stephens, Beth. "Conceptualizing Violence Under International Law: Do Tort Remedies Fit the Crime?" *Albany Law Review* 60 (1997): 579–606.

Strassfeld, Robert N. "Causal Comparisons." *Fordham Law Review* 60 (1992): 913–51.

Sundby, Scott E. "The Capital Jury and Empathy: The Problem of Worthy and Unworthy Victims." *Cornell Law Review* 88 (2003): 343–81.

Thomson, Judith Jarvis. "Causality and Rights: Some Preliminaries." *Chicago-Kent Law Review* 63 (1987): 471–96.

———. "A Defense of Abortion." *Philosophy and Public Affairs* 1 (1971): 47–66.

———. *The Realm of Rights*. Cambridge, Mass.: Harvard University Press, 1990.

———. "Rights and Compensation." In *Rights, Restitution, and Risk: Essays in Moral Theory*, edited by William Parent, 66–77. Cambridge, Mass.: Harvard University Press, 1986.

———. "Self-Defense." *Philosophy and Public Affairs* 20 (1991): 283–310.

———. "Self-Defense and Rights." In *Rights, Restitution, and Risk: Essays in Moral Theory*, edited by William Parent, 33–38. Cambridge, Mass.: Harvard University Press, 1986.

———. "Some Questions About Government Regulation of Behavior." In *Rights, Restitution, and Risk: Essays in Moral Theory*, edited by William Parent, 154–72. Cambridge, Mass.: Harvard University Press, 1986.

———. "Some Ruminations on Rights." In *Rights, Restitution, and Risk: Essays in Moral Theory*, edited by William Parent, 49–65. Cambridge, Mass.: Harvard University Press, 1986.

Toch, Hans. *Violent Men: An Inquiry into the Psychology of Violence*. Chicago: Aldine Pub. Co., 1969.

Torcia, Charles E. *Wharton's Criminal Law*. 15th ed. Deerfield, Ill.: Clark Boardman Callaghan, 1994.

Uniacke, Suzanne. *Permissible Killing: The Self-Defense Justification of Homicide*. Cambridge: Cambridge University Press, 1996.

United Kingdom Law Commission. "Consent in the Criminal Law." *Law Commission Consultation Paper*, No. 139. London: H.M.S.O., 1995.

———. "Criminal Law: Consent and Offences Against the Person." *Law Commission Consultation Paper*, No. 134. London: H.M.S.O., 1994.

———. *Eighth Programme of Law Reform*. London: H.M.S.O., 2001.

Universal Declaration of Human Rights, G.A. Res. 217A, at 71, U.N. GAOR, 3d Sess., 1st plen. mtg., U.N. Doc. A/810, December 12, 1948

U.S. Department of Justice, Office of Justice Programs, Bureau of Justice Statistics. *Murder in Families*. NCJ-143498, by Patrick A. Langan and John M. Dawson. Washington D.C.:U.S. Dept. of Justice, Bureau of Justice Statistics, July 1994.

———. *Spouse Murder Defendants in Large Urban Counties.* NCJ-153256, by Patrick A. Langan and John M. Dawson. Washington D.C.:U.S. Dept. of Justice, Bureau of Justice Statistics, September 1995.

U.S. Sentencing Commission. *1999 Sourcebook of Federal Sentencing Statistics.* 1999. http://www.ussc.gov/index.html.

———. *2000 Sourcebook of Federal Sentencing Statistics.* 2000. http://www.ussc.gov/index.html.

———. *2001 Sourcebook of Federal Sentencing Statistics.* 2001. http://www.ussc.gov/index.html.

———. *2006 Sourcebook of Federal Sentencing Statistics.* 2006. http://www.ussc.gov/index.html.

Von Hentig, Hans. *The Criminal and His Victim: Studies in the Sociobiology of Crime.* Hamden, Conn.: Archon Books, 1948.

Wagener, Hans. *Understanding Franz Werfel.* Columbia: University of South Carolina Press, 1993.

Warr, Mark, and Mark Stafford. "Public Goals of Punishment and Support for the Death Penalty." *Journal of Research in Crime and Delinquency* 21 (1984): 95–111.

Weiss, Amanda. "Criminalizing Consensual Transmission of HIV." *University of Chicago Legal Forum.* 2006 (2006): 389–408.

West, Robin L. "Authority, Autonomy, and Choice: The Role of Consent in the Moral and Political Visions of Franz Kafka and Richard Posner." *Harvard Law Review* 99 (1985): 384–428.

———. "The Difference in Women's Hedonic Lives: A Phenomenological Critique of Feminist Legal Theory." *Wisconsin Women's Law Journal* 3 (1987): 81–146.

Westen, Peter. *The Logic of Consent: The Diversity and Deceptiveness of Consent as a Defense to Criminal Conduct.* Burlington, Vt.: Ashgate Publishing, 2003.

Wexler, David B. "Patients, Therapists, and Third Parties: The Victimological Virtues of Tarasoff." *International Journal of Law and Psychiatry* 2 (1979): 1–28.

Whatley, Mark A. "Victim Characteristics Influencing Attributions of Responsibility to Rape Victims: A Meta-Analysis." *Aggression and Violent Behavior* 1 (1996): 81–95.

"When It Feels Right to Cut Off Your Leg." *Geelong Advertiser.* July 4, 2005: 15.

Williams, Joyce E., and Karen A. Holmes. *The Second Assault: Rape and Public Attitudes.* Westport, Conn.: Greenwood Press, 1981.

Wilmot-Weidman, Kimberly. "After a Three-Year Fight, Murder Is Finally Murder in Maryland." *Chicago Tribune*, November 23, 1997: 1.

Wolf, Leslie E., and Richard Vezina. "Crime and Punishment: Is There a Role for Criminal Law in HIV Prevention Policy?" *Whittier Law Review* 25 (2004): 821–88.

Wolfgang, Marvin E. *Patterns in Criminal Homicide.* Philadelphia: University of Pennsylvania, 1958.

Wozniak, Frank J. "Annotation, Validity, Construction, and Application of 'Hazing' Statutes." *ALR5th* 30:683–98. Rochester, N.Y.: Lawyers Cooperative, 1995.

Wright, R. George. "Consenting Adults: The Problem of Enhancing Human Dignity Non-Coercively." *Boston University Law Review* 75 (1995): 1397–1439.

Wright, Richard W. "Causation in Tort Law." *California Law Review* 73 (1985): 1735–1828.

Ziegler, Lane D., and Stephen S. Kroll. "Primary Breast Cancer After Prophylactic Mastectomy." *American Journal of Clinical Oncology* 14 (1991): 451–54.

INDEX

Critical Perspectives on Crime and Law

Edited by Markus D. Dubber

Wayne A. Logan, *Knowledge as Power: Criminal Registration and Community Notification Laws in America*
2009

Markus D. Dubber and Mariana Valverde, editors, *Police and the Liberal State*
2008

David Alan Sklansky, *Democracy and the Police*
2007

Markus D. Dubber and Lindsay Farmer, editors, *Modern Histories of Crime and Punishment*
2007

Markus D. Dubber and Mariana Valverde, editors, *The New Police Science: The Police Power in Domestic and International Governance*
2006